Sheets

DIVIDED WE FOUGHT

DIVIDED

A PICTORIAL HISTORY OF THE WAR

THE MACMILLAN COMPANY

WE FOUGHT

1861-1865

Picture Editors:
HIRST D. MILHOLLEN *and* MILTON KAPLAN

Caption Editors:
HIRST D. MILHOLLEN, MILTON KAPLAN *and* HULEN STUART

Author of the Text and General Editor: DAVID DONALD

NEW YORK

Acknowledgments

The authors wish to express their gratitude to the many friends who by their knowledge and advice have helped them in the preparation of this book, and in particular to those listed below:

Mrs. McCook Knox, Washington, D. C.; Mr. A. Lawrence Kocher, Williamsburg, Virginia; Miss Haydee M. Fortier, Louisiana Historical Association, New Orleans, Louisiana; Mr. James W. Foster, Maryland Historical Society, Baltimore, Maryland; Mrs. Carl Mays, Confederate Veteran, Alexandria, Virginia; Mr. J. C. Meadors, Lexington, Kentucky; Metropolitan Museum of Art, New York City; Mr. Charles van Ravenswaay, Missouri Historical Society, Saint Louis, Missouri; Mr. Floud Shoemaker, The State Historical Society of Missouri, Columbia, Missouri; Mr. J. Mack Moore, Vicksburg, Mississippi; Mr. Cyril Nast, New Rochelle, New York; Mr. Wendell Arnote, Nashville Public Library, Nashville, Tennessee; Mr. Macgill James, National Gallery of Art, Washington, D. C.; Mr. Arthur B. Carlson, The New York Historical Society, New York City; Mr. Karl Kup, The New York Public Library, New York City; The Newark Museum, Newark, New Jersey; Mr. Charles H. P. Copeland, Peabody Museum, Salem, Massachusetts; Mrs. Henry E. Raines, Confederate Museum, Charleston, South Carolina; Mrs. Barbara S. Roberts, The Pennsylvania Academy of the Fine Arts, Philadelphia, Pennsylvania; Mr. R. N. Williams, 2nd, The Historical Society of Pennsylvania, Philadelphia, Pennsylvania; Major Kenneth C. Miller, 107th Infantry, N.Y.N.G., New York City; Lieutenant Bert Sheldon, Washington, D. C.; Mr. Victor D. Spark, New York City; Senator Tom Underwood of Kentucky; Mr. Lester B. Brown, United States Naval Academy Museum, Annapolis, Maryland; Valentine Museum, Richmond, Virginia; Mr. William J. Van Schreeven, State Archivist, Richmond, Virginia; Mr. Harold Petersen, Washington, D. C.; Mr. N. Thiras, Addison Gallery of American Art, Andover, Massachusetts; Alabama Department of Archives and History, Montgomery, Alabama; Dr. George M. Anderson, Baltimore, Maryland; Mr. Edwin L. M. Taggart, Washington, D. C.; Mr. Elmer L. Mack, Bethlehem, Pennsylvania; Mr. G. H. Edgell, Museum of Fine Arts, Boston, Massachusetts; Miss Sarah M. Usher, Boston Public Library, Boston, Massachusetts; Miss Ruth Potts, Bainbridge, Georgia; Mr. L. G. Cox, Canajoharie Library and Art Gallery, Canajoharie, New York; Mr. Charles Downing Lay, The Century Association, New York City; Mr. H. Maxon Holloway, Chicago Historical Society, Chicago, Illinois; Dr. James Carpenter, Colby College, Waterville, Maine; Dr. J. Winston Coleman, Jr., Lexington, Kentucky; Dr. Huestis Cook, Jr., Richmond, Virginia; Mr. E. Maurice Bloch, Cooper Union Museum for the Arts of Decoration, New York City; Mr. Herman W. Williams, Jr., Corcoran Gallery of Art, Washington, D. C.; Mr. Howard Dearstyne, Williamsburg, Virginia; Mr. Claude C. de Brueys, New Orleans, Louisiana; Mrs. Elizabeth H. Feltman, Alexandria, Virginia; Mrs. J. E. Hays, Georgia State Department of Archives and History, Atlanta, Georgia; Mrs. Henry W. Howell, Jr., Frick Art Reference Library, New York City; Mr. James A. Hope, Watkins Glen, New York; Professor Mark DeWolfe Howe, Harvard University, Cambridge, Massachusetts; Mrs. Louis du Pont Irving, Irvington-on-Hudson, New York; the late Mrs. Mabel Jones, Macon,

Georgia; Mrs. Richard Lake, Philomont, Virginia; Miss Helen M. McFarland, Kansas State Historical Society, Topeka, Kansas; Mr. Albert Reese, Kennedy & Company, New York City; Mr. Stanley W. McClure, Washington, D. C.; Mr. Perry Coke Smith, Union League Club, New York City; Mrs. James W. Easter, Maryland Division, United Daughters of the Confederacy, Baltimore, Maryland; the late Congressman John Whitaker of Kentucky; Whitney Museum of American Art, New York City; Wildenstein & Co., New York City; Mr. F. A. LaFayette, State Historical Society, Madison, Wisconsin.

Mrs. Mary Handy Evans and Mrs. Alice Handy Cox, of the L. C. Handy Studios, Washington, D. C.; Miss Georgia Fleming, Bainbridge, Georgia, Mrs. Mamie Jennison Chestney, Macon, Georgia, and Mr. Maxim Karolik, Newport, Rhode Island, who kindly consented to our using pictures from their own private collections; Miss Josephine Cobb, of the National Archives, Washington, D. C., whose interest in the work of photographers who covered the war, and whose knowledge of Mathew B. Brady made our task less difficult; Mr. Frederick H. Meserve, New York City; Mr. Neville T. Kirk, of the United States Naval Academy, whose knowledge of naval history helped us with the identification of ships and ranks of naval officers; Mr. Harold S. Sniffen, Curator of Prints, The Mariners' Museum, Newport News, Virginia, who constantly kept us informed of new acquisitions relating to the war; Miss India W. Thomas, House Regent, and Miss Eleanor S. Brockenbrough, Assistant House Regent, of the Confederate Museum in Richmond, Virginia; the following Library of Congress Members: Mr. Jack Bishop, Sr., Mr. Frederick Goff, Miss Peggy Harmon, Miss Alice Lee Parker, Dr. Percy Powell; Mr. Donald Holmes, Chief of the Photoduplication Service of the Library, and members of his staff: Mrs. Virginia Brooke, Miss Olivera Durgy, Mrs. Emily M. Jahn, Mr. William J. Kimmel, Mr. Elmer S. King, Mr. William H. Koppy, Mr. Bernard J. McCarthy, Mrs. Jacquelyn Mitchell, Mr. Ralph E. O'Hara, Mr. Richard Rangfors, and Mr. William Younger; Colonel Willard Webb, Chief of the Stack and Reader Division; Miss Virginia Daiker, for her assistance in the reading of proof; Mr. Irwin Unger, of Columbia University, for invaluable assistance in authentication and verification of difficult dates and misplaced quotations, and for many services in speeding up the preparation of this manuscript; Mrs. Robert E. Thomas, of New York City, who gave us our title.

Publisher's Foreword

This volume must claim as its ancestor *The Photographic History of the Civil War*, published in 10 volumes in 1911 by the Review of Reviews Company under the editorship of Francis Trevelyan Miller. This famous set contains 3800 illustrations from the photographs of Mathew Brady and his assistants, and a number of other photographers. Many of these photographs were made on the actual field of battle, others in the camps or behind the lines; included also are an immense number of studio portraits. *The Photographic History of the Civil War* will always remain one of the monuments of American publishing; it can never lose its value as a source book, but by modern standards of reproduction the illustrations convey only a faint idea of the quality of the original negatives.

The set has long been out of print and will likely remain so. Yet to many students and scholars the thought must often have occurred that a single volume utilizing modern printing methods might be produced which would do justice to the material.

Obviously, if the project were to be undertaken, and if satisfactory reproductions were to be made, the chief negative collections would have to be consulted. Because of the present economics of publishing, a stringent selection would have to be made, perhaps 500 photographs in all, and these must cover all the principal events and personalities, and at the same time pass a high critical test. If this could be done and if a text could be written for the illustrations which was accurate and readable, then a volume would result which would give the present-day reader, almost as if he had participated in it himself, the shock and the tragedy of the struggle. It would also pay recognition to the accomplishment of that extraordinary group of men who photographed the war from its beginning to its end.

The noble impulse which made Mathew Brady make his record of the war is poignantly told in his own words: "My wife and my most conservative friends had looked unfavorably upon this departure from commercial business, and I can only describe the destiny that over-ruled me by saying that, like Euphorion, I felt I had to go."

From the point of view of material success, Brady's friends were undoubtedly right. The idea of photographing a war in all its phases was a daring innovation; and it entailed unknown dangers and hardship. In addition, Brady was the most fashionable photographer of his day, with palatial studios in Washington and New York. To give up this lucrative business, and risk his fortune in such a venture, must have seemed madness. There would be no ready-made market for his work, for the popular weekly newspapers had no means of reproducing his negatives.[1] It might prove, as his conservative friends counselled, his financial ruin.

Though this gloomy prediction was to prove true, Brady went, and as the war developed he trained a team of assistants to work under his supervision, and to photograph almost every important campaign. Little or nothing is known of these men. As a result, many of the finest photographs in this book bear the equivocal legend, "Mathew Brady or assistant." But Brady's was the original idea; and it was Brady who generously taught his assistants the secrets of his genius.

---

[1] Brady hoped to sell in large quantities stereographs, the double prints which can be looked at through a stereoscope. Many of these were in fact sold, but the sales did not prove sufficient even to pay the expenses of his photographic supplies.

Nothing in any later war, despite the improvement in equipment and technical knowledge, has approached the dramatic, almost three-dimensional quality, of such photographs as are reproduced on p. 343, p. 380 or p. 420.

Some years ago, Mr. Hirst Milhollen and Mr. Milton Kaplan of the Prints and Photographs Division of the Library of Congress were approached concerning the possibilities of such a volume as this. Their response was immediate and enthusiastic. They were familiar with the principal collections; Mr. Milhollen was himself a skilled photographer; and both felt sure that they would receive the utmost cooperation in the making of the prints from the keepers of the collections.

Mr. Milhollen and Mr. Kaplan felt sure too that a diligent search would uncover photographs, fully worthy of inclusion, in the museums and private collections of the South. Their discoveries, hitherto unreproduced, do much to remedy the omissions in Miller's volumes, the vast bulk of whose illustrations were photographed from the Federal side.

In addition to their searches in the South, Mr. Milhollen and Mr. Kaplan had another suggestion to make. There are in the Library of Congress two albums containing the original sketches of the battle artists, Alfred R. Waud, his brother William Waud and Edwin Forbes. A generous selection from them appears in this book and serves as an admirable complement to the dramatic but necessarily static collection of photographs.

Neither of the Wauds nor Forbes was a great battle painter. All three men were strictly campaign "sketch artists." Yet their hurried sketches are full of the panoply and febrile excitement of war. The crude reproductions made by the wood engravers of *Harper's Weekly* and *Frank Leslie's Illustrated Newspaper* which appeared week by week through the War in these magazines, give no idea of the brilliance and accuracy of the originals.

At the end of their search, Mr. Milhollen and Mr. Kaplan, assisted by Mr. Hulen Stuart whose knowledge of military detail proved invaluable, had assembled prints of almost two thousand photographs and drawings. These were subjected to a rigorous process of critical selection and reduced to about eight hundred. There for some time the matter rested.

The main body of the book was ready, an intimidating block of magnificent illustrations. The final problem was to find a text which would adequately describe its illustrations; which would in its total be an accurate military history of the war; and which in its details would be as vivid as the pictures themselves.

On the sage advice of Mr. Allan Nevins, Mr. David Donald of Columbia University was asked if he would be willing to undertake the task. After a thorough inspection of the material, he agreed. Under his hands, the book has been divided into fourteen chapters, each with its page of general introduction. The illustrations have been reduced to fit into a close pattern of less than five hundred. Using many contemporary quotations, he has written a continuous narrative which exactly conforms to the conditions imposed.

In a volume such as this, the reader will not look for a formal history of the war. For that he is recommended to the volumes by Douglas Southall Freeman and Kenneth P. Williams. What this book is, and what every picture book should be, is an aid to recognition. No piece of prose can exactly convey to us the special heroism of Brigadier General Israel Richardson leading his division up to the Bloody Lane to his own death. But let the reader look at the photograph on p. 127, and the truth is plain. Here is the portrait of the dedicated soldier, waiting with compressed lips for his opportunity, sure that his division is the best in either army.

Again and again in these pages, thanks to the skill and reverent handling of all who have worked with it, this shock of recognition or understanding will recur. In this spirit, the reader will surely turn the pages.

Contents

Abraham Lincoln.

I. Secession Meant War

"The Union Is Dissolved," screamed Charleston newspaper headlines. After decades of sectional squabbling, the South Carolinians had taken the election of a Republican President, Abraham Lincoln, as the signal for secession; and in state convention at Charleston on December 20, 1860, they solemnly voted "that the union now subsisting between South Carolina and other States under the name of the United States of America is hereby dissolved." By February 1, 1861, six other slave states had followed the example: Mississippi, Florida, Alabama, Georgia, Louisiana, Texas. When Lincoln was inaugurated, the secessionists had already chosen Jefferson Davis of Mississippi President of the Confederate States of America.

It was ironical that the election of Lincoln should have touched off the secession of the Lower South. Born in Kentucky, the new President was no abolitionist; he had no plan to revolutionize the Southern social order. Lincoln did not stand pledged to eradicate slavery in any state or even in the District of Columbia; he did not propose the abolition of the slave trade; he would not even oppose the admission of additional slave states. But had he so intended, hostile majorities in Congress and a Southern-dominated Supreme Court could effectively have curbed him.

Hotheads made no reckoning of these matters. Secession was not a product of reason so much as it was of anger and fear. For years politicians had been mumbling meaningless phrases—despotic slavocracy, nigger-loving abolitionism, manifest destiny, squatter sovereignty, Dred Scott decision, John Brown's raid, black Republican party—until the mumbo-jumbo acquired a magic significance. Fraternal affection was curdled into suspicion; bonds of unity became fetters.

In his inaugural Lincoln pleaded with his "dissatisfied fellow countrymen" to "think calmly and *well*" and to have "a patient confidence in the ultimate justice of the people"; but it was too late for reason. The formula of compromise which had succeeded in 1820 and 1850 seemed in 1860 to be appeasement and surrender. Public sentiment, North and South, was hardening. "There cannot be . . . any more compromises," wrote a Pennsylvanian; "let the issue come peaceably if possible, but let it come if it comes in blood."

For a few weeks men deceived themselves with talk of peaceable secession; but Lincoln pointed out: "Physically speaking, we cannot separate. We cannot remove our respective sections from each other, nor build an impassable wall between them." Even the most amiable agreement would have raised the gravest problems—problems of debts, of mails, of frontiers, of commerce. And the most acute of all lay in the most dangerously inflamed area in the South—Fort Sumter in Charleston harbor, still held by a tiny garrison of Federal troops. Lincoln's attempts at provisioning the fort were as ineffectual as Davis's demands for Federal withdrawal, and on April 12, 1861, the first shot was fired upon the Union flag. Secession meant war.

Jefferson Davis.

View of Charleston, South Carolina, Looking Toward the Harbor and Fort Sumter.

Lincoln's inaugural address pledged: "The power confided to me will be used to hold, occupy, and possess the property and places belonging to the government . . ." Specifically, that meant Fort Sumter, incomplete fortress on an island dominating Charleston harbor, where Major Robert Anderson, a Kentuckian loyal to the Union, commanded a garrison of about a hundred officers and men. After grave debate President Lincoln ordered a relief force to be prepared and advised Anderson to "hold out, if possible, till the arrival of the expedition."

Pledged to "independence with absolute jurisdiction over their own soil," Southerners flared up at Lincoln's proposal, and Governor Pickens of South Carolina predicted a "bloody fight." The commander of Confederate forces at Charleston, General Beauregard, received his instructions from Jefferson Davis's government: ". . . you will at once demand [Sumter's] evacuation, and if this is refused proceed, in such manner as you may determine, to reduce it."

[3]

Negroes Mounting Cannon at Morris Island for the Attack on Fort Sumter.

"Things are happening so fast," gasped Mary B. Chesnut on April 8. Her husband, a former United States Senator, had become aide-de-camp to General Beauregard. "He tells me the attack on Fort Sumter may begin to-night; depends upon Anderson and the fleet outside. . . . Anderson is burning blue lights, signs, and signals for the fleet outside, I suppose." At midnight seven guns were discharged in Citadel Square, the signal for the reserves to rally. Despite a thunderstorm, "at the corners of the streets, public squares, and other convenient points, meetings were formed, and all night the long roll of the drum and the steady tramp of the military and the gallop of the cavalry resounding through the city betokened the close proximity of the long-anticipated hostilities." Southerners flocked to the fortifications. The next day, a "floating battery, finished, mounted, and manned" was anchored off Fort Moultrie, north of Sumter; other cannon were placed on Morris Island, to the South.

On the night of April 12 Charleston was wakeful with anxiety. Colonel Chesnut was sent with a final demand for Anderson's surrender. "I do not pretend to go to sleep," wrote Mrs. Chesnut. "How can I? If Anderson does not accept terms at four, the orders are, he shall be fired upon."

Major Robert Anderson, U.S.A.

Edmund Ruffin.

Anderson refused to yield, and at 4:30 A.M. a Confederate signal shell gave "the command for immediate attack." Edmund Ruffin, aged Southern fire-eater, had been asked to fire the first cannon. "Of course I was highly gratified by the compliment," he recorded in his diary, "& delighted to perform the service—which I did. The shell struck the fort at the north-east angle of the parapet. The firing then proceeded. . . ."

[6]

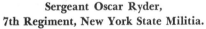

Sergeant Oscar Ryder,
7th Regiment, New York State Militia.

Private Thomas Taylor, Co. K,
8th Louisiana Infantry Regiment.

Within the fort Anderson lacked powder, guns, and men. But for thirty-four hours, until the quarters were entirely burned, the main gates destroyed by fire, the magazine surrounded by flames, he put up a vigorous defense. Then he surrendered. "I accepted terms of evacuation offered by General Beauregard," he reported to his superiors, "and marched out of the fort Sunday afternoon, the 14th instant, with colors flying and drums beating, bringing away company and private property, and saluting my flag with fifty guns."

Hostilities cleared the air. When Lincoln called for 75,000 troops, Virginia, North Carolina, Arkansas, and Tennessee followed the Gulf states into secession. The other border states remained dubiously loyal. Among the free states, however, men rallied to the flag. "At the darkest moment in the history of the republic," wrote Ralph Waldo Emerson, "when it looked as if the nation would be dismembered, pulverized into its original elements, the attack on Fort Sumter crystallized the North into a unit, and the hope of mankind was saved." In the Confederacy there was similar enthusiasm, and, as Howell Cobb said, "The anxiety among our citizens is not as to who shall *go* to the wars, but *who shall stay at home.*"

General Winfield Scott, U.S.A.

General in chief of the Union armies was Winfield Scott, seventy-five-year-old veteran of the War of 1812 and the Mexican War. By 1861 Scott was swollen and dropsical, unable to mount a horse. "I was three years old when the Constitution was adopted," he liked to remind his listeners; and, though a Virginian, he intended to maintain that Federal Union so long as there was strength in his ailing body.

Harpers Ferry—Looking Down the Potomac River.

With the defection of the upper South, Union forces were pushed back toward Washington. One outpost was the Federal arsenal at Harpers Ferry, where the Shenandoah joins the Potomac, the site only two years previously of John Brown's raid. Advised of the approach of Virginia troops, the Union commander "put piles of powder in straw in all the buildings, and quietly waited." When the Southerners arrived, his "men were run out of the arsenal and the combustibles fired. The people fired upon the soldiers, killing two, and rushed into the arsenal." Much of the property was burned, but the Confederates were able to save the valuable rifle-making machinery, which was moved to Richmond.

Similarly, the Federal navy yard at Norfolk was threatened. Unable to defend themselves, the Union forces withdrew, first firing the ships and installations. "The Merrimac, Germantown, Pennsylvania, Delaware, Columbus, and Boston were burned," reported the New York *News*, "the granite dry dock was blown up, and the entire yard actually levelled by the fire. . . ."

Old Aqueduct Bridge From the Chesapeake and Ohio Canal in Georgetown.

Washington itself seemed to be in danger. A secessionist mob in Baltimore cut rail and telegraphic communications with the Capital, and for several days no reinforcements reached the city. On April 22 Scott thought the Capital "partially besieged, threatened, and in danger of being attacked on all sides in a day or two or three."

When Federal recruits did arrive, they were placed in camps "located without regard to purposes of defence or instruction." "In no quarter were the dispositions for defence such as to offer a vigorous resistance to a respectable body of the enemy. . . . Earthworks . . . looked upon the approaches to the Georgetown aqueduct and ferry, the Long bridge . . . and some simple defensive arrangements were made at the Chain bridge. With the latter exception not a single defensive work had been commenced. . . ."

Rumors came in daily of Southern plots to seize the Capital. "The government of the Confederate States *must possess the city of Washington,*" the Milledgeville, Georgia, *Southern Recorder* openly announced. "It is folly to think it can be used any longer as the headquarters of the Lincoln Government. . . . The District of Columbia cannot remain under the jurisdiction of the United States Congress without humiliating Southern pride and defeating Southern rights."

Though the danger seemed immediate, the Federal government moved creakingly in the crisis. Only the most casual precautions were taken to guard the bridges leading from the Capital into Virginia. The Long Bridge, one mile in length and "about the width of three carriages," was "unobstructed during the day," although "for form's sake, sentinels parade to and fro." "A company of flying artillery" was "stationed on the bridge every night, near the Virginia shore, with the draw raised in front of them." So insecure were the Capital's defenses that Lincoln himself was disturbed. From a White House window he maintained a vigil, "resting the end of the telescope on his toes sublime." "It does seem to me, General," he remarked to Winfield Scott, "that if I were Beauregard I would take Washington."

Long Bridge Across the Potomac, Washington.

Private John Werth, Richmond Howitzer Battalion, C.S.A.

The first real land "battle" of the war—actually a minor skirmish—came on June 10 at Big Bethel, near Fort Monroe. "Precisely at 9 A.M.," wrote a Confederate participant, "we saw the dazzling glitter of the enemy's muskets . . . then our trusty Parrott gun opened its dark mouth and spoke in thunder tones . . . and then came the enemies shot, bursting and whizzing around our heads, and the sharp ring of the rifle."

Lieutenant John T. Greble, 2nd U.S. Artillery.

Federal infantry were repelled, but Artilleryman Greble refused to withdraw: "I never dodge! When I hear the bugle sound a retreat, I will leave, and not before." He was killed at his post. The Confederates had one dead, ten wounded, among them Private John Werth. The battle, according to the Southern chronicler, "showed to the boasting North how terribly we were in earnest, and gave . . . encouragement to the . . . weak-hearted on our side."

Major General Irvin McDowell, U.S.A.

A Scouting Party from the 1st Ohio Infantry near Fairfax Court House in June, 1861.

When Jefferson Davis moved the Confederate capital to Richmond in May, he furnished a focus for Northern war enthusiasm. "Onward to Richmond!" daily shrilled Horace Greeley's influential New York *Tribune,* and politicians picked up the cry. Yielding to pressure, President Lincoln ordered the scarcely organized Federal forces under General Irvin McDowell to advance. "At that time in the full flush of mature manhood, fully six feet tall, deep-chested, strong-limbed, clear-eyed," McDowell seemed to be "in every respect a fine and impressive soldier, but at dinner he was such a Gargantuan feeder and so absorbed in the dishes before him that he had but little time for conversation. While he drank neither wine nor spirits, he fairly gobbled the larger part of every dish within reach, and wound up with an entire watermelon, which he said was 'monstrous fine!'" His subordinates, "allowing him every professional qualification, . . . agreed that no officer who was so great a gourmand . . . could by any chance prove to be a great and successful leader of men."

In June scouting parties were pushed into Virginia, feeling out the Confederate forces near Fairfax Court House. On July 16 the main advance began. "Our men were in most excellent spirits," a Boston newspaperman reported, "and only evinced a general anxiety to *get started.*" "The sun shone brilliantly, and the fresh morning air was highly invigorating. The troops on foot started off as joyfully as if they were bound upon a New England picnic, or a clambake; and not the slightest . . . fear or uneasiness . . . seemed . . . to occupy . . . their thoughts. . . . The huge column fell into line at last, along the road. From an occasional elevation . . . we could see this immense body of men, in uniform dress, with stately tread and glistening arms, move steadily forward,—over twenty thousand strong at one point . . . all marching on—on 'to Fairfax.'"

Fairfax Court House.

At Fairfax Court House advance elements of Beauregard's army heard rumors that "McDowell was approaching with *a hundred thousand men* at his heels!" and hastily withdrew. "The enemy's flight was so precipitate," boasted McDowell, "that he left in our hands a quantity of flour, fresh beef, intrenching tools, hospital furniture and baggage." "From Fairfax," a reporter announced, "our brave army moves toward Manassas, and thence—we hope, without delay—to RICHMOND! The fever's up, and our bold troops ask only to be led, and listen earnestly for the thrilling order—'forward!'"

Ahead, at the crucial rail junction of Manassas, lay the main Confederate army, commanded by Beauregard, fresh from his victory at Sumter. Resembling in dress and appearance "a French Marshal of the Empire," he was planning Napoleonic strategy.

General Pierre Gustave Toutant Beauregard, C.S.A.

Bull Run.

Halfway between Centreville and Manassas, meandering in an easterly direction, lies Bull Run, "a small stream, . . . habitually low and sluggish" but "rapidly and frequently swollen by the summer rains until unfordable. The banks for the most part are rocky and steep, but abound in long-used fords. The country on either side, much broken and thickly wooded, becomes gently rolling and open as it recedes from the stream." On the south bank Beauregard deployed the 24,000 men in his command and waited impatiently for the reinforcements which President Davis had promised him. On July 20 he was joined by 6,000 soldiers of General Joseph E. Johnston, who had managed to elude the Federal forces appointed to hold them in the Shenandoah Valley. At once the mercurial Beauregard's spirits rose. "If I could only get the enemy to attack me, as I am trying to have him do," he wrote confidently, "I would stake my reputation on the handsomest victory that could be hoped for."

Too canny to force his way across Bull Run in the face of the main Confederate army, McDowell investigated the possibilities of a flanking movement. At first he considered going downstream to a point below Beauregard's forces, but reconnaissance and a limited action on July 18 convinced him that this plan was not feasible. Then Union scouts brought in reports of a slightly guarded ford in the opposite direction, at Sudley Springs, about three miles above the center of the Confederate position, where they said the stream could be crossed by wheeled vehicles. Ordering portions of his army to feint at the well guarded crossings, McDowell planned a surprise attack against the Confederate left flank. Before dawn on Sunday July 21, Union troops were put on the road. Confusion and mismanagement delayed them, and it was not until 9:30 that they reached Sudley Springs. The water at the ford was not deep, but the Federals, tired and thirsty, "got over very slowly, as many stopped to drink." Off to the south appeared warning "clouds of dust in the air." McDowell's plans had been detected, and Confederates were rushing to the defense.

Sudley Springs Ford.

**Burnside's Rhode Island Brigade and the 71st New York Regiment, Attacking
Confederate Batteries at Bull Run.**

Moving slowly to permit the ranks to close up, Rhode Island and New York regiments led the Union assault. Hastily summoned Confederate troops fought bitterly but were swept back. Beauregard attempted to rally them with a brief speech: "I reminded them that we fought for our homes, our firesides, and for the independence of our country. I urged them to the resolution of victory or death on that field." But artillery continued to prove more potent than eloquence, and the Union line steadily advanced. Gallantly the Confederates counterattacked, but they were forced back. "The enemy was evidently disheartened and broken," McDowell thought. "Three times was he repulsed . . . and driven back. . . . The third time it was supposed by us that the repulse was final, . . . and all were certain the day was ours."

On Matthews Hill "the scene of carnage was beyond description. Here a pile of dead and dying men; there struggling, crippled horses, and over the . . . hitherto peaceful fields, the surging, angry waves of battle still adding its victims to the long list."

Confederate Dead on Matthews Hill.

Ruins of the Henry House.

Severe fighting centered about the Henry House, on a height which dominated the battlefield. "Utterly unconscious it was to be the theatre of battle," the Henry family "made no effort to escape until it was too late to do so. Among them was an aged mother, whom the son and daughter carried to a gully, and for the first charge kept her out of the way of balls; but when the fight pressed on, they brought her in again; and when it returned they could not move her again. . . . The house was literally riddled with balls, and when the old lady was looked for, she had been sent to her long account. Many balls passed through her, and she was perfectly at rest."

The battle seemed to be a Union success, and when Jefferson Davis arrived on the field he was greeted with reports of disaster to the Confederate cause. But on the heights above Bull Run Southern troops desperately fought on. The brigade of Thomas Jonathan Jackson held on tenaciously, an inspiration to their disorganized comrades. General Barnard E. Bee rallied his depleted troops by pointing: "There is Jackson standing like a stone wall. Let us determine to die here, and we will conquer."

Alfred Ely, Congressman from New York.

The Union invasion had a holiday air about it. Sure of victory, Federal Congressmen, newspapermen, and "a few of the fairer, if not gentler sex," taking picnic baskets
in their buggies, had ridden out to see the fight. But when Congressman Alfred Ely
of New York "strolled down the road near to the scene of battle" he was captured by the
Confederates and imprisoned in Richmond.

Mrs. Spinner's House, Used as a Union Hospital During the First Battle of Bull Run.

The arrival of fresh Confederate troops from the Shenandoah Valley broke the Union assault, and the Federal line buckled. Retreat became rout, and panic swept soldiers and spectators back toward Washington. "I had read of retreats before," wrote W. T. Sherman, whose brigade had been heavily engaged in the battle, "have seen the noise and confusion of crowds of men at fires and shipwrecks, but nothing like this. It was as disgraceful as words can portray. . . ." The three-month Union volunteers who in April had so eagerly sought service now rejoiced that their time was up, and many of these summer soldiers refused to reenlist. "Nobody, no man, can save the country," Sherman lamented. "Our men are not good soldiers. They brag, but don't perform, complain sadly if they don't get everything they want, and a march of a few miles uses them up. It will take a long time to overcome these things, and what is in store for us in the future I know not."

A Union Volunteer of 1861.

Major General George Brinton McClellan, U.S.A.

II. McClellan and the Peninsula

"Circumstances make your presence here necessary," Lincoln telegraphed on July 22 to George Brinton McClellan. "Charge Rosecrans or some other general with your present department and come hither without delay." With McDowell's army transformed into "a confused mob, entirely demoralized," Lincoln was looking for a man to save Washington.

McClellan was the obvious choice. Only thirty-four years old, he had served with distinction in the Mexican War, and as American observer in the Crimean War had acquired something of a name as a military expert. When the outbreak of hostilities called him back into service, he was given command of the Department of the Ohio; and within a few weeks he drove the Confederates out of western Virginia. It was not a major campaign, but his well publicized successes came at a time when Federal armies were having few victories of any kind.

When he reached Washington, the new general in chief became the hero of the hour. He looked the part. Even "Bull Run" Russell of the London *Times* had to confess that the general was handsome. "He is a very squarely-built, thick-throated, broad-chested man, under the middle height, with slightly bowed legs, a tendency to *embonpoint*. His head, covered with a closely cut crop of dark auburn hair, is well set on his shoulders. His features are regular and prepossessing—the brow small, contracted, and furrowed; the eyes deep and anxious-looking. A short, thick, reddish moustache conceals his mouth; the rest of his face is clean shaven." McClellan radiated confidence, and Washington welcomed him as the man who had all the answers. "I find myself in a new and strange position here," he wrote, a bit boastfully, to his wife; "President, cabinet, Gen. Scott, and all deferring to me. By some strange operation of magic I seem to have become the power of the land."

The general was young, and his head was easily turned. Soon he developed a Messianic complex. "I receive letter after letter, have conversation after conversation, calling on me to save the nation, alluding to the presidency, dictatorship, etc.," he confided to Mrs. McClellan. "As I hope one day to be united with you for ever in heaven, I have no such aspiration. I would cheerfully take the dictatorship and agree to lay down my life when the country is saved. I am not spoiled by my unexpected new position. I feel sure that God will give me the strength and wisdom to preserve this great nation. . . . I feel that God has placed a great work in my hands. I have not sought it. I know how weak I am, but I know that I mean to do right, and I believe that God will help me and give me the wisdom I do not possess."

McClellan's moods oscillated between humility and elation. On the day after he arrived in Washington he announced, "I see already the main causes of our recent failure; I am sure that I can remedy these, and am confident that I can lead these armies of men to victory." "It is an immense task that I have on my hands," he told his wife, "but I believe I can accomplish it. . . . I can do it all."

Sally Port at Fort Slemmer, Arlington Heights, Virginia.

"I assumed command of the troops in the vicinity of Washington on Saturday, July 27, 1861, six days after the Battle of Bull Run," McClellan wrote. "I found no army to command; a mere collection of regiments, cowering on the banks of the Potomac. . . . Nothing of any consequence had been done to secure the southern approaches to the capital. . . . the city was almost in a condition to have been taken by a dash of a regiment of cavalry. Without one day's delay I undertook the difficult task assigned to me. . . ." On the outskirts of the city he ordered the construction of "a girdle of forts, earthworks, and camps." Around each fort was placed "a line of 'abatis,' and back of that a broad, deep ditch, or moat, partially filled with water." "One narrow draw-bridge at the sally-port or entrance of the fort" afforded the only exit, and it was predicted that any attacking party would be "more likely to find their graves in this treacherous, slippery ditch, than they were to scale the walls and capture the fort."

On the highest location about Washington, Fort Richardson was the most prominent of the new defenses. "The tents of the field and staff [officers] just crowned the summit of the slope facing toward the Potomac. A little farther down . . . in beautifully regular rows, running in terraces down the slope of the hill, were the tents of the men. . . . To the left of the camp was the fort with its girdling abatis, the white barracks just showing in a long line above the earthwork." It was "a camp not to be surpassed for beauty and comfort." From its height the soldiers could look out over the city, at "the vast proportions of the Capitol, . . . the majestic façade of the Treasury building, the unfinished shaft of the Washington monument, . . . the deep red feudal turrets of the Smithsonian . . . the gables of the Post-office and the Patent-office buildings. And then the river, broad and beautiful, sweeping past the city from the heights of Georgetown to the plains of Alexandria. . . . Beyond the city . . . every hill [was] covered with an earthwork or crested with tents."

1st Connecticut Artillery Drilling at Fort Richardson, Virginia.

Blockhouse near Aqueduct Bridge, Georgetown.

It took months to complete the fortifications, and meanwhile McClellan was fearful. "I am here in a terrible place," he informed his wife; "the enemy have from three to four times my force; the President, the old general [Scott], cannot or will not see the true state of affairs. Most of my troops are demoralized by the defeat at Bull Run; some regiments even mutinous. . . . I am weary of all this. I have no ambition in the present affairs; only wish to save my country, and find the incapables around me will not permit it. They sit on the verge of the precipice, and cannot realize what they see. Their reply to everything is, 'Impossible! Impossible!' They think nothing possible which is against their wishes." Across the river Confederate cannon on Munson's Hill seemed to threaten immediate attack. (They later were proved to be "a few Quaker guns of logs and pasteboard.") "I have, I believe, made the best possible disposition of the few men under my command," McClellan reported resignedly; "will try to make my movements as rapid and desperate as may be. If my men will only fight. . . ."

Not until September did McClellan feel reasonably secure. By "arresting all ignorant officers and men, and sending them back to their regiments; by . . . enforcing strict rules in regard to permission for leaving the camps; by prohibiting civilians and others not on duty from crossing the river or visiting the camps without permits from headquarters," he had brought "rigid discipline and order" to his Army of the Potomac. Soldiers had regular guard duty, inspection, drill. "I have a fine chance to see all the leading men of the nation here," reported one Yank happily; "and scarcely a day passes that we are not honored by a visit from 'Old Abe,' or a member of his cabinet. I was on guard at the gate of Fort Runyon, the other day, and along came two officers and simply said, 'The President,' and pretty soon along came 'Old Abe,' in a splendid carriage, accompanied by a young lady, followed by Secretaries Cameron and Seward, also accompanied by ladies. . . ."

Guards Examining Passes at Georgetown Ferry.

2nd Rhode Island Infantry at Camp Brightwood near Washington.

26th New York Infantry at Fort Lyon, Virginia.

96th Pennsylvania Infantry at Camp Northumberland, near Washington.

McClellan himself seemed omnipresent. Hours he spent in the saddle, visiting every part of his army. "I *must* ride much every day," he explained, "for my army covers much space. It is necessary for me to see as much as I can every day, and, more than that, to let the men see me and gain confidence in me." Trust him, they did. When he galloped down the lines on his black charger the soldiers cheered "Little Mac," and they sang:

"For McClellan's our leader; he is gallant and strong.

For God and our Country we are marching along."

Daily the papers described McClellan reconnoitering, drilling, and inspecting—but they could not report McClellan advancing. As months passed and the general gave no indication that he planned to use his splendid army, complaints began to register. The Confederates retained possession of the Manassas battlefield; in October they disastrously repelled a small Union force at Ball's Bluff; below the Capital they planted a battery which commanded the Potomac. Politicians protested, Lincoln prodded—and the general went into winter quarters.

Confederate Winter Barracks at Manassas.

Across the river in Virginia, the Confederates were having their own problems. During the autumn Southern forces had lived pleasantly in the open. "We have no tents and are within sound of the yankee drums," one Virginian wrote his wife. "I have never seen men so well and happy. We sleep on our arms and are constantly on duty, but the weather is fine and sleeping on the ground and breathing fresh air is very inspiriting."

Lacking resources for a fall offensive, the Southern army was obliged to go into winter quarters around Centreville and Manassas, where the soldiers erected "great villages of solidly-built log huts." "They were of round timber, laid in mud mortar, and roofed with slabs and puncheons: wooden pins being used for fastenings, even to the doors and latches." "All things considered," one of Hood's Texans reported, "our winter quarters are quite comfortable. They may lack symmetrical proportions, furniture, and now and then doors and roofs, but we have expended so much muscular energy upon them, and have taxed our combined architectural abilities so enormously, that we are . . . proud of them. . . ."

At first life in winter quarters delighted the Southern soldiers. "Barring guard and fatigue duty and the deprivation of female society," the Texan declared, "our time passes very pleasantly visiting friends in other companies and regiments and playing checkers, chess, and cards. Whist and euchre are the games most indulged in, but poker has many devotees. . . . No great amount of money is ever won or lost, for our amateur gamblers have not yet acquired the nerve of professionals, and never go beyond 'cent ante.'"

After a few weeks, however, the Confederates began to learn the meaning of boredom and hardship. Day after day, there was nothing to break "the dull monotony of camp life." Soldiers suffered from the "terribly cold and rainy" weather. Before spring the army keenly felt the shortages of man power, of arms, of supplies. Food became scarce; forage was difficult to procure; and fuel was almost non-existent. "The town was stripped and peeled. . . . Fences were gone; buildings were plundered; fields were scathed, and even the forests were hewn down."

Confederate Winter Quarters at Manassas.

"Quaker" Guns in a Confederate Fort on the Heights of Centreville.

In March, 1862, anticipating an advance by McClellan's superior forces, General Joseph E. Johnston, in direct command of the Army of Northern Virginia after the hot-tempered Beauregard quarreled with President Davis, drew back from Centreville and Manassas, and the Union troops took possession of the fortifications which had seemed so formidable. At Centreville they found "six well constructed earth forts, connected by good trenches and rifle-pits. In some of the embrasures the rebels had mounted painted logs, like cannon, looking defiance towards Washington. In one of them was mounted the smoke stack of an old locomotive. These were the Quaker guns that awed McClellan." Throughout the North an indignant laugh went up at McClellan's expense. If logs had immobilized him for a winter, what would real guns do?

McClellan, McDowell, and Their Staffs Crossing Bull Run at Blackburn's Ford.

With an escort of 2,000 cavalry, McClellan rode out to view the abandoned Confederate position. It was the old battlefield of Bull Run, where shells had twisted the "tree tops . . . in a hundred directions, as though struck by lightning." Now there was no action; merely silence. "All along . . . the road was one continuous string of huts, tents, and forts, all empty now—not a human being or animal showed themselves—not a sound save the clatter of the horses' hoofs, the shrill tones of the bugles, or the loud orders of the [Union] officers." "A column of smoke away off to the right indicated that Manassas was on fire." Confederate "machine shops, the station-houses, the Commissary and Quarter-master store-houses" were "all in ashes. On the track stood the wreck of a locomotive, and not far down the remains of four freight cars which had been burned; to the right, five hundred barrels of flour had been stove in. . . . Some fifty barrels of pork and beef had been scattered around in the mud, and a few hundred yards down the track a dense cloud of smoke was arising from the remains of a factory. . . ."

[37]

Union Charge upon Confederate Forces at the Stone Wall, Battle of Kernstown.

Instead of advancing overland against Richmond, McClellan proposed to campaign on the Peninsula, between the York and James rivers. Here, with supplies assured by Union control of the sea, he could flank the Southern forces and swiftly seize their capital.

About to embark for the Peninsula, the general had his plans upset when on March 23 Stonewall Jackson attacked Shields's division at Kernstown, in the Shenandoah Valley. "We . . . took position and were soon hotly engaged," a Confederate recalled. "There was a stone fence between two fields running parallel with the lines of battle—a Federal regiment on one side a short distance from it, and the 37th Va., about the same distance on the other side, advancing towards each other. Both regiments charged for the fence about the same time, and it was 'nip and tuck' which would reach it first; but the 37th Va., got there and, kneeling down, poured a deadly volley into the other at close quarters, and nearly annihilated it." But with superior numbers the Federals pushed Jackson back. He could be content with his defeat, for the engagement further frightened Washington, and Lincoln detached McDowell's troops from the Peninsula expedition to defend the Capital.

[38]

From the outset President Lincoln had many reservations about McClellan's proposed campaign, for he preferred a direct advance along the railroad south of Manassas. When the Confederate ironclad *Virginia* (formerly the *Merrimac*) appeared off Hampton Roads on March 8 and threatened to drive the Union fleet from the Chesapeake, he became more than ever convinced that McClellan's plan was unsafe, and Jackson's foray in the Valley renewed his fear that the defenses of the Capital had been stripped. But the President still had faith in the infallibility of the military mind, and, though he reduced the number of troops accompanying McClellan, he reluctantly allowed the Peninsula expedition to set forth.

On April 2 McClellan reached Fort Monroe. The near-by village of Hampton had been abandoned and burned by the Confederates the previous fall. "It was a nice town," a Georgia soldier reflected; "but we could not hold it so we concluded to break up the yankees from there as it would make good . . . quarters for them."

Ruins at Hampton, Virginia.

The first Confederate defense line lay across the Peninsula at Yorktown. In reality it was hastily prepared and undermanned; but to the Union soldiers the fortifications seemed "miniature mountain ranges . . . , deeply ditched, and revetted with sods, fascines, hurdles, gabions or sand bags. Along the York riverside there were water batteries of surpassing beauty, that seemed, at a little distance, successions of gentle terraces. Their pieces were likewise of enormous calibre, and their number almost incredible. The advanced line of fortifications stretched from the mouth of Warwick Creek on the South, to a point fifteen miles distant on the York . . . ; but there were two other concentric lines. . . . The remote series consisted of six forts of massive size and height, fronted by swamps and flooded meadows, with frequent creeks and ravines interposing; sharp fraise and abatis planted against scarp and slope, pointed cruelly eastward. There were two water batteries, of six and four thirty-two Columbiads respectively. . . ."

Confederate Naval Gun at Yorktown.

Reconnaissance in force by Genl Gorman before Yorktown.
Rebel Battery only three hundred yards distant behind the wood

Reconnaissance in Force by Brigadier General Willis A. Gorman Before Yorktown.

Holding the Confederate line until reinforcement could be drawn from Johnston's army was "Prince John" Magruder. Fond of amateur theatricals, the general had now every opportunity to indulge his talent. "He marched a couple of regiments through a clearing, in sight of the Federal advance guard, double-quicked them around a little forest out of sight, and then marched them through the clearing again—over and over, like a stage manager using a dozen adenoidal spear carriers to represent Caesar's legions." Reconnoitering Union officers concluded that the enemy was "in strong force and very strong position," and McClellan ordered a siege. As Johnston said, "No one but McClellan would have hesitated to attack."

For nearly a month McClellan was detained at Yorktown—completely losing any advantage that surprise might have given his Peninsula campaign. Not for this general were daring assaults and spectacular tactics; he was going to wage war by the books. Remembering "the fault of the Allies at Sebastopol," he believed that his measures were "quietly preparing the way for great success." "I have brought forty heavy guns in battery," he reported on April 23; "to-morrow night I hope to have twelve new guns and five to ten heavy mortars in battery. . . . I will not open fire unless the enemy annoys us, hoping to get all the guns in battery and the trenches well advanced before meeting with serious opposition."

[41]

Wagon Trains at Yorktown.

"The maps of the Peninsula," McClellan found, "are perfectly unreliable; the roads are wrong. . . ." From the outset his problem of supply was difficult; and it was bound to become increasingly so as he progressed up the Peninsula. His quartermaster's department struggled with demands for "horses for artillery and cavalry, . . . tents, camp and garrison equipage, forage, lumber, and all materials for camps, . . . barracks, hospitals, . . . ambulances, . . . clothes [for] the army." "Several thousands wagons, and the Richmond & York River Railroad, were employed for land-transportation; and steam-vessels, brigs, schooners, sloops, and barges, almost without number, brought the supplies."

Still McClellan demanded more supplies and reinforcements. "Wagons and troops" he called "absolutely necessary to enable me to advance to Richmond. I have by no means the transportation I must have to move my army even a few miles."

McClellan christened his headquarters near Yorktown Camp Winfield Scott, and he pitched his tent "on a magnificent plateau in the midst of . . . 30,000 men." Less than two miles from the Confederate lines, it was screened by high trees. Union siege preparations were hastened. "Steam sawmills are hard at work all round turning out material for the fortifications," reported an English newspaper man, "and my glass shows me companies of men in the distance building bridges and trains of wagons passing to and fro in all directions. It is a panorama far too grand and extended for words to describe accurately."

General McClellan's Tent, Camp Winfield Scott.

Battery No. 4 near Yorktown, Mounting Ten 13-Inch Mortars.

"I suppose ere this you have heard that we are having a fight at Yorktown at last," a Georgia soldier wrote to his family on April 16. "The enemy shelled us yesterday from their fleet and this morning they are pitching in on land. Though the enemy have shelled us for eleven days, they have injured us hardly any; I think we have lost about 4 or 5 killed and a very few wounded. I have had Bombs and Minnie Balls to whistle all around me, but fortunately they did me no harm. . . ." Laboriously McClellan brought up 13-inch mortars, each weighing 20,000 pounds; and "by the night of May 3 all the batteries were completed and nearly all armed." The big guns never fired a shot, for early the next morning the Confederates withdrew.

For hours the withdrawal was undetected, for, as the Comte de Paris remarked, "they were not early risers in the Union armies." "The disappointment was so great at the sudden departure of the Confederates that at first it could not be believed; and when the evidence was conclusive, everything had to be organized for an advance, which had not been contemplated. The troops had eaten nothing; the rations had not been distributed; many regiments had sent their wagons to a distance of several leagues to obtain them. In short, the cavalry division only took up its line of march between ten and eleven o'clock. . . ." The Confederates had escaped.

Pursuing the Confederate Troops After the Evacuation of Yorktown.

Brigadier General Philip Kearny at the Battle of Williamsburg, May 5, 1862.

"I do not want these rascals to get away from me without a sound drubbing," McClellan wrote; but when the Federals caught up with the retreating Confederates at Williamsburg the Union commander was still in Yorktown. In a confused and planless operation Union advance units were thrown back by fierce fire from the Confederate rear guard.

An urgent plea for support was sent to Phil Kearny, who had just been promoted to command a division in Heintzelman's corps. "We have the honor of saving an army!" he called to his troops, and dashed off to the front.

"Hadn't you better let Hooker go in and help you?" Heintzelman asked. "You are a stranger to your command."

And Kearny laughed: "General Heintzelman, on every occasion I can make men follow me to hell!"

The war was a great adventure, and from private to general men assumed a heroic stance. A young lieutenant colonel like William B. Hyde still wore his dress uniform and flourished his heavy cavalry saber. It was a picture-book war.

Lieutenant Colonel William B. Hyde, 9th New York Cavalry.

Embarkation of Major General John E. Wool's Division at Hampton Roads.

Discouraged by McClellan's slow progress, President Lincoln decided to look over the situation personally. Accompanied by Secretary of War Stanton and Secretary of the Treasury Chase, he arrived at Hampton Roads and reviewed the troops there under the command of General Wool, a seventy-eight-year-old veteran of the War of 1812, still full of fight. While awaiting the arrival of McClellan from the front Secretary Chase proposed a military maneuver of his own. Across the James River lay Norfolk, now a Confederate naval base, and in its harbor the *Merrimac*, which still could do heavy damage to Federal transports. Wool's troops must capture the port. In a tug Chase reconnoitered the Confederate side of the river and found "not only an available, but a most admirable, landing-place, with depth of water sufficient for the largest transport to approach to within a few feet of the shore." Lincoln too inspected the southern bank and pronounced the plan practicable. On May 10 he, Chase, and Wool (shown conferring in the foreground of the illustration) ordered an assault. When the Federals landed, they found the Confederates had hastily withdrawn, and the "mayor, with all the formality of a medieval warden, appeared with a bunch of rusty keys" to surrender the city. The *Merrimac*, now cut off from supplies, was abandoned by her crew and her magazine fired. "So ended a brilliant week's campaign by the President, recorded Chase, "for I think it quite certain that if he had not gone down, Norfolk would still have been in the possession of the enemy, and the *Merrimac* as grim and defiant as ever." New York newspapers hailed "President Lincoln's First Military and Naval Operation—Its Great Success."

Meanwhile McClellan was slowly advancing up the Peninsula. Nature itself seemed to be against him. "The weather is infamous," he exclaimed; "it has been raining all night, and is still raining heavily; no signs of stopping; roads awful. . . . The weather has delayed us terribly." "The roads were in horrible condition. In the mud and slush and deep ruts cut by the wagon-trains and artillery . . . , heavy guns became bogged and the horses were unable to drag them." "Guns and wagons sank to the axles and beyond. One officer wrote later that he saw a mule sink completely out of sight, all but its ears, in the middle of what was supposed to be a main road. He added that it was a rather small mule." Union ordnance offered particular difficulties, for the artillery was of many makes and sizes, and each gun had to have its own ammunition.

Union Ordnance Ready for Transportation from Yorktown.

Encampment of the Army of the Potomac at Cumberland Landing.

On May 13 the Union army "again pulled up stakes and moved five or six miles, and brought up at Cumberland Landing, on the Pamunkey River." "Here," recorded a Wisconsin diarist, "on a large plain, surrounded by an amphitheatre of bluffs, were collected about 70,000 of our troops, presenting from the high ground a most magnificent sight." "On all sides but the north there were tents,—high marquees for the officers, and low shelter-tents for the men. To the northward was the river with its gunboats. . . . In every other direction . . . there was a solid mass of tents and artillery and wagons, extending to a great distance. Twenty square miles were . . . covered by that camp. . . ."

Between McClellan's army and Richmond lay the Chickahominy River, ordinarily "about forty feet wide, . . . and bordered by low, marshy bottom-lands varying from half a mile to a mile in width." Heavy rains had made the river "absolutely impassable without bridges." Some troops McClellan set to constructing causeways. "The work was mainly done in the water, sometimes waist-deep, and amid mud and tangled underbrush." Other forces attempted to seize the existing bridges. A Confederate garrison at Mechanicsville, dominating the important New Bridge, drove off an initial Union attack. But when artillery joined in the assault, the Southerners hastily retreated and "in their flight left behind them a part of their knapsacks and a flag of one of their regiments." Union soldiers found the village badly mauled: "Every house shows the effect of our shot and shell. Houses are perfectly riddled, the balls entering on one side and going through on the other, and through the building in the rear. . . . Trees . . . fifteen inches in diameter, have holes through them."

Union Forces Pursuing Confederates Through Mechanicsville, May 24, 1862.

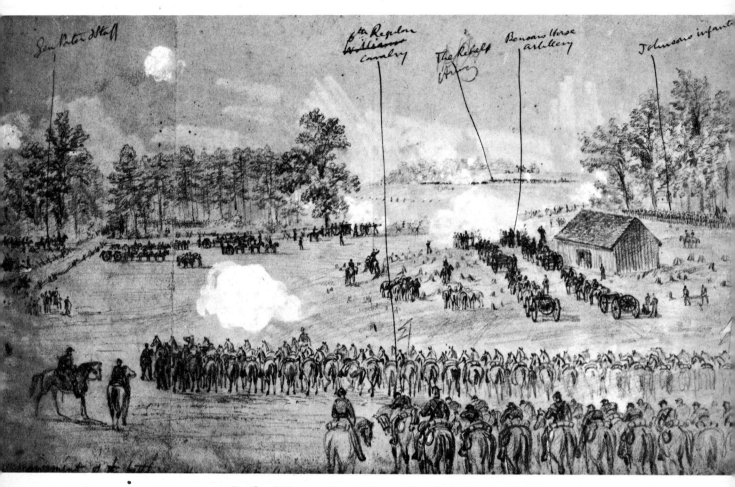

Battle of Hanover Court House, May 27, 1862, at 1:45 P.M.

McClellan kept urging that McDowell's forces be sent overland to join in the assault upon Richmond. Confederate troops at Hanover Court House were in a position to block the planned juncture, and on May 27 Fitz-John Porter was ordered to disperse them. "After a fatiguing march of fourteen miles through the mud and rain," the Federals found the Confederate picket line about noon. Captain Benson's horse artillery wheeled into position, and after an hour the Confederate line broke. Pursuing Union troops were attacked by the main body of the enemy, and Porter prepared for further battle. "A strong line of skirmishers were thrown out in advance. . . . the regiments went through the woods, at the edge of which they were halted till the line was perfectly formed and the position of the enemy ascertained. In this order the command emerged from the woods, the skirmishers firing in front. The splendid appearance of the brigade as it came into the wheat-fields, and the vigorous fire of the skirmishers, had the effect of putting the enemy to flight."

Benson's Battery, 2nd U.S. Artillery.

Cavalry and horse artillery headed the pursuit, while "those regiments preserving their first formation still steadily advanced, at shoulder arms, across the extensive fields, over a rough ravine and through the woods."

McClellan was pleased with his favorite subordinate. "Fitz did his work nobly, as I expected," he wrote. "I am quietly clearing out everything that could threaten my rear and communications, providing against the contingency of disaster, and so arranging as to make my whole force available in the approaching battle. The only fear is that Joe's [General Johnston's] heart may fail him. . . ."

Major General Erasmus D. Keyes, U.S.A.

Disturbed by Confederate operations in the Shenandoah, Lincoln on May 25 wired to McClellan bluntly: "I think the time is near when you must either attack Richmond or give up the job and come to the defence of Washington." Already McClellan had advanced his Fourth Corps, under Keyes, across the Chickahominy toward Fair Oaks, where the Confederates were waiting.

[54]

Brigadier General Benjamin Huger, C.S.A.

Johnston seized the opportunity to attack the Union army divided by the swollen river. Commanding the Confederate right was Benjamin Huger (pronounced "Hu-gee"). "He is from South Carolina, a scion of an old Huguenot family," wrote one of his men, "and . . . does not look a bit like a 'fire-eater,' as the South Carolinians are supposed to be, but a staid, even-tempered, kindly man. I like him."

Union Artillerymen in Unfinished Redoubt Before the Battle of Fair Oaks.

On the morning of May 31 Union troops north of the Chickahominy heard "the booming of the cannon . . . in all directions." Despite muddled orders and Huger's slowness, Johnston had fallen in force upon the Federals south of the river. "Bullets commenced to whiz over our heads in piping tones," recalled one Union participant; "sometimes they sounded like a very small circular saw cutting through thin strips of wood, and sometimes like great blue flies; some flew high, and some low. . . ." Keyes seemed trapped.

Desperately McClellan sought to rush reinforcements; but even the weather favored the South. "In the afternoon the gathering clouds betokened a storm, which burst . . . in a deluge of rain, mingled with the most vivid lightning and the heaviest thunder." The Chickahominy became impassable. Sumner's men finally found a bridge and "crossed its length in safety, though the swollen current already hid some of the timbers and threatened to lift them from their places." The battle was still raging about the twin farmhouses at Seven Pines. "Bullets flew in myriads around us," wrote one Union veteran, "humming deadly songs, hitting our men, and splintering the trees around us so that I thought the fine pieces of wood flew in my face."

Union Artillery at Fair Oaks Station.

Inflation of the Balloon *Intrepid* to Reconnoiter the Battle of Fair Oaks.

In this difficult terrain cavalry was almost worthless, and McClellan relied heavily upon aerial reconnaissance by Professor T. S. C. Lowe (shown to the right with his hand on the balloon). During the battle of Fair Oaks, Professor Lowe, "who had two balloons of large size, ample arrangements for the manufacture of hydrogen, and complete apparatus for the speedy inflation of his delicate globes," remained aloft almost constantly. "With the aid of good glasses," wrote a reporter who ascended during the engagement, "we were enabled to view the whole affair between these powerful contending armies. . . . Occasionally a masked Rebel battery would open upon our brave fellows. In such cases the occupants of the balloon would inform our artillerists of its position, and the next shot or two would, in every case, silence the masked and annoying customer."

On Sunday June 1, balloon observers watched "the enemy retreating toward Richmond. . . . From the scene of battle into the city of Richmond the road was literally lined

Professor T. S. C. Lowe Observing the Battle of Fair Oaks.

with ambulances, wagons, and carts, conveying dead and wounded. About twilight we saw camp-fires innumerable around the city . . . which showed us to a certainty that the main body of their army had fallen back to Richmond."

General Joseph Eggleston Johnston, C.S.A.

Burying the Dead and Burning the Horses After the Battle of Fair Oaks.

McClellan considered the battle "a glorious victory." The Confederate army was driven back, and its commander, General Johnston, struck by two balls, "fell from his horse and broke two of his ribs." To replace him President Davis immediately appointed Robert E. Lee.

For both sides the engagement was costly. After the battle the very soil around Fair Oaks seemed to one Massachusetts soldier to have "the damp, mouldy odor" of blood. "The surgeons were at work cutting off legs and arms with the most businesslike air, and near by the rebel dead, to the number of hundreds, perhaps, were being buried in a long trench, where they were laid without mark or distinction, side by side, and covered with four or five feet of earth decently and without injury."

Major General Thomas Jonathan Jackson.

McClellan's success received little acclaim in Washington; the President's mind was elsewhere. For in the Shenandoah Valley "a particularly seedy, sleepy-looking old fellow, whose uniform and cap were very dirty, and who bestrode a regular Rosinante of a horse" was terrorizing Federal commanders. He was called Stonewall Jackson.

Captain Alcibiades De Blanc and Lieutenant Robert S. Perry of the 8th Louisiana Infantry.

Washington watched in panic as Jackson fell upon the scattered Federal armies in the Valley. Outthinking, outplanning, outfighting his enemy, he would make a daring, slashing attack, and then push his men on to fresh battle before the Union commanders could catch their breath. Stripped to barest essentials, his troops marched so fast they became known as "Jackson's foot cavalry." "All Old Jackson gave us was a musket, a hundred rounds, and a gum blanket," said one Confederate, "and he druv us like hell."

Bewildered Federals fled down the Valley, toward the Potomac and toward Washington. "The pride of the Yankee army . . . that had exultingly and insolently ridden over our Valley," wrote one of Jackson's men to his wife, "was melted like snow before the sun, and the road, for miles, strewn with the choicest of viands and most valuable of goods. I am not vindictive, but . . . it seemed a just retribution for the evils they had inflicted on an innocent people. . . . We pursued the foe, that had gloried in its pride and power . . . amid the huzzas, shouts, tears, thanks, looks of unutterable delight, waving of Confederate flags and of handkerchiefs of [the] whole liberated population . . . and . . . the General, now thoroughly aroused, . . . said 'Order the whole army to press on to the Potomac.'"

Brigadier General Robert Huston Milroy, U.S.A.

Lieutenant Colonel Thomas L. Kane, 13th Pennsylvania Reserves, U.S.A.

On May 8 Jackson struck the brigades of Milroy and Schenck at McDowell; on the 23rd he hit part of Banks's forces at Front Royal; on the 25th he drove Banks himself from Winchester; and by May 29 he was threatening Harpers Ferry.

Federal forces in the Valley were not cowardly but merely confused. When the Union commander planned to abandon the field at Harrisonburg (June 6), Lieutenant Colonel Kane of the Pennsylvania "Bucktails" remonstrated: "General, think how such a stampede as this will dishearten and demoralize the army. Let me at 'em, General, with my Bucktails!"

"Just forty minutes, I'll give you, Colonel," replied the General.

"Good-bye," replied Kane. "I hope to see you again, but if I don't, take it for granted that I and my Bucktails have given a good account of ourselves."

By night his small command was decimated, and Kane himself was wounded and was a prisoner of the Confederates.

The Battle of Cross Keys, Virginia, June 8, 1862.

Lincoln saw a chance to trap Jackson, and he ordered McDowell's forces to join Frémont in the Valley. Skillfully retreating, Jackson slipped between the converging Union armies and, when they pursued, fell upon them separately. On June 8 he accepted battle from Frémont at Cross Keys. Though incorrectly dated, Edward Forbes's drawing gives an accurate view of the engagement from the Union side: 1, Blue Ridge Mountains; 2, Confederate army in the woods; 3, Cross Keys; 4, Union artillery; 5, Union infantry advancing to attack the Confederate right flank; 6, ambulances; 7, Union hospital; 9, road to Harrisonburg.

The next day Jackson struck Shields's division of McDowell's army at Port Republic (8, in Forbes's drawing), slipped through a pass in the mountains, and set off in haste to join Lee.

Brigadier General George Stoneman and His Staff.

Meanwhile, north of Richmond the Army of the Potomac lay idle. Lee was planning an offensive and sent his dashing cavalry commander, "Jeb" Stuart, out to reconnoiter. In three days (June 12–15) the Confederate horsemen rode entirely around McClellan's army, while Union cavalry under General Stoneman unsuccessfully pursued. Asked if he had "caught Stuart," one angry Federal officer replied: "No, he has gone in at the back door. I only saw his rear-guard as it passed the swamp."

Major General Fitz-John Porter, U.S.A.

Captain John C. Tidball and Staff, Battery A, 2nd U.S. Artillery.

Still expecting McDowell's army, McClellan had left Fitz-John Porter's corps north of the Chickahominy to make contact with the anticipated reinforcements. Lee, strengthened by Jackson's return, planned to fall upon the exposed wing of the Union army, and on June 26 attacked at Mechanicsville. The village itself was indefensible, and Porter's plan was "to invite a heavy attack, and then, by rapid withdrawal, to incite such confidence in the enemy as to induce incautious pursuit." Advancing Confederates were swept by Union fire, and such artillerymen as Captain Tidball coolly covered the Federal withdrawal. Confederate casualties totaled nearly 2,000; the Union loss was 360.

On the following day the Confederate assault was renewed at Gaines's Mill. "The terrible fighting,—the tornadoes of musketry, and the volleys of thunderbolts from hundreds of cannon," asserted a New York reporter, "have not been paralleled by this army, despite Williamsburg and Fair Oaks." For a time the Union line seemed to be holding. Then the magnificent John Bell Hood shouted to the Fourth Texas regiment: "Fix bayonets! Make ready! Aim! Fire! Charge!" "The timber between us and the enemy hid them from view," wrote one of Hood's men, "but we pulled triggers nevertheless, and rushed down the hill into and across the branch, at the Yankees in the first line of breastworks. They waited not for the onset, but fled like a flock of sheep, carrying with them their supports in the second and third lines."

Ruins of Gaines's Mill After the Operations of 1862 and 1864.

Union Field Hospital at Savage Station, Virginia, June 30, 1862.

McClellan now found himself isolated and surrounded in enemy country. He determined to shift his base of operations and "to make a very dangerous and difficult movement to reach the James river." The army would have to march light, and he ordered all excess supplies destroyed. Pursuing Confederates found the "whole country . . . full of deserted plunder, army wagons, and pontoon-trains partially burned or crippled; mounds of grain and rice and hillocks of mess beef smouldering; tens of thousands of axes, picks, and shovels; camp kettles gashed with hatchets; medicine chests with their drugs stirred into a foul medley. . . ." Left behind also were 2,500 wounded at the Savage Station Hospital, who fell into Confederate hands.

Union Military Bridge over the Chickahominy River.

To reach safety on the James, McClellan had to lead his weary troops across the Chickahominy and through the bottomless White Oak Swamp. "In some places all of a mile in width, and supporting on its treacherous surface a luxuriant growth," the swamp at points "presented the character of a stream. . . . In the depths of this morass, the home of almost every variety of Virginia reptiles, the soldiers worked . . . constructing the causeways. The cutting of dams above, and heavy rains . . . [converted] the whole valley into a broad lake, whose waters, pressing through the length of the swamp carried everything irresistibly before them. . . . The air seemed to be suffocating with stagnation, while beneath the pall of mist, an immense orchestra of double-bass bull frogs kept up a continual din, which at night drowned the rumble of the wagons over the corduroys."

White Oak Swamp.

Brigadier General Philip Kearny's Division at the Battle of Glendale, June 30, 1862.

As McClellan moved, Lee pursued, and there followed day after day of fighting. "In a fight, such as is represented in the picture," Alfred R. Waud wrote of his sketch of Glendale (Frayser's Farm), "it is impossible to get a view of an extended line of battle from any one point. A majority of the battles so far have been of this description, usually termed bushwhacking—very deadly but hardly affording a chance for display of tactics. For the rest, the picture describes itself, and gives a good idea of what our soldiers have to stand up to in the Virginia swamp and woods."

Reaching the James, McClellan occupied Malvern Hill. Lee ordered an assault. A Wisconsin soldier described the slaughter: "Charge after charge is made on our artillery, with a demoniac will to take it, if it costs them half their army. Down it mows their charging ranks, till they lie in heaps and rows, from behind which our men fight as securely as if in rifle pits. . . . The slaughter is terrible, and to add to the carnage, our gun boats are throwing their murderous missles with furious effect into the ranks of our enemy." At nightfall the Confederates desisted, and McClellan rapidly removed his troops to Harrison's Landing, directly under the protection of the Federal gunboats.

[74]

The Fifth Corps Under Brigadier General Fitz-John Porter at Malvern Hill, July 1, 1862.

United States Gunboats Shelling the Confederates at the Battle of Malvern Hill.

Private Edwin Francis Jennison of a Georgia Infantry Regiment, Killed at Malvern Hill.

In the Seven Days both sides suffered severely. McClellan's casualties were 15,849; Lee's, 20,135. Some regiments had almost disappeared as effective units. The 4th Michigan Infantry, for example, lost 164 men at Malvern Hill alone. "Dear Molly," wrote a Georgia soldier on July 4. "Thanks be to God I have been spared to write to you once more. . . .

A Private of Company F, 4th Michigan Infantry, U.S.A.

We have had one of the greatest battles ever fought on this continent and have driven the grand army of the north from every position they have taken. We have lost a great many men but this must needs have been. We have taken over ten thousand prisoners. I hope this will stop the war but it may not."

Major General Don Carlos Buell, U.S.A.

III. War in the West

"The Mississippi is the great problem of the Civil War," announced W. T. Sherman in 1861, "and will require large forces and good troops." Less publicized than the struggles before Richmond, the war in the West decided the fate of the Confederacy.

In 1861 the border states of Kentucky and Missouri were in a pivotal position. In Missouri civil war broke out, with Governor Claiborne Jackson struggling to lead his state into secession and Francis P. Blair, Jr., organizing the Unionists. The Federal commander at St. Louis, John C. Frémont, proved incompetent, and in August Union troops were defeated at Wilson's Creek. Not until Henry W. Halleck replaced Frémont were the Confederates driven back; and in March, 1862, they were decisively defeated at Pea Ridge, in northwestern Arkansas. Except for "bushwhacking" by guerrillas, Missouri was saved for the Union.

Meanwhile Kentucky attempted to remain neutral, though by September, 1861, the fiction had to be abandoned. Commander of all the Confederate forces in the West was Albert Sidney Johnston, of whom Jefferson Davis said: "If *he* is not a general, there is not *one* among us." Opposing Johnston in eastern Kentucky was Don Carlos Buell, the McClellan of the West, a firm disciplinarian, an admirable tactician, but a slow fighter. Hoping to liberate the large Unionist population in East Tennessee, Lincoln repeatedly urged Buell to advance; but the general found roads impassable, forage non-existent, and the enemy overwhelming.

The principal Western fighting of 1861–1862, therefore, occurred in western Tennessee. Here the key points in Johnston's defensive line were Forts Henry and Donelson, which commanded the Tennessee and Cumberland rivers where they were only eleven miles apart. If these could be seized the Union gunboats could steam up the two rivers in a vast arc behind Johnston's positions, and the Confederate front in the West would collapse. On February 6 a joint army-navy expedition commanded by U. S. Grant and Andrew H. Foote reduced Fort Henry; and Fort Donelson surrendered ten days later. It was the first major Union victory of the war.

"The blow was most disastrous," Johnston lamented, "and almost without remedy." Hastily he retreated. Buell took Nashville, and Grant's army pushed into southern Tennessee. At Shiloh on April 6 Johnston attempted to check Grant's advance, but timely reinforcements from Buell turned Union defeat into victory and drove the Southern army back into Mississippi.

Far to the south a fleet under Farragut and Porter entered the lower Mississippi, fought its way past Confederate defenses, and on April 25 reached New Orleans. Vicksburg remained the last important Confederate stronghold on the river. As Sherman had predicted: "Mississippi will be the grand field of operations."

Major General Francis Preston Blair, Jr., U.S.A.

"Leading spirit and chief adviser" of Missouri Unionists was Francis Preston Blair, Jr., Republican Congressman who later resigned to become a Union general. His father had helped Jackson save the Union in 1833; his brother was in Lincoln's cabinet. Fearing that Southern sympathizers would seize the arsenal at St. Louis, Blair, with Lincoln's blessing, secretly organized and drilled the "true and patriotic" Germans of Missouri.

Battle of Wilson's Creek. Repulse of Confederate Cavalry by Captain Totten's Artillery.

Blair's chief aide was a "little rough-visaged, red-bearded, weather-beaten Connecticut captain" named Nathaniel Lyon, who broke up the secessionist camp near St. Louis and then chased the pro-Southern governor from the capital. In July when John C. Frémont arrived to take command, it seemed that he had only to consolidate the victory.

Despite his abolitionist pronouncements which gained him vast prestige in radical circles, Frémont proved to be hopeless; certainly incompetent, his administration was also considered to be corrupt. He failed properly to support Lyon, who on August 10 met the Confederates at Wilson's Creek, in southwestern Missouri. Though (as shown in the drawing) a Confederate cavalry charge was repulsed by Union artillery under Captain James Totten, the Southerners rallied fiercely. Confederate General Sterling Price "rode up and down the line," with "white hair streaming in the wind, cheering, forming, and encouraging his ragged musketeers" to make a new attack. Lyon himself, "at the head of the column, and pretty nearly in the first fire," was fatally wounded, and the Union troops retreated in disorder toward St. Louis.

Watching Missouri affairs closely, Lincoln reluctantly concluded that Frémont was "the prey of wicked and designing men . . . [and had] absolutely no military capacity."

Major General Samuel Ryan Curtis, U.S.A.

It was months before the Union forces could resume the offensive. Meanwhile Frémont gave way to Halleck, and Samuel R. Curtis, whom Lincoln knew to be "honest, capable, faithful and patriotic" succeeded to Lyon's command. Cautiously advancing through southwestern Missouri, Curtis caught up with the Confederates just across the border in Arkansas, at Pea Ridge (also called Elkhorn Tavern).

Brigadier General Albert Pike, C.S.A.

The Confederate commander, Earl Van Dorn, attempted elaborate strategy, far too complicated for his heterogeneous force, which included half-organized regiments of Indians commanded by Albert Pike, Arkansas newspaperman, poet, Sanskrit scholar, and Mason (shown here in his Masonic regalia). The Confederate defeat (March 7–8, 1862) ended major Southern operations in Missouri and opened Arkansas to invasion.

Major General Henry Wager Halleck, U.S.A.

Halleck received credit for the victory. Author of standard works on tactics, "Old Brains" was thought to be the strategist behind the Western victories. Most of the admiration, one suspects, came from those who never saw the general, for anyone who observed "his bulging eyes, his flabby cheeks, his slack-twisted figure, and his slow and deliberate movements, and noted his sluggish speech, lacking in point and magnetism" experienced "a distinct feeling of disappointment."

Rear Admiral Andrew Hull Foote, U.S.N.

But Halleck was fortunate in his aides. One was a brigadier general from Illinois named Ulysses S. Grant. Cooperating, in command of naval operations in the Western waters, was Flag Officer Andrew H. Foote. "A strict disciplinarian, he gained to an unusual degree, the attachment and confidence of his crews"—they liked him even when he attempted to substitute a temperance sermon for their ration of grog.

Foote regarded his river operations as complementary to the army's; "they were like blades of shears," he said, "united, invincible; separated, almost useless." When his gunboats, constructed "to draw 6 feet of water, carry 13 heavy guns each, be plated with 2½ inch iron, and have a speed of 9 miles an hour," were ready, Foote joined Grant, with Halleck's authorization, in attacking the Confederate forts on the Tennessee and Cumberland rivers. First Fort Henry surrendered; then Donelson asked for Grant's terms. "No terms except an unconditional and immediate surrender can be accepted," replied Grant tersely. "I propose to move immediately upon your works."

The fall of the forts opened all of central Tennessee to the Federal fleet. Lieutenant S. L. Phelps boldly sailed his gunboats up the Tennessee to Florence, Alabama; other vessels assisted Buell in the capture of Nashville. The Confederates had lost, and the Federals had gained, an indestructible supply route.

Army Transport on the Tennessee.

The Last Charge at the Battle of Shiloh, April 7, 1862.

At Shiloh (Pittsburg Landing) Confederates struck at Grant's army. The first day of the battle, April 6, favored the assailants, though their commander, Albert Sidney Johnston, was killed. Union lines were forced back in great disorder; whole companies broke and fled. Along the Tennessee huddled "stragglers lying under cover of the river-bluff, panic-stricken, most of whom would have been shot where they lay, without resistance before they would have taken muskets and marched to the front." Only reinforcements from Buell's army saved the day.

The next morning the Union army rallied and took the offensive. Against the Confederate center Grant himself grouped six regiments for a charge which, like most other aspects of the battle of Shiloh, became a matter of controversy. Henry Lovie editorialized on his sketch: "Gen Grant present at this charge was tortured into the 'Charge of Gen. Grant' which never took place." At any rate, the attack came "with such desperate force" that the Confederates "broke and ran. Retreat at once became general. Within half an hour the whole rebel army was falling back in dismay."

The U.S.S. Cairo, Part of the Federal Fleet at the Battle of Memphis.

Along the Mississippi, meanwhile, the Union fleet was operating. Island No. 10 and Fort Pillow were reduced, and on June 6 the gunboats moved down the river to the Confederate defenses at Memphis. "Thousands of people crowded the high bluffs overlooking the river," related the Union commander. "The roar of the cannon and shell shook the houses on shore on either side for many miles. First wild yells, shrieks, and clamors, then loud, despairing murmurs, filled the affrighted city. The screaming, plunging shell crashed into the boats, blowing some of them and their crews into fragments, and the rams rushed upon each other like wild beasts in deadly conflict. Blinding smoke hovered about the scene of all this confusion and horror; and, as the battle progressed and the Confederate fleet was destroyed, all the cheering voices on shore were silenced."

Rear Admiral David Dixon Porter, U.S.N.

A Union Mortar Schooner.

Below New Orleans the Mississippi is tortuous and tricky, and the Confederates
had done their best to add to the hazards. Forts Jackson and St. Philip on opposite sides
of the river were manned; an iron chain was stretched across the channel to impede
navigation; and above this hurdle a fleet of gunboats and rams had been collected.
Commanding the Southern defenses was General Mansfield Lovell, "a lithe, brown-
haired man of forty-odd, a very attractive figure, giving . . . a promise of much
activity." The Confederates were sure that "Nothing afloat could pass the forts. Nothing that walked could get through our swamps."

But in the spring of 1862 there appeared at the mouth of the river a Union fleet
commanded by Flag-officer David G. Farragut, accompanied by a mortar flotilla under "that
brave, resolute and indefatigable officer," David D. Porter. For six days Porter's "twenty
large schooners, each mounting one heavy 13-inch mortar and at least two long 32-pound-
ers," bombarded the Confederate forts. Fort Jackson became "a perfect wreck; everything
in the shape of a building in and about it was burned up by the mortar shells, and over
eighteen hundred shells fell into the work proper." Still the defenders held out.

Major General Mansfield Lovell, C.S.A.

Commodore Farragut's Fleet Before New Orleans.

Farragut determined to run the enemy batteries. At two o'clock in the morning of April 24 the fleet was ordered to get under way. "The vessels were rather late in getting . . . into line, and did not get fairly started until half-past three A.M., and the unusual bustle apprised the garrison that something was going on. . . . The mortar-fleet rained down shells on Fort Jackson, to try and keep the men from the guns, whilst the steamers of the mortar-fleet poured in shrapnel upon the water-battery commanding the approach, at a short distance, keeping them comparatively quiet." Boldly Farragut's ships sailed upstream.

"Captain Harrison paid me the compliment of letting me pilot the vessel," recounted Lieutenant George H. Perkins of the Union navy, "and though it was a starlight night we were not discovered until we were well under the forts; then they opened a tremendous fire on us. . . . the air was filled with shells and explosions which almost blinded me as I stood on the forecastle trying to see my way, for I had never been up the river before. I soon saw that the guns of the forts were all aimed for the midstream, so I steered close under the walls of Fort St. Philip, and although our masts and rigging got badly shot through, our hull was but little damaged.

"After passing the last battery and thinking we were clear, I looked back for some of our vessels, and my heart jumped up into my mouth, when I found I could not see a *single one*. I thought they must have been sunk by the forts. Then looking ahead I saw eleven of the enemy's gunboats coming down upon us, and it seemed as if we were 'gone' sure. Three of these made a dash to board us, but a heavy charge from our eleven-inch gun settled the Gov. Moore, which was one of them. A ram, the Manassas, in attempting to butt us, just missed our stern, and we soon settled the third fellow's 'hash.' Just then some of our gunboats, which had passed the forts, came up, and then all sorts of things happened. There was the wildest excitement all around. . . . we all pitched in, and settled the eleven rebel vessels, in about twenty minutes. . . . All this time, night and day, firerafts and ships loaded with burning cotton had been coming down the river and surrounded us everywhere. . . . The river and shore were one blaze, and the sounds and explosions were terrific. Nothing I could say would give you any idea of these last twenty-four hours!"

Rear Admiral David Glasgow Farragut, U.S.N.

**Captain Theodorus Bailey and Party Landing on the Levee at New Orleans to
Demand the Surrender of the City.**

The next morning the Federal fleet lay before New Orleans; but it was not till April 29 that the mayor agreed to yield the city, and even then he refused to haul down the Confederate flag. "The city is yours by the power of brutal force," he wrote Farragut, "not by my choice, or consent of its inhabitants. . . . the people of New Orleans, while unable to resist your force, do not . . . transfer allegiance from the government of their choice . . . they yield the obedience which the conqueror is entitled to extort from the conquered."

When Union soldiers and sailors went ashore, they were greeted with proposals that "the —— Yankees" be "run up to lamp-posts." "Some cheered for Jeff Davis, Beauregard, etc., and used the most vile and obscene language toward . . . the good old flag." "Among the crowd were many women and children, and the women were shaking rebel flags, and being rude and noisy."

But in General Benjamin F. Butler, Federal military commander of the city, recalcitrant New Orleans discovered that it had met its equal. When one woman deliberately spat in a Union officer's face and another from her balcony poured slop on Farragut, Butler ordered that henceforth, if any female should insult in any manner a Union officer or soldier, "she should be regarded and held liable to be treated as a woman of the town plying her avocation." Overt resistance ceased. To this day Louisianians believe not merely that "Beast Butler" ruled the city in a high-handed and corrupt fashion, but also that the Massachusetts general himself stole silver spoons from Confederate homes in New Orleans.

Major General Benjamin F. Butler, U.S.A.

General Robert Edward Lee, C.S.A.

IV. Lee's Offensive

August, 1862, was propitious for a Confederate offensive. The Union armies were divided, and the Union generals were confused. Imported from the West "to command the whole land forces of the United States as General in Chief," Major General Henry W. Halleck was proving irresolute and inefficient—as Lincoln said, perhaps too kindly, "a first-rate clerk." McClellan's army still lay huddled at Harrison's Landing on the James, and its commander querulously demanded reinforcements. A newly constituted Army of Virginia, under General John Pope, was moving into central Virginia.

The Confederates, on the other hand, were united as never before. The Seven Days had demonstrated the caliber of their armies and of their commander. "So great is my confidence in General Lee that I am willing to follow him blind-folded," said Stonewall Jackson. "His perception is as quick and unerring as his judgment is infallible."

Lee's men had come to feel that he was something more than an ordinary mortal. "It is impossible for me to describe the impression he made upon me by his bearing and manners," declared Captain Charles M. Blackford. "I felt myself in the presence of a great man, for surely there was never a man upon whom greatness is more stamped. He is the handsomest person I ever saw; every motion is instinct with natural grace, and yet there is a dignity which, while awe-inspiring, makes one feel a sense of confidence and trust that is delightful when it is remembered that there are at present so many contingencies dependent upon his single will. . . . Lee . . . does not hesitate to avail himself of some of the aids of martial pomp, though perfectly simple in his daily life, walk and conversation. His favorite horse is a handsome grey called 'Traveler,' and the General is so fine a rider that his horse looks like a picture when ever he is seen. Then Lee wears well-fitted undress grey uniform with the handsomest trimmings, a handsome sword and cavalry boots, making him the grandest figure on any field. The men . . . have for Lee a proud admiration and personal devotion 'passing the love of woman.' He is called 'Marse Robert' and 'Uncle Bob' and whenever seen the men shout and rally around him as their darling chief for whom they would most willingly die."

The weeks after Malvern Hill posed crucial problems for the Confederate commander. If he and his magnificent army remained on the defensive, they could almost without question continue to repel any Federal forces thrown against them. On the other hand, offensive action, an invasion of the North, might afford many advantages. Such a move would certainly provide forage and food for the hungry Confederate army; it would probably relieve the tired soil of Virginia from the presence of enemy soldiers; and it might cause the Federals to relax the grinding pressure exerted by their armies in the West. Exigent political considerations also urged an advance. In Maryland there were many, it was thought, who would willingly flock to the Confederate flag, and a decided victory would strengthen the antiwar Copperhead movement throughout the North. Even more important was the fact that European recognition, with consequent aid in breaking the blockade, would probably follow a decisive Southern success on enemy soil. Of course an invasion of the North entailed great risks, but the possible gains were correspondingly large. Lee decided for action, and as a first step ordered that the army of General John Pope be "suppressed."

Railroads south of Washington were demolished by Confederates in order to forestall a Federal advance overland against Richmond. Tracks were "torn up, the rails carried south out of reach, the ties put in piles and burned. All the bridges were destroyed, the superstructures burned, and in several instances the abutments blown up."

Summoning the engineer Herman Haupt to Washington, Secretary of War Stanton directed him to rebuild the roads and railroads. Feverishly Haupt and his men worked. General McDowell "came out almost daily to watch the progress and encourage the men by his presence. He said," Haupt proudly related, "he had never heard sweeter music than the click of the hammers when we were working all night near his Headquarters, spiking rails by the aid of lanterns, the men soaked with rain and the ties laid in mud."

McDowell's Engineers Constructing a Bridge over the Rappahannock near Sulphur Springs.

Bridge on the Orange & Alexandria Railroad Repaired by Army Engineers.

Virginia Negroes said, "The Yankees can build bridges quicker than the Rebs can burn them down." Working with inexperienced soldiers, without adequate supplies, in impossible weather, Haupt constructed bridges that ignored "all the rules and precedents of military science as laid down in books." The most famous was that over Potomac Run, four stories high, and built in nine working days. It was, Lincoln said, "the most remarkable structure that human eyes ever rested upon. That man Haupt has built a bridge across Potomac Creek, about 400 feet long and nearly 100 feet high, over which loaded trains are running every hour, and, upon my word, gentlemen, there is nothing in it but beanpoles and cornstalks."

Union Artillery Advancing Toward Cedar Mountain, August 9, 1862.

In June, Lincoln summoned John Pope from the West to command the newly constituted Army of Virginia, made up of Federal forces in the region of the Shenandoah and Rappahannock. Boastful and grandiloquent, Pope issued to his new army an address as ridiculous as it was offensive: "I have come to you from the West, where we have always seen the backs of our enemies—from an army . . . whose policy has been attack and not defence. . . . I presume that I have been called here to pursue the same system, and to lead you against the enemy. . . . I desire you to dismiss from your minds certain phrases which I am sorry to find much in vogue amongst you. I hear constantly of taking strong positions and holding them—of lines of retreat, and of bases of supplies. Let us discard such

Brigadier General John Pope, U.S.A.

ideas. . . . Let us look before us and not behind. Success and glory are in the advance. Disaster and shame lurk in the rear."

"In person . . . dark, martial, and handsome," Pope was "inclined to obesity, richly garbed . . . , and possessing a fiery black eye, with luxuriant beard and hair. He smoked incessantly, and talked imprudently. . . . Although he was brave, clever, and educated, he inspired distrust by his much promising and general love of gossip. . . ." Pope is supposed to have announced he would have his "headquarters in the saddle." Ribald Confederates jeered that he was putting his headquarters where his hindquarters ought to be.

The Battle of Cedar Mountain, August 9, 1862.

When General Banks encountered the forces of Stonewall Jackson on Cedar Mountain (also ominously called Slaughter Mountain), he obeyed Pope's orders to attack. Edwin Forbes accompanied his drawing with a description of the Union assault: "At three o'clock skirmishing commenced. The cavalry again rode forward and were immediately fired on. The enemy opened with the battery in front of the house and clump of trees. . . . In a few minutes Gen. Geary's brigade filed out of the woods in our rear and came over the hill, past the batteries; the brigades of Gens. Prince, Green[e] and Gordon coming close in the rear. They took positions as follows: Geary's brigade in a cornfield . . . on the right; Prince's in front of Knapp's battery, on the right; Crawford's in the wheatfield, to the right —across which he charged and lost a great part of his command. . . . After the cannonade had continued some time, Gens. Geary and Crawford charged upon two batteries, . . . one near the white farmhouse, and the other in the corner of the [woods]. Our boys fought

Charge of Union Troops on the Left Flank of Jackson's Army at Cedar Mountain.

The Wheat Field at Cedar Mountain, Across Which Brigadier General Samuel W. Crawford's Brigade Charged Against the Confederate Left.

like heroes or devils; and although met by an immense force of the enemy, they succeeded in driving him back through one piece of woods into the open field beyond. The fighting in this woods was most terrible; men fought bayonet to bayonet. . . ."

Jackson's defeat seemed certain. "Just then while our left was wavering," related a Confederate captain, "Ewell's artillery which had gained the end of the mt. towards the enemy, opened upon their flank, while ours of the left thundered upon them in front, and Gen. Jackson ordered forward the 'Stonewall Brigade.' . . . He waved his hat and told them to Remember they were the Stonewall Brigade, and with a shout they rushed forward and hurled back the insolent foe. . . ." It was a dubious battle, but the Southerners could proudly claim, "We were left in undisputed possession of the battlefield. . . ."

On August 18 Pope was obliged to make a rapid retreat. Lee, with the whole Army of Northern Virginia, was about to trap him between the Rapidan and the Rappahannock.

"We were to retire behind the Rappahannock," wrote a member of Pope's staff. "The baggage was all loaded up, and the trains hurried off, accompanied and followed by . . . the troops. The Staff, huddled around their blazing fires, remained on the ground until midnight. The night air was excessively chilly, and the whole country was illuminated by the camp-fires left burning to deceive the enemy.

"About half an hour after midnight came the welcome order to mount; for nothing is more irksome than waiting thus with bridle in hand, hour after hour, divided between listlessness and anxiety. We had a rough ride over the open fields . . . and matters had a confused and ugly look; but the General [Pope] rode here and there, infusing some of his Western energy into the caravan, and every thing began to move. . . ."

Sigel's Corps of Pope's Army Recrossing the Rappahannock, August 19, 1862.

Repairing the Orange & Alexandria Railroad at Catlett's Station After Jackson's Raid.

Prevented from attacking directly, Lee boldly divided his army and sent Jackson's "foot cavalry" by way of Thoroughfare Gap entirely around Pope to destroy his supply base and disrupt his communications with Washington. Jackson's men ripped up the Orange & Alexandria Railroad, seized whatever Federal stores they could use, and destroyed the rest. When Union troops belatedly arrived, they saw the results of this "rebel carnival": "On the railroad track and sidelings [*sic*] stood the hot and smoking remains of what had recently been trains of cars laden with ordnance and commissary stores intended for our army. As far as the eye could reach the plain was covered with boxes, barrels, cans, cooking-utensils, saddles, sabres, muskets, and military equipments generally; hard-bread and corn-pones, meat, salt and fresh, beans, blankets, clothes, shoes, and hats. . . . Most of the buildings were burned, and many tents shared the same fate."

Railroad Stock at Manassas Junction Destroyed by Jackson's Men.

McClellan's army, recalled from the Peninsula, was landing at Alexandria, and Halleck and Haupt were desperately trying to rush the fresh troops to Pope. Jackson's raid threatened the vital railroad bridge across Bull Run, and General George W. Taylor, sent out to protect it, advanced imprudently and was mortally wounded. As his brigade "retreated in disorder along the railroad," Confederates demolished the bridge. "It is not probable that we can use the road again for some time," Haupt reported sadly, "and the army must cut its way through." But McClellan and his generals, bitterly hostile to Pope, had no such plans. Said one tipsily, "I don't care for John Pope a pinch of owl dung!" McClellan himself advised Lincoln "to leave Pope to get out of his scrape and at once use all our means to make the capital perfectly safe."

Brigadier General George W. Taylor, U.S.A.

The Second Battle of Bull Run,

Though cut off from reinforcements and supplies, Pope was not disheartened. He moved swiftly in the hope of trapping Jackson's army. "If you will march promptly and rapidly," he instructed McDowell, "we shall bag the whole crowd." On August 29 he fell upon Jackson in the first day's fighting of Second Bull Run. The devout Confederate thought afterward "nothing but the blessing and protection of Providence" had enabled him to repulse the assault, and Pope looked confidently forward to renewed battle on the next day.

But on August 29 Lee, undetected, had brought up the rest of his army by Thoroughfare Gap, the circuitous route which Jackson had used; and the next morning Longstreet was prepared to fall upon the Union flank. Edwin Forbes's panoramic sketch of the battlefield at Second Bull Run (or Manassas) locates the salient points: 1, Thoroughfare Gap, through which Lee's army marched; 2, Confederate line of battle; 3, an old railroad em-

3:30 P.M., Saturday, August 30, 1862.

bankment behind which Jackson's men were posted (this numeral, apparently omitted from the sketch, should be on the left of the Confederate line); 4, old Stone House on the turnpike used as a hospital; 5, Warrenton turnpike; 6, Baldface Hill; 7, Henry Hill; 8, Union line of battle; 9, McDowell's corps moving to the left to repel Longstreet's attack; 10, Sudley Springs road.

"The scene," wrote Forbes, "was very impressive. On the plain below lay large bodies of infantry; some in line of battle and others *en masse.* . . . Our men were weary, tired and worn out by the long marches and excitement of the past 10 days. . . . The fight was opened by our batteries in front of the hill and woods on the centre and left. It was immediately replied to by the enemy's batteries in the orchard and along the crest of the hill about three-quarters of a mile distant. After the artillery fighting had lasted some time, our infantry attacked the enemy's left flank."

Major General Samuel Peter Heintzelman, U.S.A.

The attack on the Confederate left was undertaken by Heintzelman's corps, Phil Kearny's men leading the assault. Jackson's force lay protected in a cut of an unfinished railroad, "with a field in front sloping down about four hundred yards to a piece of woods. The enemy would form in the woods and come up the slope in three lines as regular as if on drill," recalled a member of the Stonewall Brigade, "and we would pour volley after volley into them as they came; but they would still advance until within a few yards of us when they would break and fall back to the woods, where they would rally and come again. They charged in this manner three times. . . ."

Brigadier General Beverly H. Robertson, C.S.A.

By this time the Southerns were ready to do some charging themselves. Longstreet was in action against the Union left. When Beverly Robertson's cavalry arrived, "Jeb" Stuart reported proudly, "no time was lost in crowding the enemy, the artillery being kept always far in advance of the infantry lines. The fight was of remarkably short duration. The Lord of Hosts was plainly fighting on our side. . . ."

Brigadier General Thomas T. Munford, C.S.A.

With his 2nd Virginia Cavalry, Tom Munford led the assault. "Without waiting," said Robertson's report of the battle, "Colonel Munford made a brilliant and dashing charge with his regiment in line, engaging the enemy in a hand-to-hand contest, which lasted until the Twelfth Regiment had almost reached the scene of action, when the enemy commenced a general and precipitate retreat. . . ."

Defeat of Pope's Army at Bull Run, August 30, 1862.

Retreat brought chaos and blind panic. "Directly in front of our position," related a Confederate private, "the whole plain, as far as the eye can reach, is covered with the blue of the enemy—some brigades flying in disorder, others advancing in serried lines with the Stars and Stripes innumerable floating in the breeze; officers vainly endeavoring to rally their wavering ranks furiously dashing up and down the lines. Then little parties of flying soldiers [Federals] rallying are again and again led to the charge while our troops may be seen again and again on the advance; while their wild, fearful victorious yells give renewed confidence to us, strike terror to the souls of the Yankees and send them reeling back in disorder over the field. . . . Oh, the horrid scenes around us! Brains, fractured skulls, broken arms and legs, and the human form mangled in every conceivable and inconceivable manner. . . . In vain does line after line [of Federals] advance at a run. Torn and bleeding they are hurled back, scattered, routed in confusion over the plain (blue with their slain.) In vain do their officers dash in the midst of this storm of shell and bullets. The fugitives will not be rallied, but, broken and dismayed, are pursued by our victorious troops until darkness closes around."

Second Bull Run was not so complete a fiasco as First; Union soldiers had become inured to the ineptness of their commanders. Still, the troops were shaken by defeat, and many were bitter. "So long as the interests of our country are entrusted to a lying braggart like Pope," wrote one, "we have little reason to hope successfully to compete with an army led by Lee, Johnston and old 'Stonewall' Jackson."

Washington, too, was greatly perturbed. Lincoln turned to the indispensable man. "I must have McClellan to reorganize the army and bring it out of chaos," he said, adding, "McClellan has the army with him." To the dispirited columns of retreating soldiers the announcement was made: "Men, General McClellan is in command of the army!" That "was all that was necessary. Up went caps in the air and a cheer broke out which, as the news travelled, was taken up and carried to the rear of the column and the weary fagged men went into camp, cheerful and happy to talk over their rough experience of the past three weeks and speculate as to what was ahead."

Company C, 41st New York Infantry, After Second Bull Run.

Union Scouts Observing Lee's Troops Crossing the Potomac.

"General Lee had now decided . . . boldly to carry the war into the enemy's territory, or at least into the fertile plains of Maryland," wrote a Confederate cavalry officer. "After a dusty and very much impeded march . . . we reached the Potomac. . . . At White's Ford the Potomac is divided into two streams by a sandy strip of island in the middle . . . [which] offered us a momentary resting-place half-way in our passage of the river. It was, indeed, a magnificent sight as the long column of many thousand horsemen stretched across this beautiful Potomac. The evening sun slanted upon its clear placid waters, and burnished them with gold, while the arms of the soldiers glittered and blazed in its radiance. There were few moments, perhaps, from the beginning to the close of the war, of excitement more intense, of exhilaration more delightful, than when we ascended the opposite bank to the familiar but now strangely thrilling music of 'Maryland, my Maryland.'"

1st Virginia Cavalry at a Halt During the Invasion of Maryland.

Lee proclaimed his readiness to aid the people of Maryland in throwing off the "foreign yoke" which was reducing their state "to the condition of a conquered province," but most Marylanders gave him a cool reception. The Confederate army did not inspire confidence. "The rebels are wretchedly clad, and generally destitute of shoes," wrote one who observed the invaders. "The cavalry men are mostly barefooted, and the feet of the infantry are bound up in rags and pieces of rawhide. Their uniforms are in tatters and many are without hats or caps. They are very sanguine of success, and say that when they get to Baltimore they will get everything they need. . . ."

But before such a continued advance was possible Harpers Ferry had to be reduced, and Lee sent Jackson to do it. On September 15 "the entire garrison of 13,000 men . . . with their well-kept equipments, their new uniforms and beautiful banners" surrendered "to Jackson's gaunt and ragged soldiers, . . . whose tattered garments and weather-beaten features showed only too plainly the hardships they had undergone. . . . The spoils captured at Harper's Ferry were enormous."

Ruins of the Railroad Bridge at Harpers Ferry.

While Jackson was at Harpers Ferry, the rest of Lee's army had advanced toward Hagerstown. Learning that McClellan had found a copy of his orders and fearing an attack upon his divided forces, Lee decided to concentrate his army at Sharpsburg, on the Antietam Creek. It was beautiful country. "The valley thro' which we had just passed," noted a Confederate diarist, "was teeming with fertility in marked contrast with the barren fields of Virginia over which we had so recently trodden. Every where smiling fields of wheat, wide stretching acres of green corn with their yellow ears and crimson tassels met the eye; and on every hand were the pasture lands teeming with clover, timothy, and broad waving blades of nourishing grass; while every hundred yards extensive orchards, the branches of whose trees swept the ground with their luscious burdens of pears, peaches, and apples, invited . . . stragglers."

Antietam Bridge.

Sharpsburg, Maryland.

McClellan pursued, and on September 16 the armies were drawn up on opposite sides of the Antietam Creek. Lee's center was before the village of Sharpsburg.

"Such was the admirable nature of the ground chosen by Lee," recorded a Confederate diarist, "that the enemy was engaged till late in the afternoon in reconnoitering our position, and before he had completed his observations Stonewall Jackson reached the field from Harpers Ferry . . . with more than half his corps. . . .

"In the mean time about 10 A.M. the artillery of the enemy opened a furious cannonade upon our lines. . . . the wild firing of their gunners today shews conclusively that they are ignorant of our positions. Not knowing where to throw their shells, they took Sharpsburg for the object of their aim, and for nearly half the day shell and shot rained continually upon this devoted little town."

During the day Union artillery fire became more accurate, for on the hills behind the Federal position signal corps officers were making a "careful telescopic examination of all points . . . in front of Sharpsburg, and of such movements as were visible. . . . Officers were kept at their posts on this station by day and night, with but a few hours' interval, from the commencement of the battle. . . . The station was worked with peculiar labor, it being necessary to observe at times from the top of a tree, while the signals were made from a point beneath among the branches, where the flagman could only sustain himself by exertion. . . ." The surveillance was effective. A Richmond newspaper admitted: "Their signal stations on the Blue Ridge commanded a view of our every movement. We could not make a manœuvre in front or rear that was not instantly revealed to their keen look-outs. . . ."

Signal Tower on Elk Mountain Overlooking the Antietam Battlefield.

Union Artillery at the Battle of Antietam.

The artillery bombardment "was a grand and fearful spectacle," asserted a Confederate rookie, "and to me, who had never seen any continuous cannonading, it was perfectly thrilling. The men around me said it was the severest shelling they had ever witnessed. We were between the enemy and this town, and though they could not see us, I felt afraid that they would soon find us out and that took away much of the pleasure that the bombardment would otherwise have afforded me.

"Every shell went screaming, whistling, whining over our heads, and not a few burst near by us. Sometimes shell after shell would burst in quick succession over the village and we did not know whence they came or how they got there. None of our soldiers were in the town, except the cooks and a few stragglers who hid themselves in the cellars as soon as the bombardment began, and told us afterwards of the wonderful escapes they made from 'them bursting lamp-posts.'"

Confederate Dead near the Cornfield.

Antietam was in reality three separate engagements. The first, on the Confederate left, began in the afternoon of September 16, when Hooker attacked Jackson in the famous East Woods that lay before the modest white Dunker Church, about a mile north of Sharpsburg. At nightfall the first assault ceased, and exhausted enemies slept within sight of each other's lines. The next morning the Union offensive was renewed, and, advancing through a cornfield, Hooker's "compact columns of infantry fell upon the left of Lee's lines with the crushing weight of a land-slide. The Confederate battle line was too weak to withstand the momentum of such a charge. Pressed back, but neither hopelessly broken nor dismayed, the Southern troops, enthused by Lee's presence, reformed their lines, and, with a shout as piercing as the blast of a thousand bugles, rushed in counter-charge upon the exulting Federals, hurled them back in confusion, and recovered all the ground that had been lost. Again and again, hour after hour, by charges and counter-charges, this portion

Dunker Church and the Dead.

of the field was lost and recovered, until the green corn that grew upon it looked as if it had been struck by a storm of bloody hail."

"It was never my fortune to witness a more bloody, dismal battle-field," reported General Hooker, who was himself wounded. On both sides the slaughter was incredible. "War is a dredful thing," a Confederate lieutenant learned. "It is really shocking to all the senses to be upon a battle field after the battle has ceased & see the poor suffering human beings gasping in the agony of death for breath. To see thousands lying upon the field some dead others wounded & to hear the cries of the wounded for help. Then to glance at their wounds as you pass along some with an arm leg & even their nose or under jaw shot off, Oh it is revolting to humanity & why all this Can't be prevented. Oh, my God, Can't this cruel strife be brought to an end. . . ."

Major General Edwin Vose Sumner, U.S.A.

The Halt on the Line of Battle.

With "ill-regulated ardor" General Sumner had already sent part of his corps to aid Hooker; now the remaining divisions struck at the Confederate center, where D. H. Hill's thin lines were entrenched in a sunken road, soon to become famous as Bloody Lane. The Union advance was "a thrilling sight. With flags flying and the long unfaltering lines rising and falling as they crossed the rolling fields, it looked as though nothing could stop them . . . ." Soon Union observers noted the "advance line began to waver and show broken places. . . . a murderous crashing volley told of reinforcement to the enemy's line, and our own men halted and took advantage of the slight protection of a ridge of ground to regain their formation. Then came the order to advance again, and through smoke and an avalanche of fire they dashed defiantly up the ridge and poured a volley into the faces of the enemy. . . ."

Brigadier General John Brown Gordon, C.S.A.

In the sunken road the Confederates waited. Coolly John B. Gordon had his troops hold their fire till the Union line was within a few rods. "It would not do to wait another second," he recalled, "and with all my lung power I shouted 'Fire!' . . . The effect was appalling. . . . My front had been cleared; Lee's centre had been saved; and yet not a drop of blood had been lost by my men."

Brigadier General Israel B. Richardson, U.S.A.

From the Union side came the shout: "Boys! Raise the colors and follow me!" Richardson was leading his division, spearheaded by the Irish Brigade, with golden harps on its emerald flags, directly up to the sunken lane. Hatless, drawn sword in hand, Richardson himself was in the front line. His men surged forward, but the general himself fell fatally wounded.

The Bloody Lane.

The Confederate defenders abandoned the Bloody Lane. "Hastily emptying our muskets into their lines, we fled back through the cornfield," recalled one. "Oh, how I ran! or tried to run through the high corn, for my heavy belt and cartridge box and musket kept me back to *half* my speed. I was so afraid of being struck in the *back,* and I frequently turned half around in running, so as to avoid if possible so disgraceful a wound. . . . The enemy having taken our position appeared to think they had performed wonders, for instead of pursuing us and shooting us down, they began to give regular *methodical* cheers, as if they had gained a game of base ball."

In the Charge across the Burnside Bridge Antietam. 1 P.M. Sept 17th 1862. Sporbes

Union Charge Across the Burnside Bridge.

Then, belatedly, on the Union left commenced the third engagement of the battle. All morning Burnside's corps had been attempting to cross the Antietam, but the one narrow stone bridge was commanded by heights which "rose abruptly, deflecting but little from a true perpendicular. . . . With these heights manned by the enemy and the main roadway over the bridge wholly under his control, the attempt to carry it seemed but desperation, and its success almost miraculous."

"Burnside hesitated for hours in front of the bridge. . . . Attacking first with one regiment, then with two, and delaying both for artillery, Burnside was not over the bridge before two o'clock—perhaps not till three. He advanced slowly up the slopes in his front, his batteries in rear covering, to some extent, the movements of the infantry. A desperate fight was going on in a deep ravine on his right; the rebel batteries were in full play and apparently very annoying and destructive, while heavy columns of rebel troops were plainly visible, advancing . . . along the road . . . in the direction of Burnside's forces. It was at this point . . . that McClellan sent him the order" to "advance . . . at all hazards and at any cost."

**Charge of 9th New York Infantry, Hawkins's Zouaves, Against the
Confederate Right Flank at 3:30 P.M.**

"Burnside obeyed . . . most gallantly. Getting his troops well in hand, and sending a portion of his artillery to the front, he advanced with rapidity and the most determined vigor straight up the hill in front, on top of which the rebels had maintained their most dangerous battery." Union headquarters watched approvingly: "The advance was distinctly visible from our position, and the movement of the dark columns, with arms and banners glittering in the sun, following the double line of skirmishers, dashing forward at a trot, loading and firing alternately as they moved, was one of the most brilliant and exciting exhibitions of the day."

"The fight in the ravine was in full progress, the batteries in the centre were firing with new vigor, Franklin was blazing away on the right, and every hill-top, ridge and woods along the whole line was crested and veiled with white clouds of smoke. All day had been clear and bright since the early cloudy morning, and now this whole magnificent, unequalled scene shone with the splendor of an afternoon September sun."

Burnside's "splendid advance seemed to be carrying everything before it." Edwin Forbes's sketch shows the daring charge led by Hawkins's Zouaves against the Confederate right: 1, town of Sharpsburg; 2, the old Lutheran church (also shown in the photograph to the right); 3, Hawkins's Zouaves advancing; 4, Confederates retreating into the town; 5, main Confederate line of battle.

"Hawkins's Zouaves . . . found the enemy ready drawn up under cover of the hills," Forbes related, "and advanced in line of battle on the enemy's new position, about half a mile distant. The ground over which they advanced was open clover and ploughed fields, the latter very difficult and fatiguing to march in, owing to the softness of the ground. The enemy's guns, 14 in number, kept up a terrible fire on our advancing line, which never wavered, but slowly toiled along, receiving shelter, however, when they were in the hollows. They were halted a few moments to rest in the hollow nearest the enemy's position, and then were ordered to charge with a yell. As they came up the hill in front of the enemy's batteries, they received a heavy volley from a large force of infantry behind a stone wall about 200 feet in front of the enemy's batteries. Our men, though terribly decimated, gave them a volley in return, and then went on with the bayonet. The enemy did not stay to contest the ground, and . . . broke and ran, leaving their guns."

Lutheran Church on Main Street, Sharpsburg.

Major General Ambrose Powell Hill, C.S.A.

At this crucial moment, when Lee's left was badly mauled, his center broken, and his right retreating, a cloud of dust appeared on the road to the south.

Lee pointed: "What troops are those?"

A lieutenant looked through his telescope and after a breathless moment replied, "They are flying the Virginia and Confederate flags."

"It is A. P. Hill from Harpers Ferry," said Lee quietly.

With his three thousand men Hill fell upon Burnside's exposed flank and saved Lee's army. By this time it "was nearly dark . . . too late to repair errors or initiate any new movement. . . . By eight o'clock the wailing cries of the wounded and the glare of the burning buildings alone interrupted the silence and darkness which reigned over the great battle."

Civilian Volunteers Aiding the Wounded After the Battle of Antietam.

Dr. Jonathan Letterman, Medical Director of the Army of the Potomac, and His Assistants.

This "bloodiest day of the war" was "followed by the most appalling sights upon the battle-field . . . the ground strewn with the bodies of the dead and the dying . . . the cries and the groans of the wounded . . . the piles of dead men, in attitudes which show the writhing agony in which they died—faces distorted . . . begrimed and covered with clotted blood, arms and legs torn from the body or the body itself torn asunder. . . . The dead lie in heaps unburied, and the dying and wounded uncared for beside them. The faces of those who had fallen in the battle were, after more than a day's exposure, so black that no one would ever suspect that they had been white. . . . the stench which arose from the bodies decomposing in the sun was almost unendurable."

The medical corps did what it could, and civilian volunteers assisted. For hours the surgeons worked at their grisly tasks. "Some medical officers lost their lives in their devotion to duty in the battle of Antietam," reported Dr. Letterman, medical director of the Union army, "and others sickened from excessive labor which they conscientiously and skilfully performed."

Nevertheless, and necessarily, conditions were appalling. An observer found a barn, converted into "a temporary hospital, . . . crowded with victims of the day. Around, lying upon the ground, waiting to receive the surgeon's attention, are numerous wounded, imperfectly screened from night chills, rain or autumn sun. Their shelter is of the rudest kind . . . . the day closes, and night shuts the scene, leaving ten thousand men, helpless and bathed in blood, to watch the return of light, for removal and the dressing of their wounds."

Dr. Anson Hurd, 14th Indiana Infantry, U.S.A., Attending Wounded Confederates near Smith's Barn After the Battle of Antietam.

Officers of the 93rd New York Infantry Regiment After Antietam.

"In the midst of all this . . . putrefying humanity lay . . . the troops who were not dead, . . . ready to renew the conflict, but altogether strangely hilarious and recklessly at their ease. Some were cooking, and apparently enjoying their . . . breakfast although the mephitic atmosphere would have tried the stomach of a horse. Others laughed, talked, smoked, and sung snatches of droll songs. . . . Some slept."

Lincoln, McClellan, and a Group of Officers at Headquarters of the Army of the Potomac.

Lee quietly pulled his army out of Sharpsburg and retreated across the Potomac into Virgina. McClellan, who "always saw double when he looked rebelward," was loath to follow.

President Lincoln was distressed by McClellan's slowness. Letters and telegrams seemed to have no effect upon the general, who constantly demanded more troops and more supplies. Bitterly Lincoln noted that his army seemed to dwindle "like a shovelfull of fleas tossed from one place to another." When McClellan called for more cavalry horses, the President exploded: "Will you pardon me for asking what the horses of your army have done since the battle of Antietam that fatigues anything?"

On October 3 the President went in person to McClellan's camp and, "dressed in citizens clothes, wearing a high crowned hat, his long, lean figure contrasting strangely with the compact form of General McClellan," reviewed the troops. Again Lincoln urged the general to try to advance upon Richmond. "I say 'try'; if we never try we shall never succeed."

Confederates Under Major General Stuart Leaving Chambersburg, Pennsylvania, October 11, 1862.

Perhaps the final blow at Lincoln's confidence in McClellan came when the Confederate cavalry made a daring raid across Maryland and on October 10 compelled the surrender of Chambersburg, Pennsylvania. The Confederate cavalier "Jeb" Stuart, wearing his "drooping hat, caught up with a star and decorated with an ebon plume; the tall cavalry boots decked with golden spurs; the 'fighting jacket'" and riding his "magnificent charger, mud-splashed from head to foot," led the 1,800 chosen cavalrymen past McClellan's guards and returned in safety to Lee.

It was too much. Though McClellan slowly moved into Virginia, Lincoln had made up his mind. On November 5 the general was ordered to turn over command of the Army of the Potomac to General Burnside. As he read the removal order, which ended his military career, McClellan sighed, "They have made a great mistake. Alas for my poor country."

Brigadier General James Ewell Brown Stuart, C.S.A.

Major General Ambrose Everett Burnside, U.S.A.

V. Burnside and Hooker

"The change is undoubtedly for the best," wrote a young Union officer of McClellan's removal, "although nobody expects much from Burnside." It was agreed that Ambrose Everett Burnside was amiable, well intentioned, loyal, and hard-working. "In the care of his troops, in tender solicitude and untiring labors for their welfare," said a contemporary portrait album which had to include something favorable about everybody, "he is unsurpassed. . . . Always accessible to the humblest private in the ranks, he heard with unexampled patience the most trivial request . . . and replied to each with . . . hopeful encouragement." The new Federal commander had everything but ability. He himself knew he was not fit for highest command, and for once his judgment was wholly correct.

Burnside concluded that the best place in Virginia to be was wherever Lee was not, and he abruptly transferred his army to the Rappahannock, before Fredericksburg, intending a surprise dash upon Richmond. His careful and speedy preparations neglected two things: the river and the Confederates. When he finally got bridges into position, on December 13 he sent his army across a turbulent stream, through a town where sharpshooters lurked, across an open plain, over a canal, and up a hill to a stone wall, where comfortably protected Confederate riflemen took deliberate aim. In his orders for the advance Burnside had said, "I think now that the enemy will be more surprised by a crossing immediately in our front than in any other part of the river." The Confederates could scarcely have been more surprised if the general had ordered his army to commit suicide—which, in effect, he did.

After Fredericksburg even Washington saw something must be done, and Burnside was replaced with "Fighting Joe" Hooker. To Lee, watching on the south bank of the river, the substitution of a drinking incompetent for a sober one made scarcely any difference. In May, when Hooker led his army from winter quarters to fight at Chancellorsville, he was as thoroughly beaten as Burnside.

The bloody eight months after Antietam taught both armies much. Victorious Confederates, short of horses, short of forage, short of ammunition, short of men, were commencing to feel the overwhelming superiority of Union resources. Reviewing the battles, Lee could only conclude: "We had really accomplished nothing; we had not gained a foot of ground, and I knew the enemy could easily replace the men he had lost." On the other bank of the river, the "Army of the Potomac, battered about and abused, had become indifferent to results. . . . After a battle it therefore accepted a withdrawal or advance with equal complacency, maintaining the consciousness that it had done all men could do . . . ." When one commander succeeded another, remarked a Union veteran, "everybody appears entirely indifferent to the matter. Heroes of many defeats, we are not inclined to give gratuitous confidence to anyone. Whoever finally succeeds . . . has a fine chance for immortality."

Fredericksburg, Virginia.

On November 17 the first elements of Burnside's army reached the Rappahannock opposite Fredericksburg. Clearly in view across the river lay one of the oldest cities in the nation; George Washington as a boy had played in its streets. "The water-front of the city extended about a mile, with streets at right-angles, lined with substantial brick and stone buildings reaching back from the water about half that distance. The city lay on a plain away below the heights which overlooked it. At the distance of half a mile arose a formidable hill, of easy, gentle slope, . . . known by its owner's name as Marye's Heights."

Exploring Federal soldiers discovered that the river was "not fordable near the town." "There were three bridges, one opposite Falmouth, and two in front of Fredericksburg," they were told; "but all three are now destroyed except their blackened piers, which stand as melancholy monuments of the devastation of war."

By the time Burnside had prepared for a crossing, Lee's army lay waiting on the heights behind Fredericksburg. Nevertheless, on the early morning of December 11 Burnside ordered pontoon bridges to be laid. "At three," reported a New York newspaperman, "the pontoon train drove down to the water. Lumber was noiselessly piled upon the ground, and the huge boats slid from off their trucks. Then . . . a splashing in the river—a dark pathway lengthens out upon the silver surface, . . . the lusty blows of hammers re-echo from side to side. And yet no sound comes from the enemy. . . . Suddenly, Crack! crack! crack! from a hundred muskets. . . . A cry of pain comes up from the bank from the gallant engineers, mules dash off, with pontoons thundering after. . . . Suddenly, boom! goes a gun . . . musketry is lost to the ear in the mighty roar [of Union artillery]. . . . Gradually the fire slackens, and the engineers again attempt the completion of the bridge, but in vain; and after a third trial they fall back, bringing in their arms their wounded, dead, and dying."

50th New York Engineers Building Pontoon Bridges at Fredericksburg.

Across the River from Fredericksburg on the Night of December 11.

Meanwhile the Union soldiers were "in readiness to receive orders to cross the river. The men were prepared for a march, and had everything with them in case they had to remain on the other side or to push forward. . . . Turn where you would and you encountered troops. In a hollow would be hidden a brigade, with their arms stacked, and the men lying on the ground resting themselves, while the officers would be collected together chatting over the results of the terrific cannonading and the chances of a great and decisive conflict; and on the open plains lines upon lines of stacked arms showed that the word need but be given, and in a twinkling thousands of eager and trusty hands would seize them and be ready for the fight."

Burnside ordered that the Confederate sharpshooters be driven out of Fredericksburg, so that the bridges could be completed, and this time the artillery opened directly upon the city. "The roar is indescribably awful. . . . By-and-by the firing ceases, and one is almost awe-stricken with the profound silence. The mist still clings to the river, the sun struggles up red and fiery, and the air is suffocating with the odor of gunpowder. Presently the bank of fog begins to lift a little, the glistening roofs gleam faintly through the veil, then the sunbeams scatter the clouds . . . and Fredericksburg, utterly desolate, stands out before. A huge column of dense black smoke towers . . . above the livid flames, that leap and hiss and crackle, licking up the snow upon the roofs. . . . The guns renew their roar, and we see the solid shot plunge through the masonry as though it were pasteboard; other buildings are fired, and before sundown a score of houses are in ashes. . . ."

Attack on the Confederate Works at Fredericksburg, December 13, 1862.

Ruins in Fredericksburg.

Charge of Humphrey's Division at Fredericksburg, December 13, 1862.

Once over the river, the Union soldiers still had to face Lee's army, entrenched upon Marye's Heights. "As the head of the column appeared in the open," wrote one of the attackers, "the rebel batteries opened fire and pandemonium at once broke loose. . . . We marched rapidly forward . . . then came a mill race, and on the other side of it a high board fence; . . . then in full line of battle, we marched directly forward, in front of Marye's house the strongest point of the enemy's works. It seemed a terrible long distance, as with bated breath and heads bowed down, we hurried forward, the rebel guns plowing great furrows in our ranks at every step. . . . When within some three hundred yards of the rebel works, the men burst into a cheer and charged. . . . Immediately the hill in front was hid . . . by a continuous sheet of flame from base to summit. . . . we dropped down, and then flat on our bellies, opened fire while line after line of fresh troops, like ocean waves, followed each other in rapid succession, but none of them succeeded in reaching the enemy's works. . . . the attack was a failure." Hancock reported two out of every five of his veterans lost in the charge. By night the beaten Union army crept back across the Rappahannock.

Major General Winfield Scott Hancock, U.S.A.

The Mud March, January 21, 1863.

Disregarding his own obvious inadequacy, discarding the advice of his subordinates, discounting the inclement winter weather, Burnside resolved to try again, and in January he set out up the river in an attempt to flank the Confederates. The expedition became known as the "Mud March," for rains had apparently turned all of Virginia into "mud of a depth and consistency that held tight whatever penetrated it, so that release without assistance was almost impossible." "The feet of men and animals, the wheels of gun, caisson, limber and wagon had so stirred and agitated the pasty substance, that . . . in one place it was a deep, sticky loam, and in another a thick fluid-extract. Twelve horses could not move a gun. The wheels of vehicles disappeared entirely. Pontoons on their carriages stood fixed and helpless in the roadway, the wheels out of sight. . . . On the other side [of the river] the enemy had erected large boards, on which were displayed in letters plainly discernible taunting phrases. On one: 'Burnside stuck in the mud;' on another: 'Yanks, if you can't place your pontoons over yourself, we will send you a detail.'" The expedition had no results; Burnside had again proved a failure.

The Union Winter Uniform: Sergeant Major William Jackson, 12th New York Infantry,
at Stoneman's Switch, Virginia, January 27, 1863.

Major General Joseph Hooker, U.S.A.

Three Aides-de-Camp to Major General Hooker at Falmouth, Virginia:
Captains Alexander Moore, Harry Russell, and William L. Candler.

To replace Burnside, Lincoln somewhat reluctantly selected Joseph Hooker. There was much to be said in favor of the appointment. Hooker looked the part. "In person," it was enthusiastically reported, "General Hooker is very tall, erect, compactly, but not heavily built, extremely muscular, and of great physical endurance, of a light complexion, a fresh, ruddy countenance, full, clear, mild eyes, intellectual head, brown hair, slightly tinged with gray—and altogether one of the most commanding officers in his bearing and appearance in the army." He had a reputation as a fighter, though he disliked his nickname, saying, "Don't call me Fighting Joe, for that name . . . makes . . . the public think that I am a hot-headed, furious young fellow, accustomed to making furious and needless dashes at the enemy." He had performed well in battle and had been wounded at Antietam. Moreover, influential radical politicians were among his enthusiastic backers.

On the debit side, however, there were a good many counts. Hooker was vain, egotistical, boastful. He had intrigued for Burnside's removal, and he had made loud remarks about the need for a military dictatorship to straighten out the country. His soldiers observed the "many abandoned bottles, the broken and empty [wine] baskets, the frequent and suggestive popping of champagne corks" at his tent, for Hooker drank heavily. His "large and very gay looking staff" was composed of rather raffish young men. With Hooker in command, wrote a Massachusetts Adams sourly, headquarters of the Army of the Potomac became "a combination of bar-room and brothel," "a place to which no self-respecting man liked to go, and no decent woman could go."

In some ways, however, Hooker was an admirable administrator. For his "disheartened and almost sulky" men he ordered "a diet which in quantity, quality and variety was captivating, appetizing and nutritious"; and if the food never quite equaled the adjectives it at least was something more than hardtack. A regular system of furloughs was introduced for the first time. Much attention was given to drill and inspection, and Hooker from his white charger gave personal attention to details. "Our division parades . . . used to be something fine," thought one veteran, "and I recall with great clearness the steady march of our column of companies, the martial music of our bands, the thunder of our hundred drums, the glitter of our polished arms, the neatness of our uniforms, . . . as we marched by . . . in review, when we took every step with a consciousness that an inch too much or too little in its length would spoil the exact line of the company . . . and we held our shoulders back and heads up as if we had swallowed our ramrods."

General Meade, General Sedgwick (in Round Hat at Right), and Staffs at Headquarters, Falmouth.

Ambulance Train at Falmouth, Virginia, March 1863.

Hooker also attempted to reform the ambulance corps, which had achieved among his soldiers a legendary disrepute. "Officers and men of doubtful courage used every exertion to be detailed for this service," wrote one veteran, doubtless with pardonable exaggeration, "because they considered it a safe position; and, with rare exceptions, remained in the rear while the wounded were stretched upon the field and praying for assistance." One regimental commander, asked to detail ten soldiers for duty in the ambulance service, roared, "Take the most worthless cowards and stragglers that you have got; I won't insult my good and brave men by sending them to such a lot of scalawags." Once, it was said, when "the drivers bivouacked upon the road to Falmouth, they compelled the sick to leave the ambulances in the midst of a pitiless storm; and commanded them to go to their regiments, which were five miles from that point, because they wished to sleep in them during the night. . . . A formal complaint, which recited these facts, was forwarded to headquarters by the regimental surgeon; but the only notice that was taken of it was the extraordinary answer, that such conduct was customary. . . ."

Major General Hooker's Base at Aquia Creek Landing.

While training his army, Hooker was preparing to move forward; and he ordered enormous supplies to be accumulated at his Aquia Creek base. Herman Haupt was directed to be ready to reconstruct railroads and bridges as the army advanced. During the winter Haupt, who, as Secretary Chase said, had "a Major General's head on his shoulders," was not idle. "The Construction Corps," he reported proudly, "performed services of great value in perfecting organization, procuring material, and preparing for rapid advance movements whenever they should be ordered. A large number of bridge trusses were prepared in spans of 60 feet to be transported on flat cars, hauled by oxen to the sites of the bridges, and hoisted bodily into position by suitable portable machinery. These trusses were called 'shadbellies' by the workmen from their peculiar shape. . . . as my foreman . . . expressed it, he could put the bridge together about as fast as a dog could trot."

Brigadier General Herman Haupt, U.S.A.

Embarkation of the Ninth Army Corps at Aquia Creek Landing, February, 1863.

While preparing his troops, Hooker attempted to wear down Lee's small army by constant excursions and diversions. In February the Ninth Corps embarked at Aquia Creek Landing for a mysteriously unreported location; the Confederates feared a surprise attack at Charleston or Richmond. Lee was obliged to detach Longstreet's force from his already depleted army and send it below Richmond, where the Federals were menacing Suffolk. Hooker, wrote Lee in disgust, "is playing the Chinese game, trying what frightening will do. He runs out his guns, starts wagons and troops up and down the river, and creates an excitement generally. Our men look on in wonder, give a cheer, and all again subsides *in statu quo ante bellum.*"

Major General George Stoneman, U.S.A.

As another diversion Hooker in April ordered his cavalry, now consolidated into a single corps under General Stoneman, to make a raid against Lee's supplies and communications. "Let your watchword be, fight, fight, fight," Hooker directed. "If you can not cut off from [the enemy's] columns large slices, the general desires that you will not fail to take small ones."

Brigadier General Arnold Elzey, C.S.A.

Stoneman's Raiders at Kelly's Ford, Virginia.

Stoneman slipped up the river and crossed with little resistance at Kelly's Ford. Edwin Forbes's drawing illustrates the crossing: 1, Blue Ridge Mountains; 2, an old mill; 3, Kelly's Ford; 4, Rappahannock River. Leaving Averell's division behind and adroitly eluding Stuart's Confederate cavalry, Stoneman dashed far behind Lee's lines and approached the outskirts of Richmond itself, where hard-drinking Arnold Elzey had organized government clerks and workmen into a "Local Defense Brigade." At one place Stoneman burned twenty-one wagonloads of bacon; at another, 50,000 barrels of corn and wheat; and wherever possible he destroyed bridges and disrupted railroad communications. Unused to daring offensives by their own forces, Northerners extravagantly acclaimed Stoneman; but the chief effect of his raid was to deprive Hooker of proper cavalry support during the battle of Chancellorsville.

The Army of the Potomac on the Way to Chancellorsville, April 30, 1863.

In preparation for his big offensive Hooker swore off the bottle, and, grown moody and suspicious, he entrusted his plans to none of his aides. While Sedgwick made a demonstration before Fredericksburg, Hooker proposed to take the major part of his army across fords higher up the river and to fall upon Lee from the west. It was maneuver in the grand style, performed with precision. By dusk on April 30 the Federals were at Chancellorsville, and Hooker confidently proclaimed that now "our enemy must either ingloriously fly, or come out from behind his defenses and give us battle on our own ground, where certain destruction awaits him."

The Union troops continued to advance the next day, until sudden panic struck Hooker. "In the face of urgent appeals and stern protests against sacrificing such opportunities, presented by several of his most eminent generals, General Hooker, to the astonishment of his men and the wonder of the enemy," ordered his army back to defensive positions before Chancellorsville. "The major-general commanding trusts," read his order, "that a suspension in the attack to-day will embolden the enemy to attack us."

On May 2 the Federal line stretched in a semicircle below the Rappahannock. By strange error the vital and exposed right flank was entrusted to the Eleventh Corps, composed mostly of Germans who had been so often shifted from one general to another and so often defeated as to have a low morale and a lower reputation. In command now was O. O. Howard, more famed for being "strictly conscientious" and for leading "a pure, holy, and consistent life" than for any martial virtues. He had neglected instructions to guard his flank, and his "men had stacked arms and were playing cards and loitering about without any thought of danger." Then, in the quiet of late afternoon, things began to happen.

Major General Oliver Otis Howard, U.S.A.

Howard's Headquarters at Dowdall's Tavern, Two Miles from Chancellorsville, May 2, 1863.

Stonewall Jackson's 28,000 men had marched fifteen miles across the Federal front and now, yipping their high, quavering rebel yell—"an 'unearthly, fiendish yell, such as no other troops or civilized beings ever uttered,' as a Federal chaplain reported"—were charging against the exposed flank. Howard's Eleventh Corps broke and ran. "The flying Germans came dashing over the field in crowds," related a Union witness, "stampeding, . . . running as only men do run when convinced that sure destruction is awaiting them. At the same moment large masses of the rebel infantry came dashing through the woods . . . and opened a tremendous fire of musketry into the confused mass of men and animals. . . . Night was rapidly approaching, and darkness was already beginning to obscure all things . . . . May I never be a witness to another such scene! On one hand was a solid column of infantry retreating at double-quick from the face of the enemy, who were already crowding their rear; on the other was a dense mass of beings who had lost their reasoning faculties and were flying from a thousand fancied dangers as well as from the real danger that crowded so close upon them, aggravating the fearfulness of their situation by the very precipitancy with which they were seeking to escape from it. On the hill were ten thousand of the enemy, pouring their murderous volleys in upon us, yelling and hooting, to increase the alarm and confusion; hundreds of cavalry horses, left riderless . . . were dashing frantically about in all directions; a score of batteries of artillery were thrown into disorder . . . ; battery wagons, ambulances, horses, men, cannon, caissons, all jumbled . . . together in an apparently inextricable mass, and that murderous fire still pouring in upon them."

Lieutenant General Thomas Jonathan Jackson, Two Weeks Before Chancellorsville.

Couch's Second Army Corps Covering the Retreat of General Howard, May 2, 1863.

"For a moment it seemed as if no power could avert the frightful calamity that threatened the entire army." Then, almost without direction, the Union troops began to rally; and by the morning of May 3 they were holding their own. Just then Hooker was knocked unconscious. When he recovered, he groggily pulled back his men, canceled resistance, and planned retreat. "By 10 A.M.," said Lee in his report, "we were in full possession of the field."

The Confederate success had been a costly one, for on the previous night, reconnoitering, Jackson was by mistake fired upon by his own men. His arm had to be amputated, and though surgeons hoped for recovery he sank rapidly. "The charmed circle in which General Jackson and his staff moved is broken," grieved Jed Hotchkiss, his chief engineer, "and the break was a heavy one—and today [May 10] it is feared that General Jackson has reached his last days, pneumonia has attacked him, debilitated by his wound, and his physicians think the chances for his recovery are very poor—but I do pray Heaven to spare him . . . —he said himself that he did not doubt but it was for the wisest purposes that he lost his arms [sic] as the revelations of eternity would show." That afternoon Stonewall Jackson died.

At the other end of the battlefield General Sedgwick was faithfully carrying out his directive to demonstrate against the Confederate right wing. "The expected battle . . . must be one of the most sanguinary of the whole war," predicted a Southern defender on April 29. "The enemy commenced crossing, at an early hour this morning, lower down the river than before, about a mile. . . . We opposed them . . . but . . . as soon as the fog cleared away we retired to our old position and they have been massing troops in our front all day,—and had over 20,000 over, at dark, and will probably get most of their army over during the night,—and tomorrow, O! tomorrow Death will hold high carnival—but, I am sure, with God's blessing, we shall whip them." In rifle pits on Marye's Heights and behind the stone wall below, the Confederates waited.

Rifle Pits in Front of the Marye House Overlooking Fredericksburg.

Sedgwick, who liked to think of himself as a "practical as distinguished from the theoretical soldier," knew "very little of books, seldom read anything, and . . . made no pretence of proficiency in the abstruse branches of military science." But he did know his orders, and he understood that an assault at Fredericksburg would relieve Hooker. The Confederates still occupied the bloody heights behind the city, but the general was daring.

On May 3 "at twenty minutes past eleven," noted a precise Union newspaperman, "the lion-hearted men rose from their feet. Every one of the thousand spectators . . . in the rear held their breath in terrible suspense, expecting to see them all the next moment prostrate in the dust. 'Forward!' cried the General, and they dashed forward on the open plain, when instantly there was poured upon them a most terrific discharge of grape and cannister. Many lay dead, but not one faltered. . . . As they press forward, delivering the battle-cheer, which is heard above the roar of artillery, the rebel guns further to the left

The Stone Wall Below Marye's Heights, May 3, 1863.

Men of the 6th Maine Infantry.

are turned upon them. But they falter not. A moment more they have reached the stone-wall, scaled its sides, are clambering the green bank of the bluff, and precisely as the city clock struck they rush over to the embrasure of the rebel guns, and the Heights are ours. The enemy . . . fled in wild confusion. . . . 'What men are these?' was the interrogatory of one of the astonished and terrified [Confederates], as our brave boys appeared over the ramparts. 'We are Yankees, —— you; do you think we will fight now?' was the response from one of our men. . . . The Sixth Maine were the first regiment to reach the scene."

But their daring went for nothing, for with Hooker's retreat across the Rappahannock, Sedgwick too had to fall back. Chancellorsville was over, another Union disaster. "Had we been properly handled," lamented a young Federal officer, "we might have gained a great victory, but we lacked the leader and are again looking for some one worthy of the army whose energies no defeat can tame."

Major General George Gordon Meade, U.S.A.

VI. Gettysburg

"Well, boys I've been seceding for two years," exclaimed a Confederate private as he touched Maryland soil, "and now I've got back into the Union again!" It was June, 1863, and Lee had begun his second invasion of the North. Fredericksburg and Chancellorsville had given the commander a superb confidence in his men; said one of his lieutenants, "General Lee believed that the Army of Northern Virginia, as it then existed, could accomplish anything." The faith of the leader was equaled by the trust of the men. "We do not yet know where we are going nor have I any conjecture as to General Lee's plans," one of the soldiers wrote. "General Lee will look after them . . . without my aid or interference."

This expedition into enemy territory was a desperate gamble, but Lee had weighed the odds. His country was becoming impoverished, dispirited, tired. The Federal blockade was gradually starving the South. In the West, Grant was besieging Vicksburg. In Tennessee, Rosecrans was forcing Bragg back upon Chattanooga. Hooker's army was still on Virginia soil, where another victory could have no decisive results. "We should not . . . conceal from ourselves," Lee frankly warned President Davis, "that our resources in men are constantly diminishing, and the disproportion in this respect between us and our enemies . . . is steadily augmenting." An invasion of the North would at least supply provisions and forage; it might divert support from Grant; it ought to encourage war weariness among the Yankees; and, if successful, it could win European recognition for the Confederacy. There seemed to be no alternative.

Quietly Lee pulled away from Hooker's army, slipped along the Blue Ridge Mountains, crossed the Potomac, and was once more in Maryland. The news brought "excitement and terror" to the North. In Baltimore earthworks were hastily erected; in Harrisburg the state archives were packed for prompt removal; in Washington the President called for more volunteers. Meeting little resistance but progressing blindly because Stuart's cavalry were absent on another daring raid, the Confederate army moved across Maryland and into Pennsylvania.

The Army of the Potomac, under a new commander, was doggedly pursuing. To replace Hooker, Lincoln on June 27 appointed George Gordon Meade. "There is not an officer in the army," said one lieutenant, "who does not rejoice at the news. We saw enough of Hooker at Chancellorsville. . . ." Looking "more like a learned pundit than a soldier," Meade was "tall, spare, of a commanding figure and presence, his manner easy and pleasant, but having much dignity. His head is partially bald," a reporter noted, "and is small and compact, but the forehead is high. He has the late Duke of Wellington class of nose, and his eyes, which have a serious and almost sad expression, are rather sunken. . . . He has a decidedly patrician and distinguished appearance."

A man who did not underestimate the task entrusted to him or overestimate his own abilities, Meade had assumed command reluctantly. "It remains to be seen whether I have the capacity to handle successfully a large army," he wrote. He would soon have a chance to find out, for Lee's army was emerging from the mountains near a town named Gettysburg.

Charge of Union Cavalry Under Major General Alfred Pleasonton During Confederate Retirement from Upperville, Virginia, June 21, 1863.

The death of Stonewall Jackson left an irremediable gap in the Confederate army. "I do not know how to replace him," Lee lamented. Finally he decided to divide the Army of Northern Virginia into three corps. Longstreet continued to lead the First; a newly organized Third Corps was given to A. P. Hill; but most of Jackson's men fell to "Dick" Ewell, new commander of the Second Corps. Ewell had lost a leg at Groveton; but now, with a young wife and a new wooden leg, "Old Bald Head" seemed to be fully recovered.

At the same time Lee consolidated his cavalry into a single corps under Jeb Stuart. Covering the Confederate march into Maryland, Stuart fought a series of battles with Federal cavalry under Pleasonton. Because Lee wished to conceal the whereabouts of his infantry, they were all-cavalry fights, and spectators had "the rare opportunity of a full view of a cavalry charge. The two lines intermingled in apparent inextricable confusion. Sabres flashed, men yelled, horses reared. There was cutting, slashing, cheering; riderless horses dashed madly to the rear, or, lost and perplexed, ran aimlessly up and down the line." None of the battles was decisive; but for the first time Union horsemen were fighting on equal terms with Stuart's.

Major General Richard Stoddert Ewell, C.S.A.

Brigadier General John Buford, U.S.A., and Staff.

It was not till the Southerners reached Pennsylvania that the two armies made contact. Emerging from the mountains at Cashtown, advance elements of the Confederate army by accident came upon the cavalry division of General John Buford. People said of Buford, "He is of a good-natured disposition, but not to be trifled with." This "singular-looking party, . . . with a tawny moustache and a little, triangular gray eye, whose expression is determined, not to say sinister," liked to fight. Instead of retreating when he saw that the Confederates greatly outnumbered him, he put up a stiff resistance and sent word to his corps commander, General Reynolds, "We need help now."

Death of Major General John F. Reynolds at Gettysburg, July 1, 1863.

Reynolds promptly came to Buford's support. The enemy was in overwhelming numbers, he reported to Meade, but "I will fight him inch by inch, and if driven into [Gettysburg] I will barricade the streets and hold him back as long as possible." When he rode forward to inspect the disposal of his troops, the Confederates "at that instant poured in a cruel musketry fire . . . ; a bullet struck General Reynolds in the neck, wounding him mortally. Crying out with a voice that thrilled the hearts of his soldiers, 'Forward! for God's sake, forward!' he turned for an instant, beheld the order obeyed by a line of shouting infantry, and falling into the arms of . . . his aid, who rode beside him, his life went out with the words: 'Good God, Wilcox, I am killed.' "

Dead of the 24th Michigan Infantry.

"Good God," exclaimed Meade when he learned of the fighting, "if the enemy get Gettysburg we are lost!" He ordered his entire army to the assistance of Reynolds's men and directed Winfield Scott Hancock, "the greatest fighting general in the Army of the Potomac," to take command on the battlefield. Hancock arrived to find the Union line collapsed. Slowly the Federals were driven back through the town to a cemetery on the hill beyond. Here Hancock rallied the fugitives and formed new lines. When one of his officers wished to retreat farther, Hancock snapped, "Sir! *I* am in command on this field. Send every man you have got!"

But there was reason for discouragement. "Not without grief, nor without misgiving, did the officers and soldiers . . . contemplate the day's engagement. . . . Their comrades lay in heaps beyond the village whose spires gleamed peacefully in the sunset before them." The First Corps had taken nearly 10,000 men into action and by nightfall had only 2,400 left. The 24th Michigan Infantry, part of the famed Iron Brigade, had lost 399 of its 496 men.

Private Charles Comes, Company K, 8th Louisiana Infantry, Killed at Gettysburg, July 1, 1863.

Confederate losses, on the other hand, were light. Questioned during the battle about his casualties, John B. Gordon shouted, "I haven't got any, sir; the Almighty has covered my men with His shield and buckler." Lee could look forward to victory the next day. "Gentlemen," he instructed his corps commanders, "we will attack the enemy in the morning as early as practicable."

Union Artillery on Cemetery Hill.

Through the hot afternoon Meade's army was marching toward Gettysburg. From the heights of Cemetery Hill an anxious observer "could see the white-covered wagons slowly winding in and out through the forests, and the masses of blue coats toiling forward. In either direction, for miles, you could catch occasional glimpses of the same sight through the openings of the foliage. The shades of evening dimmed and magnified the scene till one might have thought the hosts of Xerxes, in all the glory of modern armor, were pressing on Gettysburgh." Zook's men, of the Second Army Corps, arrived late at night. "With few halts for rest to the music of the distant guns," related an aide, "we hurried over the dusty roads, and at 10 P.M. reached the slope of a rocky hill, about a mile and a half in the rear of the battlefield. The moment the column halted the men dropped down on the road and most of them fell asleep immediately, exhausted by the march of thirty miles on a July day over roads knee deep in dust."

But at Meade's headquarters, a "tiny farm-house, sixteen by twenty," directly in the rear of Cemetery Ridge, there could be little sleep. Before daylight the general and his aides rode out to inspect the lines. Slowly "a formidable defensive position" was prepared. The Union line, as Douglas Southall Freeman has said, was shaped like a giant fishhook. The point, facing east, was Culp's Hill; the curve, south of the town of Gettysburg, was Cemetery Hill; the long shank ran along Cemetery Ridge, almost due south; and "the loop, so to speak, where the line might be joined," was "a sharp, rugged, and almost perpendicular peak covered with original forest growth" known as Little Round Top.

West of the ridge was a valley, "a mile to two miles in width, . . . and the fields were yellow with the golden harvest," and on the opposite side a lower range, called Seminary Ridge, where the principal Confederate line was being established, running thence east through Gettysburg, parallel to the Federal position on Culp's Hill.

Headquarters of Major General Meade at Gettysburg, July 2 and 3, 1863.

Brigadier General Daniel Edgar Sickles, U.S.A.

Sickles's Corps was assigned to the Union left flank. When that general found that Cemetery Ridge just north of Little Round Top sank into low marshy ground, he pushed his divisions slightly forward, to the west, where on one end a peach orchard and on the other rocky terrain called the Devil's Den seemed to afford more protection. The advanced position formed a salient which the Confederates could attack from three

The Slaughter Pen at the Foot of Little Round Top

sides. It was afternoon of July 2 when Meade learned what had happened, and he abruptly ordered Sickles to return his men to their assigned position. "Very well, sir, I'll withdraw them," agreed Sickles, and just then the full force of Longstreet's assault hit his exposed line. "I only wish you could, sir," retorted Meade angrily, "but you see those people don't intend to let you."

"A burst of cheering, followed immediately by a violent musketry fire, told us that the rebels were charging," related Colonel Regis de Trobriand, who was on Sickles's advanced line. "It was a hard fight. The Confederates appeared to have the devil in them. . . . my men did not flinch. Like veterans . . . they had sheltered themselves behind the rocks and trunks of trees . . . and when their assailants descended into the ravine and crossed the creek, they were received, at a distance of twenty yards, with a deadly volley, every shot of which was effective. The assault broken, those . . . on the opposite slope began a rapid fire at a range still very short. On both sides, each one aimed at his man, and . . . men fell dead and wounded with frightful rapidity."

Dead Confederate Sharpshooter at Devil's Den.

Some of the severest fighting occurred at "the well-named, weird, forsaken and desolate Devil's Den," where the "ground was rocky, strewn with immense boulders, and sparsely covered with timber." Confederate sharpshooters did heavy damage to Union lines. The lad in the picture, reported the photographer, Alexander Gardner, "had built up between two huge rocks, a stone wall, from the crevices of which he had directed his shots, and, in comparative security, picked off our officers."

Slowly Sickles's line was ground back. The general himself was wounded. Meade rushed reinforcements. When Zook's men arrived, one of them related, "we halted and formed column of attack in two lines. . . . As soon as the formation was completed, we marched forward to the attack, at first over rising ground, shortly received a tremendous fire from the front . . . no word of command could be heard, and little could be seen but long lines of flame, and smoke and struggling masses of men. . . . Our men fired promiscuously, steadily pressing forward, but the fighting was so mixed, rebel and union lines so close together, . . . that a clear idea of what was going on was not readily obtainable."

"In every direction among the bodies was the debris of battle—haversacks, canteens, hats, caps, sombreros, blankets of every shade and hue, bayonets, cartridge boxes—every conceivable part of the equipment of a soldier of the blue or grey mingled with the bodies of Yankee and rebel, friends and foes. . . . They were in every possible position, with arm uplifted, with clenched fist and menacing attitude, some with the smile of peace. . . . Some were in the act of tearing a cartridge, others just loading or reaching for the rammer. . . . Corpses strewed the ground at every step. Arms, legs, heads, and parts of dismembered bodies were scattered all about, and sticking among the rocks, and against the trunks of trees, hair, brains, entrails and shreds of human flesh. . . ."

Dead of the 1st Minnesota Infantry.

Major General Gouverneur Kemble Warren, U.S.A.

Little Round Top.

Just as Longstreet's attack struck Sickles, General Warren, Meade's acting chief of staff, made a horrifying discovery. Climbing Little Round Top, "the key to our left flank," he found "not a man on the hill." It was a desperate moment, for in the woods below, Warren "saw the gleam of a line of muskets nearly a mile long, already arrayed to outflank our line." Off he dashed for troops. On the road he met the 140th New York Infantry and commandeered them, panting, "Bring them up on the double-quick—don't stop for aligning! I'll take the responsibility." Lifting his guns bodily over the rocks, Hazlett followed with his battery. The 20th Maine Volunteers rushed to the rescue. "Up the steep hillside we ran, and reached the crest," wrote one of them. "Shells were crashing through the air above our heads . . . but our men appeared to be as cool . . . as if they had been forming a line upon the parade ground in camp. . . . Our regiment was mantled in fire and smoke. . . . The air seemed to be alive with lead. The lines at times were so near each other that the hostile gun barrels almost touched. . . . Our line is pressed back. . . . Our ammunition is nearly all gone. . . . The order is given 'Fix bayonets!' . . . 'Charge bayonets, charge!' . . . The rebels were confounded at the movement. We struck them with a fearful shock. They recoil, stagger, break and run, and like avenging demons our men pursue. . . ." Little Round Top was saved.

Battle of Gettysburg at 10:00 A.M. on July 3, 1863, viewed

While Longstreet was fighting on the Union left, Ewell was busy at the extreme right, and Edward Johnson's division advanced far up Culp's Hill. Night left the armies in position, and the third day of the battle (July 3) opened with Federal General Slocum's attempt to drive back the Confederates from the right. Edwin Forbes's drawing gives an unusual view of the Union position from the rear (the east). The Federal line ran along the ridge in the background; beyond lay the valley and Seminary Ridge. The details of the sketch require a key: 1, Culp's Hill, where Slocum's Twelfth Corps was repelling Johnson's renewed attack; 2, Wolf's Hill; 3, Cemetery and cemetery gate, held by Howard's Eleventh Corps (compare the drawing on page 176); 4, Baltimore turnpike leading to Gettysburg, filled with infantry, ammunition wagons, and ambulances; 5, Powers Hill, Slocum's headquarters (where Meade also made his headquarters later in the day during Pickett's charge); 6, Knapp's Pennsylvania Battery shelling between Culp's Hill and Wolf's Hill,

[184]

from Junction of Gettysburg Turnpike and Taneytown Road.

enfilading Johnson's line of battle; 7, General Slocum and staff; 8, reserves ready to attack Johnson's division; 9, smoke from guns of the Twelfth Corps, on Culp's Hill; 10, Wadsworth's Division, First Corps; 11, batteries on Cemetery Ridge, Wadsworth's division; 12, batteries on the Cemetery and on the plateau in front, First and Eleventh Corps; 13, bursting caisson, Hancock's Second Corps; 14, Ziegler's Grove (objective of Pickett's charge in the afternoon); 15, infantry supporting guns on the ridge; 16, road to Taneytown (running generally south); 17, ambulances going to the front; 18, reserve artillery; 19, brigade marching between Culp's Hill and Wolf's Hill to attack Johnson's flank; 20, point to which Johnson's division had penetrated on the previous night (July 2); 21, Union batteries replying to Confederate guns on Seminary Hill; 22, Gettysburg (beyond the ridge and to the right).

Pickett's Charge.

In the afternoon the Confederates made their final assault. Reluctantly Longstreet summoned Pickett, of the "graceful build, dark, glossy hair, worn almost to his shoulders in curly waves, of wondrous pulchritude and magnetic presence," and ordered him to cross the valley, ascend the ridge, and break the Union line. "I will lead my division forward, General Longstreet," said Pickett gallantly, and he prepared his men to charge. After a furious artillery barrage, they advanced. One of the survivors recorded his emotions. "We rise to our feet. . . . Some are actually *fainting* from the heat and dread. . . . Onward—steady—dress to the right . . . how gentle the slope! steady—keep well in line—there is the line of guns we must take—right in front—but how far they appear! . . . Now truly does the work of death begin. The line becomes unsteady because at every step a gap must be closed. . . . Close up the ranks when a friend falls, while his life blood bespatters your cheek. . . . Still we press on—oh, how long it seems. . . . Our men are falling faster now. . . . Volley after volley of crashing musket balls . . . mow us down like wheat before the scythe. . . . Thirty more yards and the guns are ours."

Major General George Edward Pickett, C.S.A.

Brigadier General Alexander Stewart Webb, U.S.A.

The Confederates reached the summit and in an instant "the larger portion of Webb's Brigade . . . was breaking . . . and . . . falling back, a fear-stricken flock of confusion." But Webb was "on foot in the midst of the men. Entreaty, command, expostulation, encouragement, were employed. Webb was everywhere." His men rallied and, reinforced, pushed the assailants back. From the Union line roared the cry, *"The crest is safe!"*

[188]

Colonel James Lawson Kemper, C.S.A.

All three of Pickett's brigadiers charged with their men. Armistead was killed; Garnett was hit. "I was close enough to the enemy to distinguish features and expressions of faces," wrote Kemper. "I fell just about the time our men began to give back." The charge had failed, and with it the Confederacy. "The army did all it could," Lee said sadly. "I fear I required of it impossibilities."

Three Confederate Soldiers Captured at Gettysburg.

Retreating into the mountains, the Confederates made for Virginia. Meade had repelled the invader and had captured thousands of prisoners, but he pursued slowly. By the time he reached the Potomac, Lee was safe on the other side. "We had them within our grasp," mourned Lincoln. "We had only to stretch forth our hands & they were ours. And nothing I could say or do could make the Army move."

[190]

VII. From Gettysburg to Grant

On August 1, 1863, the Gettysburg campaign officially closed. It had been a disastrous summer for the South. The invasion of Pennsylvania had proved to be a failure. Grant had taken Vicksburg. In East Tennessee, Bragg was pressed so hard that Lee had to send Longstreet's corps to his rescue. And once again the Army of Northern Virginia was on home ground, in the area where the war had done its worst. "The people in this neighborhood," reflected a Confederate captain, "are in a most deplorable condition. . . . their fences and outhouses are destroyed and not a pig left to drive away the wolf of hunger. Many must starve to death."

Meade slowly followed Lee into Virginia; but pressure from Lincoln and Halleck could not persuade him to risk another battle—except on his own terms. "If Bob Lee will go into those fields there and fight me, man for man," Meade told his critics, "I will do it this afternoon." When Halleck pointed out that "Bob Lee" was not likely to be so foolish, Meade retorted angrily, "If you have any orders to give me, I am prepared to receive and obey them, but I must insist on being spared the infliction of such truisms in the guise of opinions as you have recently honored me with, particularly as they were not asked for."

With one army dispirited and the other diffident, there could be no major operations during the fall. "It seems likely," thought one of Meade's lieutenants, "we shall be led in a plodding, ordinary sort of way, neither giving nor receiving any serious blows, a great pity." There were skirmishes and maneuvers, advances and retreats, feints and raids, which had no particular purpose and achieved no particular results. In late July the Army of the Potomac crept forward into central Virginia; when Lee threatened to come between it and Washington, it hastily retreated. In November, Meade advanced again over the same terrain, found the Confederates heavily entrenched, and again withdrew. The Union army's tactics, reflected Colonel Theodore Lyman, who was serving as a volunteer aide to Meade, were about as effective as trying "to catch a sea-gull with a pinch of salt."

In December both armies went into winter quarters. "The troops burrowed in the earth and built their little shelters, and the officers and men devoted themselves to unlimited festivity, balls, horse-races, cock-fights, greased pigs and poles, and other games such as only soldiers can devise." In the Federal camp, Lyman observed, "There is about as much appearance of an enemy near at hand, as there would be on Boston Common."

Though superficially alike, the rival winter quarters had a fundamental difference. The pictures of Meade's camp give the impression of rough plenty. For the Union army there was always more—more men, more food, more horses, more ammunition. One would give a great deal for comparable pictures of Lee's troops during this bleak winter of Southern defeat. Troops were going barefoot and in tatters; rations had been cut again; cavalry horses were starving for lack of forage. In their hearts many Southerners were coming to see that the North must win, once it found a general.

Capture of Confederate Guns by General Custer near Culpeper Court House.

On September 13–15, as Meade followed Lee into Virginia, the Confederate rear guard was attacked by Union cavalry near Culpeper. "Just in the outskirts," wrote Theodore Lyman, "the Rebels had planted two batteries, as a last check, and behind were drawn up their supports of cavalry. Our cavalry were coming out of the woods, on all sides, moving on the town in the form of a semi-circle. . . . Then there suddenly appeared a body of our cavalry, quite on the left of the town, who made a rush, at full speed, on three cannon there stationed, and took the whole of them with their caissons. This was a really handsome charge and was led by General Custer, who had his horse shot under him. This officer is one of the funniest-looking beings you ever saw, and looks like a circus rider gone mad! He wears a huzzar jacket and tight trousers, of faded black velvet trimmed with tarnished gold lace. His head is decked with a little, gray felt hat; high boots and gilt spurs complete the costume, which is enhanced by the General's coiffure, consisting in short, dry, flaxen ringlets!"

There was further fighting at Raccoon Ford, just as the Confederates were crossing the Rapidan. "As we got in sight of it," Lyman reported, "the prospect was not cheering. The opposite bank, partly wooded and partly covered with cultivation, rose in steep, high hills, which completely commanded our side of the river. It was a fine sight to see the column splashing along the wood road, lying between fine oak trees; but the fine sight was presently interrupted by a shell, which exploded about 100 yards ahead of me and right among the horses' legs, without touching me! . . . After some difficulty we got some guns in position and drove off those opposed. Then General Kilpatrick's division went to a better ford below, and tried to get over there; but the Rebels opened on him with . . . a hard fire. . . . Whereupon both parties stopped and stared at each other. . . ." The next day the Confederates withdrew farther to the south.

General John Buford's Attack on Confederates at Raccoon Ford.

Culpeper, Virginia.

Meade made his headquarters at Culpeper Court House, which he found "beautifully situated at the foot of the Blue Ridge, with the mountains in view, with pure air and plenty of good water; the best country in Virginia we have yet been in." But to Federal troops it seemed "eminently a 'deserted village.' Its dwellings were all closed and apparently tenantless. No resident, male or female, was seen on the highways, and of the twenty stores and groceries none seemed to be doing business. Two hotels . . . still pretended to accommodate travellers. There were four churches, a large institute for girls, an academy for boys and several other schools. The buildings were of brick and frame, the latter largely predominating. . . . The population had numbered about 1500."

In October, Union headquarters learned that the Confederate army was "performing some fancy antics" again. By threatening to come between Meade and Washington, it compelled the Federals to retreat north to Centreville, near the old battlefield of Bull Run. Then Lee once again withdrew to the south, destroying railroads and bridges as he went. "Every rail was removed for miles, and having been placed across piles of burning ties was rendered temporarily unserviceable. Every bridge, too, was thoroughly destroyed. . . ." "His object," wrote the frustrated Meade, "is to prevent my advance, and in the mean-time send more troops to Bragg [in East Tennessee]. This was a deep game, and I am free to admit that in the playing of it he has got the advantage of me." Once more Union engineers had to rebuild the road south.

Building a Railroad Bridge Across Cedar Run near Catlett's Station, Virginia.

Capture of Confederate Fortifications at Rappahannock Bridge, November 7, 1863.

On November 7 Meade's "great, black columns of infantry" were again at the Rappahannock. Lee was expecting them. He hoped to attack Meade in superior force by permitting part of his army to cross at Kelly's Ford while holding the rest of the Union force north of the river at Rappahannock bridge, where Early occupied a strong position. The plan failed. In a surprise night attack nearly all Lee's men north of the river were captured. Meanwhile at Kelly's Ford, after an artillery barrage had broken the Confederate line, Meade's infantry waded waist-deep across the cold river and charged on the retreating Southerners. "It is absolutely sickening," wrote one Confederate officer, "and I feel personally disgraced by the issue of the late campaign. . . ."

Captain Jacob Henry Sleeper's 10th Massachusetts Battery at Kelly's Ford, November 7, 1863.

Going into Bivouac at Night.

Meade pushed farther south to Mine Run, where a major battle threatened; but, finding the Confederate position too strongly fortified, he withdrew and presently went into winter quarters.

The weary Army of the Potomac welcomed every opportunity to rest. Edwin Forbes watched the soldiers eagerly preparing for camp at night. In "anticipation of the evening meal" they "would step out of the column and confiscate all fence-rails available. They made a ludicrous appearance as they trudged along, with a gun on one shoulder, and a fence-rail on the other. . . . different brigades march[ed] to allotted positions, and the work of pitching camp soon began. Knapsacks and traps were unslung, and in a short time the hill-sides were covered with little 'pup' tents. The noise of axes . . . filled the air, and camp-fires began to blaze along in all directions. As it grew dark, the tents looked like thousands of Japanese lanterns. . . . The country was covered by a dense cloud of smoke, lit up by the glow of the fires, and the many sounds from the camp mingled in one great roar. . . . Jubilant spirits prevailed, and the jests and laughter in the face of so much danger seemed strange."

"'Beef on the hoof' was the soldiers' name for the fresh beef furnished them, and the herds of cattle from which it came were no inconsiderable portion of the army's supplies. The Commissary Department usually furnished a certain number of steers to each moving column, and it was a pleasant sight to watch the droves with their escorts as they traveled along the road. A stalwart white ox, with eyes too gentle to suggest slaughter, would sometimes be in lead, and around his neck would be hung blankets, a cartridge-box and other accoutrements of the guard. Often a soldier would sit astride the animal in lead and guide him with a long pole, while the rest of the herd would be kept in order by a series of vigorous shouts. When a herd reached camp at night-fall, it would be driven into an adjacent field, where it was carefully guarded during the night and where it could rest and feed till the column moved again."

Beef for the Army.

Night Action at Morton's Ford, Virginia, February 6, 1864.

From time to time the tranquillity of winter quarters was interrupted by rather mean-ingless excursions. On February 6 unexpected orders were issued by Meade for simul-taneous demonstrations at Raccoon and Morton's fords. "Well, who would have thought of marching out of comfortable winter quarters, to go poking around the Rapidan!" ex-claimed Theodore Lyman. "To Morton's Ford is some ten miles but you might as well call it fifty, such is the state of the roads. Mud, varying from fetlocks to knees, then holes, runs, ditches and rocks—such was the road. . . . Here we had thrown across a division. . . . The enemy had offered a good deal of opposition, with a skirmish fire and with artillery; despite which the whole division had waded the stream, up to their waists (cold work for the 6th of February!), and were now in line, behind some ridges; while a heavy skirmish line covered their front. Enclosing them, almost in a semi-circle, were the Rebel earthworks. It looked a shaky position for us! . . . Our artillery opened . . . and, in course of an hour or so, night set in, and the firing ceased, our line holding its own every-where." It was hard to see that the expedition had any purpose or any accomplishments.

Brigadier General Judson Kilpatrick's Raid on Richmond.

A far more daring exploit was the expedition undertaken in February-March by General Kilpatrick ("Kill-cavalry," the infantry called him). It was not one of Meade's ideas, but the cavalry officer seemed to have direct White House approval for his raid. "The idea," Lyman learned, "is to liberate the prisoners [in Richmond], catch all the rebel M.C.'s that are lying round loose, and make tracks to our nearest lines. I conceive the chances are pretty hazardous. . . ." The raiders actually reached the outskirts of Richmond, "and, as the spires and houses of the city came in view, cheer upon cheer went up from our men. Riding rapidly toward the city, the outer line of works was entered." But Colonel Dahlgren was killed, Kilpatrick himself was delayed, and "as the shrill whistle of the locomotive told of the bringing up of reenforcements from Pickett's brigade," Kilpatrick reluctantly withdrew. Back in camp it was charged that the general had proved to be "a frothy braggart, without brains and not over-stocked with desire to fall on the field," and some rejoiced that "Kill has rather dished himself."

Union Picket Line at Rappahannock Station, January 20, 1864.

Except for such interruptions, winter duty was unrelieved monotony. Pickets had to be maintained against spies and surprise. In early 1864 Edwin Forbes sketched the Union line above the Rappahannock River at Beverly Ford. "In the foreground was a line of rude picket huts, tenanted by groups of soldiers, while within short distance men on duty were passing up and down with guns at a shoulder. Across the Rapidan, about fifteen miles to the south, was a range of hills on which Gen. Lee's army was camped, and from which with the aid of a glass faint columns of ascending smoke could be discerned." Picket duty was not pleasant, for Virginia can be cold and bleak during the winter. "The men out on picket," recalled one veteran, "need the thickest clothing to keep the life current flowing. The cold stars overhead, the ice-bound earth—tramp, tramp, through the long hours of the longest nights of the winter, walks the picket on his beat till the relief comes, and the sentry returns."

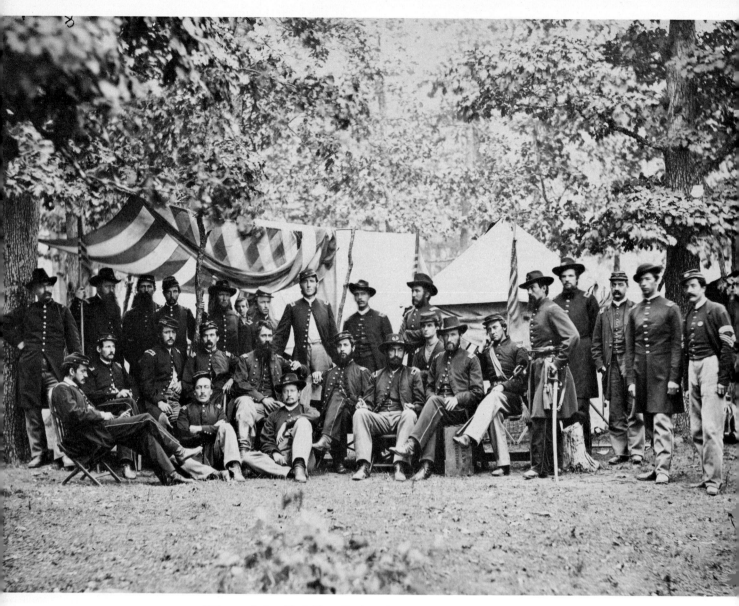

Officers of the 93rd New York Infantry near Germantown, Virginia.

"As a rule," wrote Theodore Lyman, "I am much pleased with the aspect of our officers, high and low. They are cleanly and have a firm, quiet bearing. You can often pick out those who have been through the thick of it, by their subdued and steady look." Some privates had a different view, for, as one of them said of his officers, "They get all the glory and most of the pay and don't earn ten cents apiece on the average, the drunken rascals."

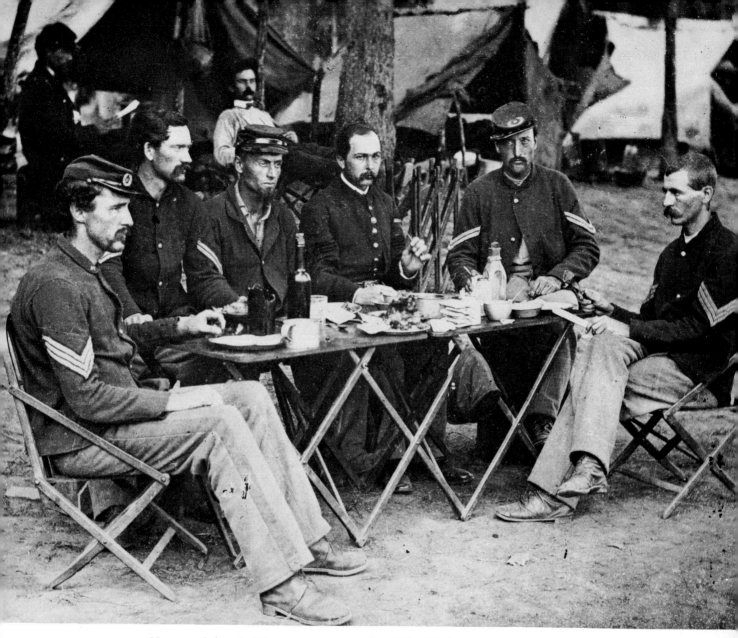

Noncommissioned Officers, Company D, 93rd New York Infantry, at Mess.

"A daily ration for a soldier was as follows: Hard bread, or (hard tack) 16 ounces; soft bread was sometimes, when in camp, issued in place of the hard bread, and the amount was 22 ounces per day. Beef, (salt or fresh) 20 ounces. Pork or bacon, 12 ounces. And to every 100 men per day there was issued, beans, 15 pounds; rice, 10 pounds; ground coffee, 8 pounds. In place of coffee 1½ pounds tea; sugar, 15 pounds; vinegar, 4 quarts; soap, 4 pounds; salt, 3¼ pounds; pepper ¼ pound, and candles, 1¼ pounds." In the postwar years some veterans recalled, "Our meat was generally good, soft bread fresh and nice, coffee and other groceries as good as you will get at the groceryman's." At the time, however, they were more likely to write home, "The boys say that our 'grub' is enough to make a *mule* desert, and a *hog* wish he had never been born."

Union Drummer Boy at Beverly Ford, Virginia, August 11, 1863.

Drum Corps, 93rd New York Infantry, near Germantown, Virginia.

Drummer boys sounded the daily calls on drum, fife, or bugle and "were in their special element at a grand review, when they appeared with white gloves and shining brasses." Twelve-year-old Johnnie Walker, wrote a private of the 22nd Wisconsin Regiment, "is drummer for the band, and when they play at dress parade every evening lots of gentlemen and ladies come from the city to hear them play and see the little drummer and when we are marching, and the ladies see the little soldier-boy they always give him apples, cakes or something. . . . When we are marching Johnnie always keeps up with the big men, and is always singing and laughing but when he gets tired the big Colonel . . . will let Johnnie have his horse to ride. Everybody in the regiment likes Johnnie because he is a good little boy, is always pleasant and polite and not saucy like a great many boys. His mother sent him a suit of clothes made exactly like officer's clothes, and Lieutenant Baumman says he will get him a pair of shoulder straps with silver drum sticks upon them."

A Group of Zouaves at Brandy Station, Virginia.

Exotically clad Zouave units had been the rage at the beginning of the war, but by 1863 their finery was becoming sadly tarnished. An English observer found them "miserably shabby. Were they genuine Turks, most appropriately might they be commanded by Seedy Pasha. . . . Grubby and clumsily twisted are their turbans; faded their fez-caps; torn the tassels which used to droop therefrom; braidless the once brave jackets; cleft in unseemly rents, or branded with disgraceful patches, the baggy breeches. The whilom bright yellow jackets have grown dirty brown, like a portmanteau too long in use; and the once white gaiters have come to be of no color at all."

"There are perfect shoals of womenkind now in the army," found Theodore Lyman in February, 1864, "a good many, of course, in Culpeper, where they can live in houses. The rest of them must live a sort of Bedouin life." An English visitor was pleased with "this pleasurable invasion." "Many of the officers had sent for their wives," he found; "and some of the officers' spouses had, I dare say, come down to the camp without being sent for. . . . Their influence softens and humanises much that might otherwise be harsh and repulsive. In their company, at least, officers who should be gentlemen do not get drunk . . . ." Lyman, on the other hand, was not enthusiastic about these army ladies. "Such a set of feminine humans I have not seen often; it was Lowell factories broken loose and gone mad."

Headquarters of the 1st Brigade, Horse Artillery, at Brandy Station.

By 1863 the standard army tent was the "A, or Wedge Tent," so called because of its shape. "Four men was the number usually assigned to one of them; but they were often occupied by five, and sometimes six. These tents when stockaded were quite spacious and comfortable. . . . In stockading a tent . . . the most common way . . . was to build . . . walls 'cob-fashion,' notching them together at the corners. . . . The chinks between the logs were filled with mud, worked to a viscous consistency, which adhered more or less tenaciously according to the amount of clay in the mixture. It usually needed renewing after a severe storm. The chimney was built outside. . . . It stood sometimes at the end and sometimes in the middle of one side of the stockade. It started from a fireplace . . . built of brick, of stone, or of wood. . . . When built of wood, the chimneys were lined with a very thick coating of mud. They were generally continued above the fireplace with

Camp of the 18th Pennsylvania Cavalry near Brandy Station.

Winter Quarters of Telegraphic and Photographic Departments at Brandy Station.

split wood built cob-fashion, which was filled between and lined with the red clayey soil of Virginia. . . . Very frequently pork and beef barrels were secured to serve this purpose, being put one above another, and now and then a lively hurrah would run through the camp when one of these was discovered on fire. . . . Many of these huts were deemed incomplete until a sign appeared over the door. Here and there some one would make an attempt at having a door-plate of wood suitably inscribed; but the more common sight was a sign over the entrance bearing such inscriptions, rudely cut or marked with charcoal, as: 'Parker House,' 'Hole in the Wall,' . . . 'Astor House,' 'Willard's Hotel'. . . ."

In such quarters the armies sat down to wait until spring. "The life here is miserably lazy," Lyman complained; "hardly an order to carry, and the horses all eating their heads off. . . . If one could only be at home, till one was *wanted,* and then be on the spot; but this is everywhere the way of war; lie still and lie still; then up and manœuvre and march hard; then a big battle; and then a lot more lie still."

Major General Ulysses Simpson Grant, U.S.A., in the Fall of 1863.

VIII. The Toughest of Tough Jobs

"He habitually wears an expression as if he had determined to drive his head through a brick wall, and was about to do it," wrote a Union officer of General Grant. A good many observers in 1862–1863 were saying the same thing about the general who kept stubbornly attempting the impossible. After Halleck was called to Washington, Grant was left in command of Union forces in western Tennessee and in Mississippi. The Confederates before him were under Earl Van Dorn and John C. Pemberton, able aides of Joseph E. Johnston, who had general command of Southern defenses in the West. The Confederates had one principal objective—to defend Vicksburg. Should Vicksburg be lost, said Pemberton, it "meant the loss of the valuable stores and munitions of war collected for its defense; the fall of Port Hudson [in Louisiana, the only other Confederate stronghold on the river]; the surrender of the Mississippi River, and the severance of the Confederacy." Grant's assignment was, accordingly, to take Vicksburg.

But that city, on high bluffs commanding the Mississippi, well "fortified and defended at all points," was a position "impregnable against any force that could be brought against its front." It was, Charles A. Dana wrote, "the toughest of tough jobs." Grant first attempted an overland approach, pushing south through Mississippi; but the difficulties of supplying his forces from one rickety rail line running through hostile countryside discouraged the venture. When Van Dorn in a brilliant raid destroyed Grant's base of supplies at Holly Springs, the overland approach was abandoned. Meanwhile General Sherman had been sent down the river with part of Grant's troops; his direct assault on Vicksburg was also a failure.

In Washington pressure was growing for Grant's removal. The Northwest was indignant at his inability to open the river, a vital trade route. General Halleck, never friendly to Grant, became even cooler toward this independent-minded subordinate. Men ran to Lincoln with tales of Grant's incompetence, his imbecility, his inebriation. Reluctantly the President yielded, to the extent of authorizing John A. McClernand, a former Democratic Congressman from Illinois, to raise an army in the Northwest for use against Vicksburg. Such a move would, he thought, be a welcome chance to get more men into the army; and perhaps he wished to spur Grant on.

At the beginning of 1863, therefore, Grant's position was clear. Most of his army lay at Young's Point, on the west bank of the Mississippi just above Vicksburg. A frontal assault on the city would be suicidal. To withdraw his troops up the river to Memphis for a fresh start would be an admission of defeat, and would have serious repercussions on the whole Union cause as well as on his own career. The general looked over the situation and made up his mind. "There was," he concluded, "nothing left to be done but to *go forward to a decisive victory.*"

Brigadier General John Aaron Rawlins, U.S.A.

Grant's adjutant, Rawlins, frankly admitted "that he had no technical knowledge of war"; but he had what was more important—a knowledge of Grant. "He . . . watches over him day and night," reported Dana, "and whenever he commits the folly of tasting liquor hastens to remind him that at the beginning of the war he gave . . . his word of honor not to touch a drop as long as it lasted." As Grant admitted, Rawlins came to be "more nearly indispensable to him than anyone else."

Major General John Alexander McClernand, U.S.A.

After McClernand arrived with his freshly recruited troops, he found himself relegated to the somewhat obscure position of corps commander under Grant. "He was naturally a proud, austere, and imperious man, who took but little pains to conceal his feelings and acted always with noticeable reserve and hauteur toward Grant." Ultimately Grant felt obliged to relieve him of his command.

Everybody had a plan for capturing Vicksburg. All the plans centered about one problem—how "to secure a footing upon dry ground on the east side of the river from which the troops could operate against Vicksburg." Some worked on a canal which would by-pass the city; others hoped to get below it by flooding backwaters and bayous; still others favored a naval expedition through the swamps above Vicksburg. All were equally unsuccessful; Grant regarded them as mere "experiments with which the winter was whiled away."

In the spring of 1863 the general revealed his own plan. It was a bold one. Requesting the navy to run its gunboats and transports past the Confederate river batteries, he marched his army to a point below Vicksburg, had it ferried over to the eastern side, abandoned his base of supplies, and planned to live upon the countryside. "I was going into the enemy's country," Grant realized, "with a large river behind me and an enemy holding points strongly fortified above and below." Now his army could only go forward.

Big Black River Station, Mississippi.

Battlefield of Big Black River, Mississippi.

Grant moved swiftly to prevent the scattered and surprised Confederate forces from concentrating. First he struck out for Jackson, the capital of Mississippi, where he drove back Johnston's forces. Then, turning rapidly to the west, he marched along the single railroad line toward Vicksburg. At Champion's Hill, Pemberton put up a fight but was thrown back. Again the next day, May 17, at the crossing of the Big Black River, he tried to hold Grant. "Their rifle pits were quite numerous," a Union sergeant reported, "but they were all on low ground, so that when the word was given the Yankees rushed over them with the greatest ease. The rebs may be drawing us into a trap, but as yet we have not a moments' fear of the result, for when Grant tells us to go over a thing we go, and feel safe in going." In disorder Pemberton's army fled to the defenses of Vicksburg as he lamented, "Just thirty years ago I began my military career . . . and today—the same date—that career is ended in disaster and disgrace." For the Union forces pursued at once. "On the road to Vicksburg," the sergeant commenced his diary entry, "resolved to capture the city or get badly whipped."

Brigadier General Martin Luther Smith, C.S.A.

Vicksburg was prepared for assault. Under the expert direction of M. L. Smith, later Lee's chief engineer during the Wilderness campaign, a semicircle of fortifications had been constructed with both ends resting on the river. "Fatigue parties were set to work making . . . repairs and connections; at the same time all field-artillery, Parrott guns, and siege pieces on the river front were moved to the rear line [facing Grant], platforms and embrasures were prepared for them, and ammunition was placed in convenient and protected places." When the Union troops appeared, they found "long lines of rebel earthworks following the zig-zag courses of the hills, and black field guns . . . menacing from their port-holes." The Confederate fortifications, thought Union general Thomas Kilby Smith, were "masterpieces of . . . military engineering."

The Siege of Vicksburg.

On May 19 the Federals attempted a direct assault upon the Vicksburg fortifications. "God! what a charge it was!" exclaimed Kilby Smith. "We had to work in on foot, over tangled abattis, up precipitous hills, and against ramparts bristling with cannon and rifle; the pits behind filled with soldiers ready with the hand grenade, and under a constantly enfilading fire. . . . My men came on so gallantly; not one to falter. I turned back to see them swept down in ranks. . . . We did all mortal man could do—but such slaughter!"

After another futile assault on May 22, the Union army settled down to besiege the city. Day after day there was constant bombardment. The firing, thought one Confederate defender, "can be compared to men clearing land—the report of musketry is like the chopping of axes and that of the cannon like the falling of trees."

As the Confederates continued to hold out, the Union commander undertook to sink a mine under their entrenchments. On June 25, reported a Federal artilleryman, "all hands were anxiously waiting, each desirous of witnessing the result. . . . All at once a dead heavy roll, a hundred shouts, and you could see nothing but a black cloud of dirt and powder smoke, throwing the earth 30 or 40 feet in the air, and about half of the wall rolled over the ditch as if turned by a ponderous plow. Instantaneous with this was the crack of a hundred cannon . . . while the infantry advancing with a yell . . . rushed up the breastworks. . . . Our men tried hard to . . . take possession of the fort, but it was too much." The siege went on.

U.S.S. Cricket.

From the river Porter's fleet assisted in the siege, and such "tinclads" as the little *Cricket*, with its "six twelve-pound boat-howitzers (smooth bores), and . . . forty-eight officers and men," joined his mortar boats in keeping up a constant bombardment. Shells "were thrown high in the air from a distance of four miles, describing nearly a half-circle in their flight, and either bursted into large fragments hundreds of feet above the earth, or, failing to explode, buried themselves deep in its surface, where they frequently blew up and tore immense holes in the ground. . . ."

Within the city people took to caves for protection. "Our new habitation," wrote one Vicksburg lady, "was an excavation made in the earth, and branching six feet from the entrance, forming a cave in the shape of a **T**. In one of the wings my bed fitted; the other I used as a kind of a dressing room. . . . We were safe at least from fragments of shell— and they were flying in all directions; though no one seemed to think our cave any protection, should a mortar shell happen to fall directly on top of the ground above us. We had our roof arched and braced, the supports of the bracing taking up much room in our confined quarters. The earth was about five feet thick above. . . ."

Though the beleaguered Confederates had to hoard their ammunition, they used their guns effectively. Federals especially dreaded one rifled eighteen-pounder, nicknamed "Whistling Dick" from the peculiar sound made by its shells. So long as such guns were part of the city's water batteries, Porter's fleet did not have free run of the river. "About half after nine o'clock," one Confederate defender wrote proudly on May 27, "the mortars commenced playing us more rapidly and at ten four gunboats advanced up the river and engaged the lower batteries, and soon we discovered from the smoke above that a boat was advancing from that direction. There was great commotion in the city—the women and children and even men ran for their rat holes thinking there would be a general attack in front . . . but all were soon undeceived. Our detachment was on the gun, we were ordered to it and soon we were at our posts eager for the fray. . . . The iron-clad then ran as near under the guns of the upper batteries as possible as entirely out of our range. Firing shot after shot she was soon repulsed and . . . we gave her all we had to spare. Cheer after cheer from the men told us that some good had been done; for the monster had become companion to the fishes under the waters of the great Mississippi."

"Whistling Dick."

The Landing at Vicksburg.

By the end of June, Pemberton saw that he could not hold out much longer. Johnston's forces lay too far away to relieve the siege. "General Starvation" was in command at Vicksburg. "We live on peas, mostly," one diarist recorded, while another reported that soup made from mule meat "was quite rich in taste and appearance." On June 28 a letter signed "Many Soldiers" reached Pemberton, complaining "Our rations have been cut down to one biscuit and a small bit of bacon per day. . . . If you can't feed us you had better surrender us, horrible as the idea is. . . . The army is now ripe for mutiny, unless it can be fed." Pemberton in despair asked for Grant's terms, and on Independence Day the Federal army marched into the captured city.

"Admiral Porter, with his fleet, came 'rounding to,' and soon the shore was close hemmed in by the steamers which now lined the levee. Bands were playing, troops were marching to and fro through the streets, and the cannon opened the National salute at noon, which was kept up by the gunboats till after 2 o'clock p.m."

The one remaining Confederate stronghold on the river was Port Hudson, already under siege by N. P. Bank's army. The defenders occupied a formidable position, a little Vicksburg. First Banks had ordered an assault "in the hope that some stroke of luck might give him the victory." John W. De Forest described a part of the attack: ". . . a sheet of red flashes lit up the dimness, followed by crashes of musketry and the yells of combatants. Then came the roar of artillery, the crackling of shells, and the whistling of grape. We could hear the humming, shrieking, and hissing of the projectiles as they passed over our heads; we could feel the shuddering of the trees against which we leaned, as they were struck; we were conscious of a falling of severed leaves and branches." When the charge failed, the Federal troops settled down to a bloody siege, "forty days and nights in the wilderness of death."

The Confederate defenders gallantly held out until they learned of the fall of Vicksburg, and then they too surrendered. Now, as Lincoln said, the Father of Waters ran "unvexed to the sea."

Captain Clayton Cox's Battery, 1st Regiment Indiana Heavy Artillery, Port Hudson, Louisiana.

The Autocrat, Flagship of Brigadier General Alfred W. Ellet's Marine
Brigade, Patrolling the Mississippi.

On July 16 the steamboat *Imperial* quietly landed at a wharf in New Orleans, direct
from St. Louis with a commercial cargo, having sailed down the Mississippi "undisturbed
by a hostile shot or challenge from bluff or levee on either shore." "Now that the Mississippi
is open from St. Anthony's to the Gulf," a New York newspaper editorialized, "the army
and navy to a great extent relinquish the care of the river to Ellet's Marine Brigade. . . .
The steamers are built peculiarly, and are garrisoned by cavalry, infantry and artillery.
Their business is to keep the river open and aid in other operations, naval and military."

The river was opened, and the Confederacy was severed; but there remained much
strength in the divided halves. In the intense interest in the great struggles in the East,
one sometimes forgets that there was also still a war in the West. General N. P. Banks, who
had succeeded the notorious Butler at New Orleans, was ambitious to crush the Confederate armies remaining in western Louisiana and in Texas. "A handsome, soldierly-looking
man, though rather theatrical in his style of dress," Banks "wore yellow gauntlets high up
on his wrists, looking as clean as if they had just come from the glove-maker; his hat was
picturesque, his long boots and spurs were faultless, and his air was that of one used to
command. In short," wrote Admiral Porter, "I never saw a more faultless-looking soldier."

Major General Nathaniel Prentiss Banks, U.S.A.

Lieutenant General Richard Taylor, C.S.A.

The U.S.S. Osage, Part of the Red River Expedition.

In the spring of 1864 Banks obtained the reluctant cooperation of Porter for an expedition up the Red River toward Shreveport. At first the soldiers and the steamboats advanced without much opposition, for Kirby-Smith, commander of all Confederate forces in the trans-Mississippi states, wished to lure Banks far inland and to fall upon him with reinforcements brought from Arkansas and Texas. But General Richard Taylor, who led the Southern troops in western Louisiana, was "a passionate, high-tempered man, [with] but little sense of subordination," and he decided to fight the advancing Union army despite his orders. "It is not the first time I have fought with a halter around my neck," he said; and on April 8 he struck at Banks's advancing columns near Sabine Crossroads. At first the Federals resisted. "Suddenly there was a rush, a shout, the crushing of trees, the breaking down of rails, the rush and scamper of men. Men found themselves swallowed up . . . in a hissing, seething, bubbling whirlpool of agitated men. . . . The line of battle had given way. Gen. Banks took off his hat and implored his men to remain. . . . but it was of no avail." Although the next day Banks won a victory, he decided to retreat down the river and abandon the expedition.

The U.S.S. Signal Towing Material for the Bailey Dam.

Porter was warned that he had better get his fleet back down the river if he wished to save it. But the Red River was behaving like a Confederate. The water, falling rapidly, was not deep enough for the Union gunboats to pass the shoal-ridden descent. Porter had bragged that his gunboats could go "wherever the sand was damp"; now he found them stranded. Then somebody discovered a Lieutenant Colonel Bailey who proposed by constructing temporary dams across the river to float the gunboats over the rapids. When Porter was told of the scheme, he said, "If you can dam better than I can, you must be a good hand at it, for I have been damning all night." At once soldiers were put to work. "The dam is being pushed in every possible way," reported one enlisted man. "Trees are cut and dragged in the river, and bags filled with earth are thrown in to fill up the spaces. Stones are so scarce that brick houses not in use are torn down and used for ballast." After eight days' work the water was high enough for most of the vessels to float downstream to safety.

That was the end of Banks's expedition. For the rest of the war General Kirby-Smith was left virtually unmolested in his trans-Mississippi command. He had accepted it as an "exile"; by the end of the war it was almost his private empire.

Lieutenant General Edmund Kirby-Smith, C.S.A.

Major General George Henry Thomas, U.S.A.

IX. Campaign for Chattanooga

"Recollect that East Tennessee is my horror," wrote Sherman. "That any military man should send a force into East Tennessee puzzles me." The general's dislike of this formidable mountainous terrain was understandable; yet there were excellent reasons why Northern and Southern armies should contend for the barren ground of eastern Tennessee. The inhabitants of the mountain regions were opposed to Jefferson Davis's government and stanchly loyal to the old Federal Union. Neither Richmond nor Washington could afford to ignore this potential fifth column in the center of the South. Furthermore, East Tennessee was strategically important. The rail hub of the Confederacy, Chattanooga, had connections extending east to Lee's army in Virginia, west to Johnston's forces in Mississippi, and south to important supply bases in Georgia. Here it was, thought Charles A. Dana, "that the heart of rebellion was within reach."

The armies that fought for this critical region were drawn chiefly from the Western states. "A fine-looking lot, strong, lean, long-limbed fighters," they were as brave and as hardy as the soldiers of Grant or Lee; yet for nearly three years their campaigns resulted in nothing more than the senseless shedding of blood. The fault was not in the men but in their leaders. After June, 1862, the principal Confederate commander was Braxton Bragg, tense, punctilious, arrogant, a martinet and a dawdler. Rapidly he became "the subject of hatred and contempt" among his own men; his subordinates' antagonism toward him was "the worst conceivable."

For a long time the Union forces were equally unfortunate. After Shiloh, Buell commanded the Army of the Cumberland; but, stubborn and slow, he permitted Bragg to march past him in September, 1862, on an invasion of Kentucky, timed to coincide with Lee's expedition into Maryland. "The two armies are running a race for the Ohio River," wrote a Union officer, as Buell hastily pursued the Confederates. "At this time Bragg has the lead." The whole campaign was a tragedy of errors. By lingering at Frankfort to install a puppet Confederate governor, Bragg wasted his advantage; by fighting against their commander's orders, Buell's forces precipitated an unplanned and indecisive battle at Perryville (October 8, 1862).

When Bragg slipped back unmolested into Tennessee, it was clear that a new Federal general was needed, and Lincoln chose W. S. Rosecrans, suspected to have military ability and known to have influential political connections. If Buell was slow and cautious, Rosecrans was slow and careless; and, if his battle with Bragg at Murfreesboro (also called Stone's River—December 30, 1862, to January 2, 1863) proved anything, it was that neither army was competently commanded.

For Bragg there was no replacement in sight; but already one could discern within the Union army the coming man. George H. Thomas was known to be "an officer of the very highest qualities, soldierly and personally." Wrote Dana: "He had more the character of George Washington than any other man I ever knew . . . a noble character." Affectionately known to his soldiers as "Uncle George" or "Old Pap," before many months Thomas would become known to the world as the "Rock of Chickamauga."

Pauline Cushman.

Every part of the Army of the Cumberland was superior to its commanders in chief. By order of General Mitchel, Pauline Cushman, beautiful actress of French-Spanish ancestry, was "expelled" from Nashville as an ardent secessionist. Welcomed by the Confederates, she served as a Union spy and accumulated maps and drawings of major military importance until arrested by Bragg's men.

Major General Ormsby MacKnight Mitchel, U.S.A.

The "indefatigable" Mitchel was one of the ablest of Buell's divisional commanders. In a daring raid this astronomer-turned-soldier seized Huntsville, Alabama, controlling the Memphis & Charleston Railroad. But his dash was too much for Buell—as was his vanity, for Mitchel seemed "determined to make all understand that he was the greatest of living soldiers." He was obliged to request transfer to another department.

**Charge of Brigadier General James S. Negley's Division Across Stone's
River, at 4:00 P.M., January 2, 1863.**

Under peremptory orders from Washington, Rosecrans, who replaced Buell, began
slowly to advance southeast from Nashville. On the last day of 1862 he met Bragg's army
near Murfreesboro. In the first day's battle the Confederates drove the Union line back
upon itself, like an inverted V. Two days later Bragg renewed the attack, sending
Breckinridge against the Federal left, "routing two brigades of the first line and driving
them pell-mell to the river and across it." "The shot roll up the Murfreesboro pike like
balls on a bowling alley," reported one awed officer.

Union General Negley shouted: "Who'll lead the way? Who'll save the Left?"

"The Nineteenth Illinois!" volunteered Colonel Joseph R. Scott, proudly.

"The Nineteenth it is then! By the left flank march!"

"Scott put his cap on his sword and shouted 'Forward!' His men lay down and fired
one volley, then rose, fixed bayonets, and started upon that grand charge which saved
the day. . . . Into the river they plunged waist deep, although a whole rebel division
was disputing the passage; up the precipitious bank, bristling with bayonets; baring
their heads to the pitiless leaden rain; against bayonet and shot and shell . . . they
swept on."

Bragg withdrew, leaving the field in Federal possession. A few days later a Union
officer saw on the battleground "Nationals and Confederates, young, middle-aged, and

Private Morton Wood Williams of a Georgia Regiment, Killed at Murfreesboro.

old, . . . scattered over the woods and fields for miles. . . . Farther on we find men with their legs shot off; one with brains scooped out with a cannon ball; another with half a face gone; another with entrails protruding. . . . Many Confederate sharpshooters lay behind stumps, rails, and logs, shot in the head. A young boy, dressed in Confederate uniform, lies with his face turned to the sky and looks as if he might be sleeping."

Ruins of Nashville & Chattanooga Railroad Bridge and Construction of a Pontoon Bridge over the Tennessee River at Bridgeport, Alabama, August, 1863.

Credit for the quasi-victory went to Rosecrans; but, as months passed and the general made no further advance, many wondered whether their praise had not been misdirected. Washington became increasingly irate with the ineffectual general, and Charles A. Dana was sent to investigate. "While few persons exhibited more estimable qualities," Dana reported, "I have never seen a public man possessing talent with less administrative power, less clearness and steadiness in difficulty, and greater practical incapacity than General Rosecrans."

Finally, in June, 1863, the general was ready to advance; and by shrewd maneuver he compelled Bragg to retreat toward Chattanooga. When the Confederates crossed the Tennessee River, they burned the railroad trestle at Bridgeport; but the Federals were ready for the emergency. For weeks their pontoniers had been training. "Twice each week," a Union diarist noted, "they unload the pontoons from the wagons, run them into the water, put the scantling from boat to boat, lay down the plank, and thus make a good bridge on which men, horses, and wagons can cross. . . . They can bridge any stream between this and the Tennessee in an hour, and can put a bridge over that in probably three hours."

Major General William Starke Rosecrans, U.S.A.

Brigadier General James Abram Garfield, U.S.A.

Confederates Opening Fire upon Federal Cavalry at Reed's Bridge over the Chickamauga.

Bragg withdrew from Chattanooga, and Rosecrans talked jubilantly of his bloodless victory, the success of which he attributed in great measure to his chief of staff, James A. Garfield, "ever active, prudent, and sagacious," who possessed "the instincts . . . of a great commander."

Such rejoicing was premature, for Bragg had merely retired some ten miles to Chickamauga Creek, where he was expecting Longstreet's Corps from the Army of Northern Virginia, being rushed by "passenger, baggage, mail, coal, box, [and] platform" cars to his aid. On September 18 they arrived, and at once Hood's men were ordered to seize Reed's bridge, on the Federal left. "I had my horse to leap from the train," remembered Hood, who was still suffering from a wound received at Gettysburg, "mounted with one arm in a sling, and, about 3 p.m., joined our forces . . . in line of battle. . . . In a short time we arrived at Reid's [sic] bridge across the Chickamauga, and discovered the Federals drawn up in battle array beyond the bridge, which they had partially destroyed. I ordered forward some . . . artillery, opened fire. . . . Our opponents quickly retreated. We repaired the bridge, and continued to advance till darkness closed in. . . . Meantime the main body of the [Confederate] Army crossed the Chickamauga at different points . . . ."

Sergeant John Clem, 22nd Michigan Infantry.

The next day the real Confederate assault commenced. In the imperiled Union line everybody had to fight. Little Johnny Clem, twelve-year-old drummer boy of a Michigan regiment, "had three bullets through his hat. . . . A rebel Colonel . . . mounted on horseback, encountered the young hero, and called out, 'Stop, you little Yankee devil!' By way of answer the boy halted, . . . fired, and the officer fell dead from his horse." For his courage Clem was later made a sergeant.

Battle of Chickamauga.

The second day's fighting was indecisive, but on September 20 the Confederates renewed the assault, and in smashing blows broke the Union right, crumpled the center, and struck hard at the left, where the imperturbable Thomas held firm. As Longstreet's Virginia veterans approached, Thomas gave the order "to aim carefully and make every shot count, and the deadly work began. The front ranks melted away under the rapid fire of our men," related a Northern officer, "but those following bowed their heads to the storm of bullets and pressed on, some of them falling at every step, until, the supporting touch of elbows being lost, the survivors hesitate, halt, then turning, start back with a rush that carries everything with them to the rear—all who escape the bullets as deadly in the wild retreat as in the desperate and orderly advance. This was all repeated again and again, until the slope was so covered with dead and wounded men that . . . we could hardly see the ground." "The wildly neighing horses, wild and frightened, were running in every direction; the whistling, seething, crackling bullets, the piercing, screaming fragments of shells, the whirring sound of shrapnel and the savage shower of cannister, mingled with the fierce answering yells of defiance, all united in one horrid sound. The ghastly, mangled dead and horribly wounded strewed the earth. . . . The dead were piled upon each other in ricks, like cord wood, to make passage for advancing columns. The sluggish stream of Chickamauga ran red with human blood."

John Ross House at Rossville, Headquarters of General Granger During the Battle of Chickamauga.

All day the battle continued, and by afternoon Thomas's position was becoming desperate. "About four o'clock," related one of his officers, "we saw away off to our rear the banners and glittering guns of a division coming toward us, and we became agitated by doubt and hope. Are they friends or foes? The thunder, as of a thousand anvils, still goes on in our front. Men fall around us like leaves in autumn. . . . The approaching troops are said to be ours, and we feel a throb of exultation."

They were the Union reserves, under Granger and Steedman. "Rude, rough, and tough," Granger was "a man without any sense of fear— . . . thoroughly indifferent to the dangers of battle." Without being ordered, he and Steedman had decided they were needed at the front, and they came. "They brought with them the reserve corps of twenty-five thousand men—fifteen thousand of them enlisted men, and the other ten thousand were Steedman and Granger themselves."

The Union army had been saved, and Thomas was able to lead a melancholy retreat into Chattanooga, but the battle was clearly an impressive Confederate victory. Dana telegraphed to Washington, "Chickamauga is as fatal a name in our history as Bull Run."

[240]

Major General Gordon Granger, U.S.A.

Union Soldiers Encamped at Citico Creek, East of Chattanooga.

In a cup-shaped valley hemmed in by high ridges, Chattanooga, which had seemed to be a Union prize, proved to be a trap. When Rosecrans retreated into the city the Confederates entrenched themselves on Missionary Ridge, Orchard Knob, and Lookout Mountain; and at night the beleaguered Federal army looked out upon a "grand semicircle" of Confederate fortifications "lighted up with the enemy's little camp fires." The Tennessee River was still in Federal hands, but below Chattanooga were rapids known as the "Suck" which most boats could not pass.

Very shortly the Union army began to realize that it was under siege. General John Beatty reported "much suffering among the men." "They have for weeks been reduced to quarter rations, and at times so eager for food that the commissary storerooms would be thronged and the few crumbs that fell from broken boxes of hard bread carefully gathered up and eaten. Men have followed the forage wagons and picked up the grains of corn that fell from them, and in some instances they have picked up the grains of corn from the mud where mules have been fed. The suffering among the animals has been intense. Hundreds of mules and horses have died of starvation."

In this crisis Rosecrans acted, as Lincoln said, "like a duck hit on the head"; and the President appointed Thomas to succeed him. At the same time Grant was made commander of all Federal armies between the mountains and the Mississippi; and he rushed to the aid of his besieged troops. He telegraphed Thomas to hold Chattanooga at all hazards, and that general tersely replied, "I will hold the town till we starve."

Grant acted to prevent that eventuality. By a virtual miracle of transportation, Secretary Stanton sent General Hooker, with a strong detachment from Meade's Army of the Potomac, over a circuitous route to the Tennessee front. Grant used this force to push up the river from Bridgeport to a point at the foot of Lookout Mountain, just above the "Suck" in the river. With Hooker's troops in this position, food and supplies could be sent by rail to Bridgeport, by wagon from that point to Hooker's camp, and by steamboat thence into Chattanooga itself. The soldiers called this devious system the "cracker line," because it brought them food. "The capacity of the railroad and steamboats was not sufficient," Grant wrote later, "to supply all the wants of the army, but actual suffering was prevented."

Union Army Transports on the Tennessee River Below Chattanooga.

Major General John White Geary, U.S.A.

It was not until Bragg personally saw the Union soldiers in the valley below Lookout Mountain that the obtuse Confederate commander would credit their presence. Then he ordered an assault. At midnight, October 28, the Southerners struck at Geary's division of Hooker's force, and were driven back in some confusion. The attack was badly planned and worse executed, for "a strong feeling of jealousy" between Longstreet's

[244]

Brigadier General Evander McIvor Law, C.S.A.

brigadiers, Jenkins and Law, paralyzed the action. Law held back, saying "that he did not care to win General Jenkins's spurs as a major-general." Then, at the critical moment, Federal wagon mules, restive at the midnight firing, broke loose and rushed straight toward the Southerners "with trace-chains rattling and whiffle-trees snapping over the stumps of trees." The Confederates retreated, and the "cracker line" was safe.

Colonels Orlando M. Poe and Orville E. Babcock at Fort Sanders, Knoxville.

Bragg was still so confident of success that he felt able to undertake an auxiliary expedition while starving out Chattanooga. In early November he dispatched Longstreet, with whom he was already in violent controversy, against a Federal army under Burnside, which had taken Knoxville and was threatening Confederate control of the upper valley. Burnside wisely retreated to Knoxville itself, where Captain O. M. Poe was rapidly constructing fortifications. "Rifle-pits and breastworks are springing up around the soon to be beleaguered city," a Federal diarist reported. "Forests are being cleared, the sluices and creeks on the north are being damned up, and the plain in front will soon . . . be breast-deep in water. Captain Poe is every inch the soldier, and there is a general feeling pervading the army and people that our defences could scarce be in abler or wiser hands. His calm deportment, systematic vigor, and quiet earnestness inspire every one with confidence."

Longstreet decided to assault the Federal fortifications, the most formidable of which was Fort Sanders, with a "ditch . . . twelve feet wide and about eight [feet] deep, and the parapet . . . about twelve feet high." After preliminary skirmishing, the Confederate general sent "an avalanche of men" against the position on November 30. "Whole ranks stumbled over wires stretched from stump to stump, and fell among the dead and dying; yet still over their prostrate bodies marched the doomed heroes of that forlorn hope. At last the ditch was reached, and the slaughter became butchery." When the Confederates "jumped into the ditch and tried to scramble up the slope of the earthwork," they found the walls wet and slick from the winter rains. "Some got to the top, only to be shot down or captured. The guns flanking the ditch raked it with double charges of cannister. Shells were lighted and thrown as hand-grenades into the practically helpless crowd below. Those who had not entered the ditch soon wavered and fell back, at first sullenly and slowly, then in despair running for life to cover." Longstreet's assault was "an utter and disastrous failure."

Union Soldier Guarding the Bridge at Strawberry Plains near Knoxville.

Pulpit Rock, the Summit of Lookout Mountain.

Major General Peter Joseph Osterhaus, U.S.A.

Back in Chattanooga, Grant felt strong enough to strike. On November 24 Hooker sent Osterhaus's division up "steep, ragged, rocky" Lookout Mountain. "Climbing over ledges and shoulders," the Federals furiously repulsed their enemy. In the afternoon fog enveloped the mountain, and all one could see of this "battle above the clouds" was the flash of muskets, "like swarms of fire flies." During the night the Confederates withdrew.

Missionary Ridge from Orchard Knob.

The next day the fighting resumed on all fronts. It was a new experience for the veterans of the Army of the Cumberland to fight a planned battle. "During the day," related General Beatty, "as we listened to the roar of the conflict, I thought I detected in the management what I had never discovered before on the battlefield—a little common sense. . . . The struggle . . . seemed more like a series of independent battles than one grand conflict. There were few times during the day when the engagement appeared to be heavy and continuous along the whole line. There certainly was not an extended and unceasing roll, as at Chickamauga and Stone River, but rather a succession of heavy blows. Now it would thunder furiously on the extreme right, then the left would take up the sledge, and finally the center would begin to pound; and so the National giant appeared to skip from point to point . . . striking rapid and thundering blows here and there, as if seeking the weak place in his antagonist's armor." That was the way Grant had planned it. On the right Hooker was to take Lookout Mountain; on the left Sherman was to flank Missionary Ridge, the enemy's strongest position; then in the center Thomas was to advance beyond Orchard Knob.

About four o'clock, thinking "that the enemy had sent a great mass of their troops to crush Sherman," Grant ordered Thomas to take the Confederate skirmish line at the foot of Missionary Ridge. While the two generals watched from Orchard Knob, the men advanced. The Confederates were pushed back, and the mission was accomplished. But "it was evident that something more must be done. With such a storm of iron hail falling thickly around, it was impossible to remain—they must either advance or retreat." "The cannonade from the summit now grew terrific," remembered a participant, "and as the charges of canister poured over the heads of our men, they sounded like flocks of wild geese sweeping past, while from behind rocks, logs and earthworks, poured an incessant stream of musketry fire." The Federal troops hesitated. Then General Phil Sheridan "dashed forward on his black charger to the foot of the ridge, dismounted, threw his cape to his orderly, and running forward among us, shouted, 'Boys, we are going to take the ridge. Forward and help your comrades.' That settled the question. . . . Those defending the heights above grew more and more desperate as our men approached the top. . . . they thrust cartridges into guns by handsfull; they lighted the fusees [sic] of shells and then rolled them down; they seized huge stones and threw them, but nothing could stop the force of the desperate charge, and one after another the regimental flags were borne over the parapet and the ridge was ours."

Battle of Missionary Ridge, November 25, 1863.

Brigadier General Braxton Bragg, C.S.A.

From Missionary Ridge, Bragg had looked scornfully down upon the approaching Union line, thinking his position "one which ought to have been held against any assaulting column." Then his men broke, and he rushed forward, shouting, "Here is your commander!" But the Confederate soldiers, who hated him as a "merciless tyrant," replied with the favorite army gibe, "Here's your mule!" and kept on running.

**Confederate Soldiers Captured at the Battle of Chattanooga Awaiting
Transportation to Northern Prisons.**

Bragg was the worst defeated general in Confederate history. The Union success
was total. "Glory to God!" wired Dana to Washington, "the day is decisively ours."
"Prisoners taken yesterday reported this morning at 3,500, but probably not over 3,000
with 52 cannon, 500 stand small-arms, 10 flags. Among prisoners large proportion officers from colonels down. . . . The storming of the ridge by our troops was one of the
greatest miracles in military history. No man who climbs the ascent by any of the
roads that wind along its front can believe that 18,000 men were moved up its broken
and crumbling face unless it was his fortune to witness the deed. It seems as awful as
a visible interposition of God. Neither Grant nor Thomas intended it. . . . The unac-
countable spirit of the troops bore them bodily up those impracticable steeps, over the
bristling rifle-pits on the crest and the thirty cannon enfilading every gully. . . . The
generals . . . caught the inspiration of the men, and were ready themselves to undertake impossibilities."

Gideon Welles, United States Secretary of the Navy.

X. High Seas and Harbors

"I knew I had done my duty faithfully, honestly, and as well as I knew how," boasted Gideon Welles at the end of the war. Four years of uninterrupted victory gave Lincoln's "Old Man of the Sea" a right to be proud. On the land the conflict raged with varying fortunes, and the Confederates often took the offensive; at sea Federal successes were so regular as to seem routine, for it was, from beginning to end, a Union war.

On many fronts the Federal navy was successful. A vital part of its war assignment has been repeatedly noticed in these pages—the work of the gunboats and transports on the inland waters. The assault on Forts Henry and Donelson, the capture of Vicksburg, and the raid up the Red River could never have been carried out but for the navy's cooperation. As usual, the navy thought the land forces hogged too much of the credit for these ventures—and, as usual, the navy was perhaps right.

On the high seas the Federal fleets had responsibilities all their own. The most tedious, but the most important, was to keep a constant vigil along the intricate Southern coast, intercepting blockade runners with their precious cargoes of arms, medicine, and supplies for the starving South. Desperately the Confederates sought to throw off the throttling grasp, and with rams, torpedoes, and ironclads boldly but unsuccessfully challenged the Federal fleets. Toward the end of the war the blockade was working with marked effectiveness; it had become, wrote Mrs. Chesnut of Charleston, a "stockade, which hems us in with only the sky open to us."

More dramatic than blockade duty was the pursuit and capture of Confederate privateers and raiders, such as the *Sumter* and the *Alabama,* which ranged over the oceans and threatened to sweep the United States merchant marine from the seas.

Finally, the Federal navy pioneered in amphibious operations against Southern ports, both to strengthen the blockade and to provide bases for Union troops far behind the Confederate lines. Not a single important Southern port from Virginia to Texas escaped assault; and the capture of Fort Fisher, North Carolina, in January, 1865, put an iron curtain over the last remaining Southern window on the world.

For all these successes popular acclaim went, of course, to the admirals—Farragut, Porter, Du Pont, Foote. But, as more astute observers realized, "It is the Department that makes success or invites disaster." To Gideon Welles, the Connecticut landlubber whose appointment had been greeted with the sneer that he did not "know the stem from the stern of a ship," and to his assistant secretary, Gustavus Vasa Fox, the chief credit belonged. Proudly Fox could write of the victory he had helped to engineer: "I have endeavored in this war to preserve the organization of the navy, and to carve out work for it which should be purely naval, depending entirely upon the power of its ordnance, the skill of its officers, and the unflinching courage of its sailors. I know the arm thoroughly, and in the dark hours of preparation, I laughed at the public abuse, knowing the victories the navy would give to the country. We have won. . . ."

U.S.S. Sabine off Fortress Monroe.

In 1861 the United States navy was just commencing a technological revolution. "The fact that sailing vessels were soon to be laid aside was still far from general recognition, especially among officers of conservative tendencies; the three great weapons . . . , the rifled gun, the ram, and the torpedo, were almost unknown in the service; and iron armor was still an experiment." Of the ninety vessels in the American navy more than half were sailing ships. A sail frigate, like the *Sabine,* reputed to have been the first Union blockader in the South Atlantic, still had its uses; but for combat purposes it was "now as obsolete as the galleys of Themistocles."

Many of the officers seemed as antiquated as their ships. The younger men complained that there were so many "ante-diluvians," "would-be heroes, and men of art" in the service that the Department could exhibit a complete collection of *marine fossils for the Naval Archives.*

When Lincoln was inaugurated there was only one steam vessel at Washington—the *Pawnee*. The other twenty-five steamers in commission were scattered all over the globe. But even when gathered together the little squadron of five screw-frigates (like the *Merrimac*, abandoned at Norfolk navy yard), six sloops of the first or *Hartford* class, four large side-wheelers, and eight sloops of the second or *Pawnee* class could really be considered only "as the nucleus of a fleet."

It seemed to be almost farcical for President Lincoln to order a blockade of Southern ports with so small a fleet; but on April 19 he announced firmly that "a competent force will be posted so as to prevent entrance and exit of vessels from the [Confederate] ports." At first it was a paper proclamation; but increasing naval strength slowly made the Federal blockade effective. "As fast as we can augment our force, or spare vessels from other points," Secretary Welles told his flag officers, "we shall endeavor to reenforce your command. . . . By cutting off all communication we not only distress and cripple the States in insurrection, but by an effective blockade we destroy any excuse or pretext on the part of foreign Governments to aid . . . those who are waging war upon the Government."

Quarterdeck and Starboard Battery of U.S.S. Pawnee.

Blockade Runners in Port at St. George, Bermuda Islands.

The Nashville Running the Blockade off Wilmington, North Carolina, April 24, 1862.

Wreck of a Blockade Runner off Sullivan's Island, South Carolina.

Havana, Matamoras, Nassau, and St. George, on Bermuda, were the principal ports from which blockade runners made their furtive dashes through the ever tightening Union surveillance. To these ports prosperity came in unprecedented share. At St. George one could see "eight or ten . . . blockade runners lying in the harbor," whose crews were "a reckless lot, and believed in eating, drinking and being merry, for fear they would die on the morrow and might miss something."

The typical blockade runner was "a long, low side-wheel steamer of from four to six hundred tons, with a slight frame, sharp and narrow, its length perhaps nine times its beam. It had feathering paddles, and one or two raking telescopic funnels, which might be lowered close to the deck. The hull rose only a few feet out of the water, and was painted a dull gray or lead color, so that it could hardly be seen by daylight at two hundred yards. . . . Anthracite coal, which made no smoke, was burned in the furnaces." Taking advantage of surprise, of their semi-invisibility, and of their pilots' familiarity with tricky coastal waters, the runners tried to slip through the Union squadrons on moonless nights. Pursued, many were run onto shoals, where the waves beat them to pieces or Union guns demolished them. But so profitable was the dangerous business that a ship could pay for itself if it completed two or three runs.

Admiral Raphael Semmes, C.S.N.

Most blockade runners were privately owned, but raiders were a part of the Confederate fleet. Raphael Semmes, commander of the *Sumter* and of the *Alabama*, fought not for profit but in behalf of the South's "glorious struggle for the right of self-government, and in defence of her institutions, her property, and everything a people hold sacred." "May we prove ourselves in this struggle worthy . . . of our great cause!" he prayed.

**Captain John Ancrum Winslow (Third from Left) and His Officers on the Deck of
the Kearsage After Sinking the Alabama.**

Around the world Semmes ranged, stationing himself for periods of about two months on the main trade routes and preying upon United States merchant ships which passed. After taking from them "everything we needed, Boston bread and crackers of the freshest, beef and pork, cheese and good butter, dried and canned fruits and sundries," the Confederates, who had no home port to which they could bring their prizes, would frequently fire the captured vessels, watching the flames run "up the tarred rigging like demons to the mastheads, with burning lanyards flying to the gale."

For years the Federal navy tried to capture the "pirate," but with no success. Semmes was too swift, too shrewd. Finally, however, in June, 1864, the *Kearsage* cornered the *Alabama* in Cherbourg harbor and, when she emerged, fought her in the English Channel. "As we approached her, within about one thousand two hundred yards," Captain Winslow reported to Welles, "she opened fire, we receiving two or three broadsides before a shot was returned. The action continued, the respective steamers making a circle round and round at a distance of about nine hundred yards from each other. At the expiration of an hour the Alabama struck, going down in about twenty minutes afterward. . . ."

Franklin Buchanan, C.S.N.

"We have an iron vessel here," a Georgia private excitedly wrote to his grandfather. It was the former *Merrimac*, resurrected from the ruins of Norfolk navy yard, refurbished with an ironclad deck, and rechristened the C.S.S. *Virginia*. Commanded by Commodore Franklin Buchanan, she appeared in Hampton Roads on March 8, 1862, and rammed and blasted the Federal fleet there. The *Cumberland* sank; the *Congress* burned; and three other ships ran aground to escape a similar fate. "Our vessel, The Virginia, has invented a new way of destroying the blockade," the Georgia soldier exulted. "Instead of raising it she sinks it or I believe she is good at both, for the one she burned was raised to a pretty considerable height when the magazine exploded."

The next day the *Virginia* reappeared to continue the destruction, only to find a peculiar vessel, looking like a cheesebox on a raft, awaiting it. It was the *Monitor*, creation of John Ericsson, which had steamed down from New York and, without having completed its trial runs, was ready to pit its ironclad deck and its revolving turret against the *Virginia*'s strength. "I laid the *Monitor* close alongside the *Merrimac*, and gave her a shot," Captain Worden told President Lincoln later as he showed him over the ironclad. "She returned our compliment by a shell weighing one hundred and fifty pounds, fired when we were close together, which struck the turret so squarely that it received the whole force. Here you see the scar, two and a half inches deep in the wrought iron, a perfect mold of the shell. . . . It did not start a rivet-head or a nut!"

Effect of the Fire from the C.S.S. Virginia on the Turret of the U.S.S. Monitor.

The Crew on the Deck of the Monitor.

On the *Virginia* "all was bustle, smoke, grimy figures, and stern commands, while down in the engine and boiler rooms the sixteen furnaces were belching out fire and smoke." Finding she could not sink the *Monitor*, the Confederate ironclad tried to ram her. But "she got the worst of it," declared the *Monitor*'s chief engineer. "She gave us a tremendous thump, but did not injure us in the least." Looking for easier prey, the *Virginia* approached the *Minnesota,* only to find the *Monitor* intervening. The Confederate trained her stern gun on the Federal ironclad "when she was only twenty yards from its muzzle and delivered a rifle-pointed shell which dislodged the iron . . . sheltering the *Monitor*'s conning-tower, carrying away the steering-gear . . . and blinding Captain Worden."

When Worden recovered, his first question was, "Have I saved the *Minnesota*?"

"Yes," was the reply, "and whipped the *Merrimac*!"

"Then," said Worden, "I don't care what becomes of me." The *Virginia* had limped back to its base at Norfolk, damaged but not demolished. It never again ventured into combat, and when the Confederates abandoned Norfolk they blew up the ironclad to prevent its falling into Union hands.

Rear Admiral John Lorimer Worden, U.S.N.

The battle of the ironclads marked the arrival of a new era in naval construction. Fox thought the *Monitor* "absolutely impregnable" and favored building a fleet of turreted ironclads. One by one the other navy men were convinced. After the Fort Fisher expedition, Admiral Porter concluded that the larger monitors, like the *Onondaga,* were "a most perfect success" and claimed that they "could certainly clear any harbor on our coast of blockaders in case we were at war with a foreign power." To self-righteous Gideon Welles, who had assumed the serious responsibility for authorizing the first monitor, such reflections seemed to have the unfair advantage of hindsight. "The fight with the Merrimac made for them rapid converts," he confided to his diary. "When the first turret vessel, the Monitor, was building, many naval men and men in the shipping interest sneered at her as a humbug, and at me as no sailor or judge, until she vindicated her power and worth in that first remarkable conflict. Then I was abused by party men because I had not made preparations for and built more."

The Monitor Onondaga on the James River.

The C.S.S. Stonewall in the Potomac After the Civil War.

Without a single ship of war at the start of hostilities, without shipbuilding facilities, without a merchant marine, without a seagoing population, the Confederate navy had to depend heavily upon European assistance. The *Alabama* was the most renowned of the South's European-built warships, but the *Stonewall*, constructed in France late in the war, was for a time a more serious threat to the Federal fleets. "A ram with armored sides (four or five inches), a 300-pounder rifled Armstrong gun in the casemated bow, and a fixed turret aft containing two rifled 70-pounders," the vessel was "truly an ugly antagonist." On her maiden voyage the *Stonewall* encountered two Federal warships off the coast of Spain, but though she flaunted her Confederate flag, the wooden ships could not be persuaded to fight so formidable an antagonist. Exultant, the *Stonewall*'s captain steered for America, sure of his ability to raise the blockade. But when he arrived at Havana he learned that the war had ended. Surrendered to the United States by the Spanish authorities, the *Stonewall* was ultimately sold to Japan.

Wherever they could, Confederates prepared coastal defenses against anticipated attacks. Fort Pickens, off Pensacola, Florida, was never surrendered by the United States, and at the outbreak of the war the Confederates tried to erect batteries on the surrounding sand hills, "at the water-line and partly concealed amidst the woods which fringe the shore as far as the navy yard of Warrington, near Pensacola." "Arms glanced in the blazing sun where regiments were engaged at drill, clouds of dust rose from the sandy roads, horsemen riding along the beach, groups of men in uniform, gave a martial appearance to the place in unison with the black muzzles of the guns which peeped from the white sand batteries from the entrance of the harbor to the navy yard." So impressive were General Bragg's fortifications that an English observer doubted "very much whether the fort and the fleet combined can silence his fire"; but later he was privately informed by the general that "his batteries were far from being in a state, either as regards armament or ammunition, which would justify him in meeting the fire of the forts and the ships."

Confederate Water Battery at Warrington, Pensacola Bay, Florida.

Bombardment of Confederate Batteries at Aquia Creek, Virginia, June 1, 1861.

After the secession of Virginia, when Union defenses were pushed back to Washington, the Confederates established batteries at Aquia Creek, in effect blockading the Potomac. From the President down, Northerners were irate. "If it is not a state secret," demanded Commodore Hiram Paulding, "let me . . . ask why the Batteries on the Potomac are permitted to exist and fire with impunity upon all who pass them!—Do we want guns or men or is there a mysterious or secret purpose in allowing so great a nuisance to exist?" When the army refused to act, the navy tried to take the matter in hand. For several days in May and June a small flotilla was sent to bombard the annoying batteries. "The Freeborn approached to within two miles from the shore, and fired four or five shots," it was reported, "when the Pawnee entered into the conflict, taking a position nearer to the land. For the first two hours, the fire from the shore batteries was sharp, but was returned with more expedition by the Pawnee. During the engagement, she fired 160 shells, one of which was seen to explode immediately over the heads of the Confederates who were working the battery. . . . The railroad depot and buildings on the shore . . . are all destroyed. The damage to the beach battery is not considered permanent, as the Confederates can soon repair it." In fact, within a few days the battery was as strong as ever, and the Southerners held the position until Johnston voluntarily withdrew.

Landing of the Federal Troops at Hatteras Inlet, August 28, 1861.

In August, 1861, the Federal navy felt ready to undertake the first of its coastal landing operations, and the Cape Hatteras region of North Carolina was selected because the intricate channels and abominable weather made an offshore blockade almost impossible. The principal entry to the North Carolina sounds was Hatteras Inlet, where the Confederates had two forts, "Hatteras and Clark, separated by a shallow bay, half a mile wide. Of these works Fort Hatteras was the larger, and together they mounted twenty-five guns."

Flag Officer Silas H. Stringham commanded the naval expedition, and he was accompanied by about nine hundred troops under the flamboyant Benjamin F. Butler. "The bombardment was commenced at a distance of about two and a half miles by the Minnesota on Wednesday [August 28], at 11 A.M., and she was soon joined by the entire fleet. When the bombardment opened, the landing of troops from the transports, by launches and small-boats, commenced, under cover of the guns of the Harriet Lane and Monticello. By this time the wind had come up so that the surf ran high, and though the greatest efforts were made, only about three hundred of the forces were landed. Every boat was either broken

Second Day's Action at Hatteras Inlet.

up or beached, and notwithstanding nearly one thousand men had been placed on schooners, it was considered too dangerous to attempt to land them, and they were returned to the transports. When the bombardment had continued about three hours, the flag of Fort Clark came down, and the rebels retreated to Fort Hatteras. . . . Soon after our forces on shore occupied the abandoned fort and waved the Stars and Stripes from the ramparts."

The next morning "the Susquehanna opened the ball, and in a few minutes the entire fleet concentrated its fire on Fort Hatteras. Our forces on shore were now in Fort Clark, spectators of the scene. Fort Hatteras did not return the fire for nearly half an hour, and its shots all fell short. The bombardment was continued without intermission, when, at half-past eleven, our shells began to range on the magazine—a white flag was displayed on the fort—our men at Fort Clark, with loud shouts, started on a double quick, and were met on the beach by a flag of truce. . . . General Butler, who had entered the inlet on the steamer Fanny, demanded an unconditional surrender. These terms after a Council of War, were accepted."

As Admiral Porter pointed out, "the reduction of these works was not a very great achievement for a squadron mounting 158 guns"; yet to Northerners discouraged by repeated defeats on land it seemed a very great victory. The commander of the *Pawnee* was extravagant in thinking "the capture of this place the most important event of the war"; but it did put an end to blockade running in that vicinity.

50th Pennsylvania Infantry at Beaufort, South Carolina.

The South Atlantic Blockading Squadron needed some secure base, and in November, 1861, an army-navy expedition was sent against Port Royal, South Carolina, halfway between Charleston and Savannah. Three times Admiral Du Pont's fleet steamed into the harbor, blasted Fort Walker on Hilton Head, then turned in an ellipse to present another broadside. The Confederate defenders retreated pell-mell, and Du Pont's victory was, as he said, "more complete and more brilliant than I ever could have believed."

Port Royal then became the headquarters of the fleet, and Hilton Head and Beaufort were occupied by troops brought along under General Thomas West Sherman, one of the few army officers with whom the navy successfully and amicably cooperated. Du Pont praised the general as "a *soldier* every inch of him." "A more arduous, onerous and responsible but thankless work," thought the admiral, "no public officer ever went through, and none ever brought to such a task more true and unselfish devotion."

Such army-navy harmony was almost unparalleled. Shortly Sherman was replaced by the uncooperative Hunter and the unyielding Gillmore, and the usual interservice rivalry was renewed. By 1863 Fox was urging the admirals not to wait for army support in coastal operations. "The sublimity" of a purely naval assault, he told Du Pont, "is beyond words to describe, and I beg of you not to let the Army spoil it. The immortal wreath of laurel should cluster around your flag alone."

Brigadier General Thomas West Sherman, U.S.A.

Fort Marion, St. Augustine, Florida.

Many of the smaller Southern ports surrendered without a fight. When Commander C. R. P. Rodgers approached St. Augustine in March, 1862, he found a white flag "hoisted upon one of the bastions of Fort Marion." "The Mayor . . . informed me," he reported to his superiors, "that the place had been evacuated the preceding night by two companies of Florida troops, and that they . . . placed the city in my hands. . . . About fifteen hundred persons remain in St. Augustine, about one fifth of the inhabitants having fled. . . . There is a great scarcity of provisions in the place; . . . and much poverty exists. In the water-battery at the Fort, are three fine army thirty-two-pounders of seven thousand pounds, and two eight-inch sea-coast howitzers of fifty-six hundred pounds, with shot and some powder. There are a number of very old guns in the Fort, useless and not mounted."

Savannah, Georgia.

At Savannah the Confederates planned to put up a resolute defense. The city itself lay far up the Savannah River, whose entrance was protected by Fort Pulaski. Early in 1862 it became clear that the Federals intended to assault the fort. "You can see from the ramparts some 60 or 70 Yankee vessels," a Georgia defender wrote to his wife. "You can see their tents & hear their drums from our Island over on the S C side, we are almost surrounded by them—& may I think very probably will be very soon cut off from Savannah . . . ." Aside from the impending danger, the officer was agreeably "disappointed as to our quarters & conveniences" in Fort Pulaski. "The men sleep in the casemates that is where the cannon are, which to explain it to you is a brick house each man is furnished with lumber to build him a bed with, it is perfectly dry, clean neat, warm & safe—each company has a large kitchen made out of brick 20 by 40 ft. with a large table & benches one large fire place with three closets . . . —in short officers & men are better & more comfortably situated, than we are at home."

Ruins at Fort Pulaski.

"As to taking the fort," the Georgia officer boasted, "they never can do it by fighting. We are perfectly protected, neither shell or balls can hurt us." While talking of success, the Southerners prepared for defeat. "They are about fifty to our one, with superior arms, vessels &c. Their heavy cannon & morters are frowning upon us from some seven Batteries & an innumerial quantity of Boats—all intended for our destruction—the destruction of men, that have never wronged them or sought to devest them of a right—what a comment upon this enlightened & Christian age. . . . the Garrison is determined . . . to strike untill the walls of our Fort is battered down or we fall, If the Fort is taken we want them to find nothing to take but crumbled & ruin walls & mangled corpse. . . . There is something sad & melancholy in the preparation for Battle. . . . the floor is covered around each gun with sand not for health or cleanliness but to drink up human blood as it flows."

For all the Southerners' proud defiance the Federal batteries, when opened on Pulaski on April 10, proved too much to take. "The bombardment continued without intermission for thirty hours," Union General David Hunter reported; "the Fort was breached in the south-east angle, and at the moment of surrender . . . we had commenced preparations for storming. The whole armament of the Fort, forty-seven guns, a great supply of . . . ammunition, . . . have fallen into our hands; also three hundred and sixty prisoners."

Ruins Inside Fort Pulaski.

Admiral Dahlgren's Signalmen Receiving a Message from the Georgia Shore.

The fall of Fort Pulaski closed the Savannah River to blockaders; but Savannah itself, protected from ocean assault by the tortuous river channel, was not taken, nor was the strongly fortified Fort McAllister on the Ogeechee River to the south. For these undertakings the navy needed land support. It did not arrive promptly—not, in fact, until December, 1864, when W. T. Sherman's veterans marched across Georgia to the sea. Nearing the coast, Sherman "saw that the first step was to open communications with our fleet, supposed to be waiting for us with supplies and clothing." On December 13, looking anxiously toward the sea, Sherman discerned "a faint cloud of smoke, and an object gliding, as it were, along the horizon above the tops of the sedge toward the sea, which little by little grew till it was pronounced to be the smoke-stack of a steamer coming up the river. 'It must be one of our squadron!' Soon the flag of the United States was plainly visible. . . . Soon we made out a group of officers on the deck . . . signaling with a flag, 'Who are you?' The answer went back promptly, 'General Sherman.' " That night Sherman was piloted out to the fleet, where he made plans for supplying his army. It is perhaps needless to observe that, without Federal command of the ocean, his march to the sea would have been not merely pointless but suicidal.

In an emotional sense, Charleston, South Carolina, was the most important port in the South. Among Northerners there seemed to be "no city so culpable, or against which there is such intense animosity." Fox thought it "the centre of this wicked rebellion," and he repeatedly urged its capture to signal the sure fate of secession. Calmer heads in Washington were dubious about an assault, and President Lincoln "thought it would fail." Nevertheless, in April, 1863, Secretary Welles authorized a gigantic expedition, consisting of "fifty-two steamers . . . and the most formidable ironclad force that ever went into battle," to seize the Carolina citadel. "A desperate stand will be made at Charleston," the Secretary predicted, "and their defenses are formidable. . . . We shall not get the place, if we get it at all on this first trial, without great sacrifice. . . . What man can do, our brave fellows will accomplish, but impossibilities cannot be overcome."

Water Battery at Fort Johnson in Charleston Harbor.

Brigadier General Roswell Sabine Ripley, C.S.A.

Palmetto Battery, C.S.A., Charleston.

To an assailant Charleston presented a position of appalling strength. Months before, General Ripley, in charge of the Confederate defenses, had guessed "that the long-threatened attack on Charleston was immediately impending" and had taken "every possible precaution . . . including the concentration . . . of all available troops." Forts and batteries guarding the harbor were improved and alerted. Guarding the north entrance was Sullivan's Island, where Fort Moultrie, "very materially strengthened" with "massive ramparts of sand" and flanked by "the heavy batteries of Bee and Beauregard," commanded the main channel. To the south Fort Wagner, on Morris Island, and Fort Johnson had been rebuilt. "The new works were of earth and of the most approved construction. . . . A large bomb-proof was also visible; it was reported to be very strong, with heavy traverses." Other fortifications were located nearer Charleston itself, and "in the city, the principal battery was at White Point, which . . . terminates the tongue of land on which the city stands." "In fact," a British army officer noted, "both sides of the harbor for several miles appear to bristle with forts mounting heavy guns."

Interior of Fort Sumter.

At the entrance of the harbor lay Fort Sumter itself, rising "conspicuously . . . in mid-channel." "It was . . . pierced for two tiers of guns," a *New York Times* reporter observed, "but the lower embrasures had been filled in to strengthen it. From the top of the fort frown the barbette guns, which comprise all the heaviest portion of its armament . . . and it is easy to see that the ordnance is of the most formidable character."

The Outer Wall at Fort Sumter.

Across the main channel between Sumter and Moultrie the Confederates stretched "entanglements to foul the propellers, and torpedoes to break the bottoms of the monitors." "They were marked by rows of casks very near together. To the eye they appeared almost to touch one another, and there was more than one line of them." "The interior channels were reported to be obstructed . . . by . . . rows of piles . . . and floating torpedoes."

[283]

Captain John Rodgers, U.S.N.

Deck of the U.S.S. Catskill.

Fox urged Du Pont to send his fleet, "supreme and superb, defiant and disdainful," straight into Charleston harbor to "demand the surrender of the Forts, or swift destruction." On April 7, 1863, nine ironclads, headed by the monitor *Weehawken* under that "man of genius" Captain John Rodgers, steamed up the main channel. "When the *Weehawken* had reached within six hundred yards of Fort Sumter, a long, broad, brilliant flame suddenly leaped from its side, with all but simultaneous intense glares from Cumming's point and Moultrie, followed instantaneously by immense volumes of smoke and a rain of projectiles that fairly hid the turrets of our craft with countless spouts of water thrown by striking shot and shell. Again and again this appalling scene was enacted. . . ." Finding it could not pass the obstruction, the *Weehawken* turned back, and the fleet retreated from the worst naval disaster of the war. Damage was extensive, and the myth of the monitors' invulnerability was destroyed. "I was surprised," reported the commander of the *Catskill*, which had been near the end of the attacking line, "to find . . . that these vessels could be so much injured in so short a time. . . ." "No ship had been exposed to the severest fire of the enemy over forty minutes, and yet in that brief period . . . five of the ironclads were wholly or partially disabled." The assault was not renewed, for the officers agreed as to "the utter impracticability of taking the city of Charleston by the force under [their] command."

Rear Admiral John Adolphus Bernard Dahlgren on Board the U.S.S. Pawnee in Charleston Harbor.

Secretary Welles became convinced that Admiral Du Pont was "determined Charleston shall not be captured by the Navy," and he felt "the necessity of selecting a new commander." He chose John A. Dahlgren, a favorite of President Lincoln's, renowned as an inventor of improved artillery and as an efficient chief of naval ordnance. Everybody agreed that this "light-complexioned man of perhaps forty years of age, slight and of medium

"Powder Monkey" on the Deck of the U.S.S. New Hampshire off Charleston.

height, pale and delicate featured," had great theoretical and administrative ability; but nobody knew whether he could command a fleet. Some thought him "a diseased man on the subject of preferment & position," but Welles hoped that Dahlgren's very ambition might make for success when the attack on Charleston was renewed—this time with support from the army.

Brigadier General Quincy Adams Gillmore, U.S.A.

Federal Troops Manning the Parrott Guns at Battery Meade, Morris Island.

The army had observed the navy's discomfiture with poorly concealed glee, and in June the new commander of the Department of the South, General Gillmore, presented his own plan for attack. He proposed to land on Morris Island and, under the flanking fire of the gunboats, to take Fort Wagner, which commanded the southern shore of Charleston harbor. Dahlgren from the first "was not sanguine of General Gillmore's success" and predicted to his diary, *"The attack will not be what it should be."* Before long the two commanders were wrangling bitterly.

During the night of July 9 Gillmore's troops went ashore on the southern end of Morris Island and "moved in column along the low beach; the iron-clads shelling the ground ahead of them." The assault on Fort Wagner was repulsed, and Gillmore settled down for a siege. To his alarm he found his position under fire not merely from Wagner but from Sumter as well. Dahlgren's fleet came to his rescue with a blasting fire against Sumter, where the east wall was "battered in, and the parapet undermined. . . . Guns were dismounted. . . . The fire was very damaging; . . . and the shot swept through the fort." Fourteen times the Confederate flag on the ramparts was shot down. But when Dahlgren demanded the surrender of the fort, he got the reply, "Come and take it."

The "Swamp Angel."

Held up by Fort Wagner, General Gillmore threatened to bombard Charleston itself unless the Confederate defenders of Morris Island surrendered. When the Southerners refused, he assigned Colonel E. W. Serrell the difficult task of erecting a battery on the marshy island, which was "a bed of soft, black mud, from sixteen to eighteen feet in depth, overgrown with reeds and grass, traversed by numerous and deep and tortuous *bayous,* and subject to daily overflow by the tides." By driving "piling down the twenty feet to the sand substratum," Serrell was able to support the eight-inch 200-pounder Parrott rifle gun, nicknamed the "Swamp Angel," which on August 22 threw shells filled with Greek fire into Charleston itself. The Confederates at once protested to Gillmore, "Your firing a number of the most destructive missiles ever used in war in the midst of a city taken unawares and filled with sleeping women and children will give you a bad eminence in history," but the "Swamp Angel" continued to fire until on its thirty-sixth round it exploded. "No military results of great value were ever expected from this firing," General Gillmore wrote callously. "As an experiment with heavy guns, to test their endurance under the severest trial to which they could possibly be subjected in actual service, the results were . . . highly interesting and novel."

Colonel Edward W. Serrell, 1st New York Engineers.

Ruins of Charleston, Seen from the Circular Church.

Gradually the Confederates were driven back from the outer defenses of the harbor. Fort Wagner was captured; Sumter was silenced. Through the winter of 1863–1864 the Federals kept up an annoying if ineffectual fire upon Charleston itself. "It fairly makes me dizzy," Mrs. Chesnut exclaimed, "to think of that ever lasting racket they are beating about people's ears down there."

Still, surprisingly little damage was done to the city. "The shelling . . . continues," wrote one inhabitant on July 21, 1864, "and I understand that no less than 7000 shell have been thrown. It is marvelous that in such a bombardment so few people have been killed or wounded but the damages to property in the lower part of the city begin to be considerable. I rode down King Street a few days ago to South Bay and then around East Bay Battery to Water Street and up through Water and Church Streets to Broad and was surprised to see the number of houses that have been struck, particularly on King, Church and Broad

Streets. The Mills House had eleven holes in it. Old Mr. Righton's on Water Street had seven and numbers have two or three. They have not yet, however, knocked down a single building of any kind, and as today completes 11 months since they began you can form some idea as to the job before them when you have worked out the following Sum in the Rule of Three—If in eleven months they have not knocked down a single building, how many Centuries will it take to destroy the City?"

Charleston was thus besieged but not destroyed, and it remained a Confederate stronghold until Sherman's approach forced its abandonment.

A Destroyed Confederate Gun Mount on the Battery in Charleston.

Expedition Leaving the Chesapeake Bay for Fort Fisher, December 13, 1864.

Far more important than Charleston from a purely naval point of view was Wilmington, North Carolina, on the Cape Fear River. For months Admiral David D. Porter urged an expedition against Fort Fisher, which protected the intricate entry to that river; but he had to wait till troops could accompany him. "It was no use to attack Fort Fisher without them," Porter said, "for, although we might disable the guns, we could not take possession of the place. . . . All I wanted of the army was to occupy the works after I had finished with them."

It was not until December, 1864, that the "grand naval and military expedition" got under way. "The fleet," an uncensored newspaperman revealed, "consists of 65 war vessels, including some of the most formidable ships in the navy. Six of these are iron-clads. Upward of a hundred transports accompany the expedition. There is also good supply of picket-boats provided with torpedo machines. . . . Altogether the fleet mans 820 guns." Without much difficulty the fleet got around Capes Henry and Hatteras, but on December 22 "it came on to blow hard from the southeast, and when the sun went down the sight was a grand and threatening one. The seven monitors . . . held on well at their anchors, but would disappear entirely from sight as the heavy seas swept over them. The ships soon began to drag, and all hands were kept on deck during the entire night ready to do what was possible in case of collision. When daylight came the monitors were still in place, but the rest of the fleet was scattered over a space of sixteen miles. . . ." Not until the 23rd was Porter ready to attack.

A Group of United States Marines at the Washington Navy Yard.

Once again the marines and soldiers aboard the fleet were commanded by Benjamin F. Butler, who had conceived a novel way to reduce the fort. Instead of assaulting it, he proposed the "scheme of knocking down Fort Fisher by blowing up a vessel filled with powder." The navy men were dubious; but as Porter "had plenty of bad powder and worthless vessels" on hand he agreed to the experiment.

One hundred and fifty tons of powder was placed on board the *Louisiana*, and the old hulk was towed alongside the fort late at night. A delayed fuse was lighted, and the fleet waited. "Half past one came, and no explosion, and we were fearful of some mishap; but just as the bells struck two o'clock it came. At first a gentle vibration, then the masts and spars shook as if they would come down about our ears; and then came the low rumble like distant thunder, while the sky to the westward was lighted up for a few seconds, and then great masses of powder smoke hung over the land like thunder clouds."

Confident that the walls had fallen, Butler's flagship came "in at full speed, heading straight at Fort Fisher. . . . There was a flash from the fort and a prolonged roar, and all the guns on that face of the work opened on his ship." Fort Fisher was totally uninjured. Later, when Union officers asked captured Confederates about the effects of the explosion, they were told: "It was dreadful; it woke up everybody in Fort Fisher!"

Discouraged by his failure, Butler withdrew the troops and declared that Fort Fisher was impregnable. But Porter wrote Grant, "Send me the same soldiers with another general, and we will have the fort." In January, 1865, another expedition was ready, and this time the troops were under hard-fighting General A. H. Terry. On January 15, while the fleet bombarded the fort, the soldiers, assisted by four hundred marines and sixteen hundred sailors, attacked from the land. "At three o'clock the order to charge was given," a blue jacket remembered, "and we started for our long run of twelve hundred yards over the loose sand. The fleet kept up a hot fire until we approached within about six hundred yards of the fort and then ceased firing. The rebels seemed to understand our signals, and almost before the last gun was fired manned the parapet and opened on us with . . . muskets. . . . Under the shower of bullets the marines broke before reaching the rifle pits that had been dug for them, and did not appear again as an organization in the assault. Most of the men and many of the officers mixed in with the column of sailors, and went on with them. About five hundred yards from the fort the head of the column suddenly stopped, and, as if by magic, the whole mass of men went down like a row of

Interior of Fort Fisher.

Ruins at Fort Fisher.

falling bricks; in a second every man was flat on his stomach. The officers called on the men, and they responded instantly, starting forward as fast as they could go. At about three hundred yards they again went down, this time under the effect of canister added to the rifle fire. Again we rallied them, and once more started to the front under a perfect hail of lead, with men dropping rapidly in every direction. We were now so close that we could hear the voices of the rebels. . . . The officers were pulling their caps down over their eyes, for it was almost impossible to look at the deadly flashing blue line of parapet. . . ." The Confederate fire was too grueling, and sailors, unused to land fighting, could not manage the ditch that lay before the parapet. Badly battered, they retreated, leaving many wounded on the sand, where they were drowned by incoming tides.

But as the defenders "gave three cheers, thinking they had gained the day, they received a volley of musketry in their backs." Terry's troops, attacking from the opposite side of the fort, "had been successful in gaining the highest parapets." For hours the Confederates resisted furiously, but that night they were forced to surrender "the last stronghold of the Southern Confederacy on the Atlantic coast."

Grant's Army Crossing the Rapidan at Germanna Ford, May 4, 1864.

XI. In the Wilderness

On April 21, 1864, Richard Henry Dana, Jr., while registering at Willard's Hotel in Washington, observed "a short, round-shouldered man, in a very tarnished major-general's uniform. . . . There was nothing marked in his appearance. He had no gait, no *station*, no manner, rough, light-brown whiskers, a blue eye, and rather a scrubby look withal. A crowd formed round him, men looked, stared at him, as if they were taking his likeness, and two generals were introduced. Still, I could not get his name. . . . Who could it be? He had a cigar in his mouth, and rather the look of a man who did, or once did, take a little too much to drink. I inquired of the bookkeeper. 'That is General Grant.' I joined the starers. I saw that the ordinary, scrubby-looking man, with a slightly seedy look, as if he was out of office and on half-pay, and nothing to do but to hang round the entry of Willard's, cigar in mouth, had a clear blue eye and a look of resolution, as if he could not be trifled with, and an entire indifference to the crowd about him. Straight nose, too. Still, to see him talking and smoking in the lower entry of Willard's in that crowd, in such times,—the generalissimo of our armies, on whom the destiny of the empire seemed to hang!"

Reluctantly Grant had come East, and Lincoln turned over to his new lieutenant general the honor and responsibility of commanding all the Federal armies. "All he wanted or had ever wanted," he told Grant, "was some one who would take the responsibility and act, and call on him for all the assistance needed, pledging himself to use all the power of the government in rendering such assistance."

For the first time there emerged a plan of total war against the South. Grant ordered all the Northern armies to advance simultaneously. In the West, Sherman was to drive against Joseph E. Johnston's forces and toward Atlanta; Banks was to move upon Mobile (though because of the Red River fiasco that part of the plan miscarried); Sigel was to operate in the Valley of Virginia; and a newly constituted army under Benjamin F. Butler was to land south of the James and operate against Lee's rear. The principal offensive again fell to the Army of the Potomac, which Meade commanded, but which Grant himself accompanied in its forward movement. When President Lincoln was informed of these plans for a general movement all along the line, he "seemed to think it a new feature in war." Grant explained that the troops by advancing "would compel the enemy to keep detachments to hold them back, or else lay his own territory open to invasion." Lincoln characteristically replied, "Oh, yes! I see that. As we say out West, if a man can't skin he must hold a leg while somebody else does."

"Lee's army will be your objective point," Grant instructed Meade. "Wherever Lee goes, there will you go also." At dawn on May 4, through a Virginia countryside where spring was in the air and "there were the little green leaves just opening, and purple violets . . . by the wayside," the Army of the Potomac began its advance. Across the pontoon bridges at Germanna Ford it marched, into the tangled Wilderness, where Lee's veterans were waiting. Grant sent back word to Washington, "If you see the President, tell him, from me, that, whatever happens, there will be no turning back."

Wadsworth's Division in Action in the Wilderness.

The Wilderness was rightly named. "It was covered by a dense forest, almost impenetrable by troops in line of battle, where maneuvering was an operation of extreme difficulty and uncertainty. The undergrowth was so heavy that it was scarcely possible to see more than 100 paces in any direction." Here for the first time Lee had a chance to test Grant.

Bringing up Hill's and Ewell's corps with great rapidity and ordering Longstreet's to join them, the Confederate general hoped to reenact Chancellorsville. The first day's fighting was confused. Men lost their way, regiments became detached, and by nightfall Union and Confederate lines "lay like a worm fence, at every angle." Early on the morning of May 6 the Federal troops renewed the assault—only to rush headlong into Longstreet's men, just arrived at the front. "Half or three-fourths of an hour of alternating success and repulse," a newspaperman on the Union left reported, "and General Wadsworth orders a charge to recover his command from a slight wavering. He is cheered loudly by his men, who love the gray haired chieftain. One horse is shot under him. He mounts a second and spurs to the front, hat in hand, and we should have won then, but his men saw him fall. He was shot through the head, . . . and his body fell into the hands of the enemy."

Brigadier General James Samuel Wadsworth, U.S.A.

Wounded escaping from the burning woods of the Wilderness —

Wounded Soldiers Escaping from the Burning Woods of the Wilderness, May 6, 1864.

By midmorning the front was momentarily stabilized, and Longstreet, wearing "his once gray uniform . . . changed to brown, [with] many a button . . . missing; his riding-boots . . . dusty and worn," was at Lee's headquarters urging a movement by an unfinished railway cut against the left flank of the Union army. Lee agreed, and Longstreet set off; it was to be Chancellorsville all over again.

On the Federal left Hancock thought he was winning. "We are driving them, sir," he exclaimed happily; "tell General Meade we are driving them most beautifully." Then the thunder broke on his unprotected flank. "The streams of wounded came faster and faster back; here a field officer, reeling in the saddle; and there another, hastily carried past on a stretcher." Longstreet's flanking movement was "an ideal success."

So, for the moment, it seemed. But Longstreet himself came under crossfire from the main Confederate line, and a bullet pierced his throat; it would be months before Lee's "Old War Horse" would again see active service. Lee undertook to continue the attack, but the momentum of the charge had been lost. Fires broke out in the woods and "advanced on all sides through the tall grass, and, taking the dry pines, raged up to their tops." There were screams as the flames licked the clothing of the wounded. "Some were carried off by the ambulance corps, others in blankets suspended to four muskets, and more by the aid of sticks, muskets, or even by crawling." But for many there was no rescue.

Lieutenant General James Longstreet, C.S.A.

General Grant and Staff on the Way to Spotsylvania Court House, May 7, 1864.

For Lee the battle had been costly, but Grant had been checked. If he behaved as had previous commanders of the Army of the Potomac, Grant would retreat across the river, and the Confederates once more could take the offensive. This, however, was not Grant's idea. Before the fighting in the Wilderness was over he was planning his next aggressive move. "I am now sending back to Belle Plaines all my wagons for a fresh supply of provisions, and ammunition," he wrote to Halleck, "and propose to fight it out on this line if it takes all Summer."

Disillusioned soldiers of the Army of the Potomac had seen heroes come and go, and they had no heart for cheering generals these days—particularly if the general happened to be a taciturn and unprepossessing Westerner. But when they learned that Grant had ordered not a retreat but an advance toward Spotsylvania, soldiers, "weary and sleepy after their long battle, with stiffened limbs and smarting wounds, now sprang to their feet. . . . Wild cheers echoed through the forest, and glad shouts of triumph rent the air. Men swung their hats, tossed up their arms, and pressed forward to within touch of their chief." Always practical, Grant merely remarked: "This is most unfortunate. The sound will reach the ears of the enemy, and I fear it may reveal our movement."

Brigadier General Fitzhugh Lee, C.S.A.

Lee had already anticipated Grant's movement and had ordered his army toward Spotsylvania. When the first Federals arrived, only the cavalry of Fitzhugh Lee, fighting nephew of the great general, were in place. As Fitz Lee was slowly forced back, advance units of Southern infantry came in sight. "Run for our rail piles," shouted a cavalryman; "the Federal infantry will reach them first, if you don't run." "Our men sprang forward as if by magic," recalled one of Kershaw's brigade. "We occupy the rail piles in time to see a column . . . moving toward us, about sixty yards away. Fire . . . is poured into that column. . . . [It] staggers and then falls back."

May 11th 1864   The   The Wilderness, on the Brock road

Union Troops in the Wilderness Clearing a Space Where Guns Could Work.

By the evening of May 8 both armies again faced each other, this time near Spotsylvania. Painfully the generals had learned that a spade is as much a soldier's tool as a musket. Wherever the armies bivouacked now, they at once erected temporary fortifications. Rifle pits, reported Charles Francis Adams, "scar the whole country all along the road of these two armies. You see them confronting each other in long lines on every defensible position and you never seem to get through them. A rifle pit, in fact, is in the perfection to which they are now carried in these armies, nothing more nor less than most formidable fortifications, alive with infantry and bristling with artillery. The instant our infantry, for instance, get into position, they go to work with axes and spades and in a very short time there springs up in front of them a wooden barricade, made out of fence rails, felled trees or any material in reach of men who know what danger is and feel it near them; and in rear and front of this a trench is dug, the dirt from the rear being thrown over to the front, so as to bank it up and make it impenetrable to musketry and, except at the top, to artillery. This cover is anywhere from four to six feet high, is often very neatly made, and is regularly bastioned out, as it were, for artillery. As fast as a position is won, it is fortified in this way. For defence the same thing is done."

The Center of the Union Position at Spotsylvania, May 9, 1864.

During the night both Union and Confederate commanders ordered probing attacks upon the enemy's lines. "There was a heavy crash of musketry, and a wild, savage yell," remembered one Maine veteran. "The confusion was indescribable; it was only with the greatest difficulty that we could tell friend from foe. . . . It was a struggle at close quarters, a hand-to-hand conflict, resembling a mob. . . . The air was filled with . . . shouts, cheers, commands, oaths, the sharp reports of rifles, the hissing shot, dull, heavy thuds of clubbed muskets, the swish of swords and sabres, groans and prayers." The next morning General Sedgwick, inspecting the battle line, noticed one of his men dodging Confederate bullets. "Why, what are you dodging for?" asked the old regular. "They could not hit an elephant at that distance." The next second he was killed by a Confederate sharpshooter.

Edwin Forbes's drawing gives a clear picture of the Union center just after Sedgwick's death: 1, position of the Confederate army; 2, Union troops behind breastworks facing the enemy; 3, Alsop house; 4, road to Spotsylvania Court House; 5, Sedgwick's corps; 6, point where General Sedgwick was killed; 7, Spotsylvania Court House (behind trees); 8, General Warren's Fifth Corps; 9, General Hancock's Second Corps; 10, reserve batteries; 11, General Grant and staff; 12, fence-rail breastwork thrown up by Union skirmishers while advancing; 13, coehorn mortar battery; 14, road on which Sedgwick's body was brought from the field.

The Struggle for the Salient, May 12, 1864.

The most vulnerable part of Lee's line was a salient in the center which the soldiers called the "Mule Shoe," because of its shape. In a few days it would bear the ominous name, "The Bloody Angle." On May 10 Colonel Emory Upton "with a heavy column of picked men, made a most brilliant assault with the bayonet. . . . The men rushed on, without firing a shot, carried the breastworks in the face of cannon and musketry, and took 900 prisoners. Some of the men, who faltered, were run through the body by their comrades!" Upton was compelled to withdraw, but for his gallantry Grant commissioned him brigadier general.

Two days later Hancock tried to reduce the salient. Moving through "mist and fog . . . so heavy that it was impossible to see farther than a few rods," his men silently seized the apex of the Angle and, having cut Lee's army in two, began "rushing like a swollen torrent through a broken mill-dam." Then John B. Gordon arrived at the "utterly hopeless" scene—and ordered a counterattack. Just at that moment Lee himself appeared, mounted on Traveller and apparently ready to lead the charge himself. "General Lee to the rear," the men shouted. "General Lee to the rear!" As Traveller was led back by loving hands, Gordon shouted "Forward!" and his men swept on, "pouring their rapid volleys into Hancock's confused ranks, and swelling the deafening din of battle with their piercing shouts. . . . Hancock was repulsed and driven out."

Major General Emory Upton, U.S.A.

Confederate Soldier of Ewell's Corps Killed in the Attack of May 19, 1864.

Again Grant had been taught that he could not carry Lee's entrenched positions by direct assault. The Confederates had a similar lesson to learn about their foe. On May 19, thinking that Grant was withdrawing, Lee ordered Ewell to reconnoiter. The Confederates met the untried division of General Robert O. Tyler, which had never before seen battle. "If you keep on like this a couple of years," the veterans had jeered at them, "you'll learn all the tricks of the trade."

After May 19 there were no more taunts. Badly chewed up, Ewell was lucky to escape as Hancock and Warren hurried up with reinforcements. "As you see," Tyler proudly told them, "my men are raw hands at this sort of work, but they are behaving like veterans." Both sides had lost heavily. "A staff-officer, passing over the ground after dark, saw . . . a row of men stretched upon the ground, looking as if they had lain down in line of

[*310*]

battle to sleep. He started to shake several of them, and cried out: 'Get up! What do you mean by going to sleep at such a time as this?' He was shocked to find that this row consisted entirely of dead bodies lying as they fell, shot down in the ranks with the alinement perfectly preserved."

Except for Ewell's reconnaissance, fighting at Spotsylvania had been terminated by five days of merciful rain. Not even ambulances could run over the impassable roads. "All offensive operations necessarily cease until we can have twenty-four hours of dry weather," Grant wrote. Both commanders used the interlude to count the costs of the battles just ended and to request reinforcements. Although the Federals had lost 28,202 in killed and wounded since Grant crossed the Rapidan, and the Confederates perhaps 17,250, the Union could bear a war of attrition better than the South. "How long this game is to be played," Meade wrote, "it is impossible to tell; but in the long run, we ought to succeed, because it is in our power more promptly to fill the gaps in men and material which this constant fighting produces."

Confederate Soldier of Ewell's Corps Killed in Attack of May 19.

Grant sent his wounded away to Belle Plain and to Fredericksburg, whence they could be transported to Washington hospitals. At Fredericksburg, reported a member of the Sanitary Commission, "the stores on both sides of the streets are full [of wounded]— filthy shops, old shoe stores, old blacksmiths' rooms, men lying on the floor without even straw under them, and with their heads on old bits of cast iron." At Belle Plain things were equally bad. Secretary Welles found it "a rough place with no dwelling,—an extemporized plankway from the shore some twenty or thirty rods in the rear. Some forty or fifty steamers and barges, most of them crowded with persons, were there. Recruits going forward to reinforce Grant's army, or the wounded and maimed returning from battle. Rows of stretchers, on each of which was a maimed or wounded Union soldier, were wending towards the steamers which were to bear them to Washington, while from the newly arrived boats were emerging the fresh soldiers going forward to the field."

Union Troops Wounded in the Wilderness Campaign Relaxing at Fredericksburg.

Wilderness Dead at Fredericksburg.

Charles Francis Adams, attached to Meade's headquarters during the Wilderness fighting, acutely summarized the results of the campaign: "These two great armies have pounded each other nearly to pieces for many days; neither has achieved any real success over the other on the field of battle. Our loss has probably been greater than theirs, for ours has been the offensive; but we have a decided balance of prisoners and captured artillery in our favor. The enemy, I think, outfight us, but we outnumber them, and, finally, within the last three days one witnesses in this Army as it moves along all the results of a victory, when in fact it has done only barren fighting. For it has done the one thing needful before the enemy—it has advanced. The result is wonderful. Hammered and pounded as this Army has been; worked, marched, fought and reduced as it is, it is in better spirits and better fighting trim today than it was in the first day's fight in the Wilderness. Strange as it seems to me, it is, I believe, yet the fact, that this Army is now just on its second wind, and is more formidable than it ever was before."

Jericho Mills on the North Anna River, Where Warren's Fifth Corps Crossed, May 23, 1864.

"In the Wilderness," wrote Grant's aide, Horace Porter, "the manoeuvers had been largely a game of blindman's-buff; they now became more like the play of pussy-wants-a-corner." Repeatedly Grant tried to turn Lee's right flank, so as to come between the Confederate army and Richmond and force the Southern general to risk a battle. "All of our manoeuvres," Grant wrote, were "made for the very purpose of getting the enemy out of his cover." By May 23 the armies were on opposite banks of the North Anna River, and Grant ordered Gouverneur Warren's Fifth Corps across at Jericho Mills. "The current was very swift," wrote one of the advance guard, "and the water nearly up to our arm-pits, which made the crossing a very difficult task to perform, but it was soon accomplished, and we then formed a line of battle to guard the men who were employed in building a pontoon bridge across the river." Before A. P. Hill was ready to attack, the Federal soldiers had crossed the river and were building earthworks. "General Hill," said Lee reproachfully, "why did you let these people cross the river? Why did you not drive them back as General Jackson would have done?"

Lee's defenses were still too strong, and Grant had to make another flanking move, this time arriving south of the Pamunkey River, just before Cold Harbor. Richmond lay within sound of Federal guns—but before it stretched Lee's army, still intact. "At daylight on June 2 the headquarters [of Grant] were moved . . . to a camp near Bethesda Church, so as to be nearer the center of the line. . . . The pews had been carried out of the church and placed in the shade of the trees surrounding it. . . . The ubiquitous photographers were promptly on the ground, and they succeeded in taking several fairly good views of the group. A supply of New York papers had just been received, and the party, with the exception of the general, were soon absorbed in reading the news. He was too much occupied at the time in thinking over his plans for the day to give attention to the papers. . . ."

Grant (Leaning over the Bench) in Council of War at Bethesda Church, June 2, 1864.

Throwing Up Breastworks near Hawes's Store at the Battle of Cold Harbor.

Both armies had settled down to the sober and unheroic work of death. "Your typical 'great white plain,' with long lines advancing and manoeuvering, led on by generals in cocked hats and by bands of music," wrote a weary Union officer, "exist not for us." "At Cold Harbor," a Confederate lad related, "our brigade worked all night with only bayonets, cups, two or three picks, and as many shovels to throw up a breastwork, and next day several of us excavated sleeping-places in the rear." Behind the earthworks, a newspaperman observed, the men "work all day, and never once stand upright; load the pieces upon their hands and knees, extending the rammers out of the embrasures, while others ply shovels to replace the earth knocked away by hostile projectiles. . . . You must be wary, and you must promptly drop on your knees when you see a puff of smoke. . . . You will have sufficient time to drop down into safety, for the smoke will puff out white and distinct a quarter of a minute before the sound of the discharge reaches you or the ball whizzes by or thuds in the thrown-up dirt."

Coehorns at Cold Harbor.

In the Federal lines, Theodore Lyman wrote his wife, there was "a good deal of artillery, so that there was the noise of battle from morning to night. We took in some cohorn mortars, as they are called. These are light, small mortars, that may be carried by two or three men, and are fired with a light charge of powder. They throw a 24-lb. shell a maximum distance of about 1000 yards. As these shells go up in the air and then come down almost straight, they are very good against rifle-pits. General Gibbon says there has been a great mistake about the armies of Israel marching seven times round Jericho blowing on horns, thereby causing the walls to fall down. He says the marching round was a 'flank movement,' and that the walls were then blow down with cohorns. Some of the heavy artillerists of the German regiment were first sent to fire these mortars; but it was found that they could give no definite account of where the projectiles went, the reason of which was that, every time they fired, the officer and his gunners tumbled down flat in great fear of Rebel sharpshooters!"

Brigadier General John Gibbon, U.S.A.

Brigadier General Francis Barlow's Charge at Cold Harbor, June 3, 1864.

For June 3 Grant ordered a frontal assault upon Lee's entrenchments. His men knew it would be suicidal; and, the night before, they sat up "calmly writing their names and home addresses on slips of paper, and pinning them on the backs of their coats, so that their dead bodies might be recognized upon the field." At 4:30 A.M. the advance began. The "steel-cold General Gibbon" pushed his division forward, followed closely by Hancock's second division under young Frank Barlow, looking "like a highly independent mounted newsboy; . . . attired in a flannel checked shirt; a threadbare pair of trousers, and an old blue *képi*." Incredibly, Barlow's men swept over the first line of Lee's works. Waud's sketch shows the Seventh New York Heavy Artillery at the moment of success. Some of the Federals tried to turn captured guns upon the enemy, while others (in the foreground) were disarming prisoners.

Desperately Lee followed the fighting. He had not one regiment in reserve. As he listened intently, the firing told him that his line had been bent but not broken. Barlow and Gibbon were thrown back, and the Union army retreated under murderous fire. "Our men have . . . been foolishly and wantonly sacrificed," Upton wrote bitterly; "we were recklessly ordered to assault the enemy's intrenchments, knowing neither their strength nor position. Our loss was very heavy, and to no purpose."

"I pass much of my time noticing Grant . . . ," Charles Francis Adams wrote on the day after Cold Harbor. "For the last few days he has evidently been thinking very hard. I never noticed this before. Formerly he always had a disengaged expression in his face; lately he has had an intent, abstracted look, and as he and Meade sit round on our march I see Grant stroking his beard, puffing at his cigar and whittling at small sticks, but with so abstracted an air that I see well that they are with him merely aids to reflection. In fact as he gets down near Richmond and approaches the solution of his problem, he has need to keep up a devil of a thinking. Yesterday he attacked the enemy and was decidedly repulsed. He always is repulsed when he attacks their works, and so are they when they attack his. The course of the campaign seems to me to have settled pretty decisively that neither of these two armies can, in the field, the one acting defensively and the other offensively, gain any great advantage. Fighting being equal, it becomes therefore a question of generalship. To capture Richmond Grant must do with Lee what he did with Pemberton, he must outgeneral him and force him to fight him on his own ground. This all of us uninformed think he could accomplish by crossing the James and taking Richmond in the rear, and accordingly we are most eager that that should be done. Grant seems to hesitate

Grant's Troops at Charles City Court House, June 13, 1864.

Union Cavalry Guarding the Evacuation of Port Royal, Virginia, May 30, 1864.

to do this and to desire to approach by this side. His reasons of course we do not know, but they yesterday cost this army six thousand men. Feeling that we cannot beat the rebels by hard, point-blank pounding before Richmond, we are most anxious to find ourselves in some position in which they must come out and pound us or give way. The south bank of the James seems to hold out to us hopes of supplies, rest and success. . . ."

It was a bitter decision for Grant to make, for a change of base would be a tacit admission that his bloody summer's campaign had been a failure. But on June 11, after ordering the evacuation of supply bases and the destruction of lines of communication behind him, Grant announced, "The movement to transfer this army to the south side of the James River will commence after dark to-morrow night."

Lieutenant General Grant at City Point, August, 1864.

XII. Before Richmond

In 1864 events moved like an old newsreel crazily projected backward. Grant's campaign had begun in the Wilderness, within sight of Chancellorsville, where Hooker had been defeated only twelve months before. He was checked at Spotsylvania, close to the scene of Burnside's disastrous repulse. At Cold Harbor some of his veterans could identify landmarks remembered from their Peninsula campaign with McClellan in 1862. And when Grant shifted his base to the James River, as McClellan before him had done, Lee again sent an expedition down the Valley to threaten Washington. By fall it seemed that the war had become an insane parody of itself.

War-weariness and depression spread over the land. The very appearance of the armies in the field reflected the fatigue. Gone were the fine uniforms, the epaulettes, the shining sabers. The picture-book war was over. "The men look dirty and tired," Charles Francis Adams thought; "they toil along in loose, swaying columns and are chiefly remarkable for a most wonderful collection of old felt hats in every stage of dilapidation. Their clothes are torn, dusty and shabby; few carry knapsacks and most confine their luggage to a shelter-tent and blanket which is tied in a coil over one shoulder." They fought as loyally and as doggedly as ever, but the glamour was gone. War had become a grim, unending business of slaughter.

The weariness of the soldiers was reflected in defeatism behind the lines. In the North many had opposed the war from the start, and Lincoln's emancipation policy had made Copperheads of more. Bloody draft riots in 1863, even at a time when Lee had invaded Pennsylvania and John Hunt Morgan was raiding the Great Lakes states, showed the strength of Northern antiwar sentiment. Grant's remorseless but fruitless campaign further encouraged defeatism. Even Secretary Welles admitted, "Grant has not great regard for human life," and newspapers bluntly called him "The Butcher." In the summer Democrats nominated General McClellan for President on a platform which denounced the war as a failure.

In the Confederacy, too, there was bitterness and disillusionment. Farms had been looted, cities had been pillaged, lives had been sacrificed to no apparent purpose. Inflation starved the city dwellers, and small farmers protested that it was a rich man's war and a poor man's fight. Failure made President Davis increasingly unpopular, and he was denounced as a "miserable, stupid, one-eyed, dyspeptic, arrogant tyrant." Even his Vice President encouraged the defeatists. As Federal armies advanced they were welcomed by the Union-loving population of the mountain areas; and in the low country the Negroes flocked about them, having learned that Lincoln's troops brought freedom.

But as both sides staggered drearily into a fourth winter of war there were no signs of surcease. It seemed that the armies might fight each other to death. But when Grant was told that the war was becoming a Kilkenny cat affair he remarked grimly, "Our cat has the longer tail."

General Butler's Headquarters on the James River.

While Grant was battering overland toward Richmond, he had sent Benjamin F. Butler's army by sea to make a landing on the James below the Confederate capital. Like Butler himself, the venture took on a comic-opera aspect. "He *is* the strangest sight . . . you ever saw," Theodore Lyman wrote; "it is hard to keep your eyes off him. With his head set immediately on a stout shapeless body, his very squinting eyes, and a set of legs and arms that look as if made for somebody else, and hastily glued to him by mistake, he presents a combination of Victor Emmanuel, Aesop, and Richard III, which is very confusing to the mind. Add to this a horse with a kind of rapid, ambling trot that shakes about the arms, legs, etc., till you don't feel quite sure whether it is a centaur, or what it is, and you have a picture of this celebrated General."

Butler's expedition was as poorly organized as his body. When he landed, Petersburg had almost no defenders and Richmond itself had been stripped to reinforce Lee. But instead of advancing at once he halted to engage in acrimonious note writing to his two corps commanders. They agreed, Butler complained, "upon but one thing and that was, how they could thwart and interfere with me."

Poor judgment led Butler to concentrate his troops on the Bermuda Hundred, between the James and Appomattox rivers. By the time he did get moving, Beauregard had arrived with the reserves, and the Confederate general quickly pushed the Army of the James back behind the narrow neck of this peninsula and erected fortifications to keep him there. "Having hermetically sealed itself up at Bermuda Hundred," the army was, as Grant tartly complained, "as completely shut off from further operations directly before Richmond as if it had been in a bottle strongly corked."

In this "bottle," as comfortably protected as if he had been back in his Massachusetts law office, Butler conducted a mock war while Grant was bloodily battling his way south. He was strong on alerts, alarms, reconnaissances. Daily he inspected fortifications. Upon the slightest provocation he constructed bridges. To the south of the Appomattox, Butler had managed to hold on to City Point, and he spent many happy days supervising the building of a fortified pontoon bridge to connect the divided portions of his command.

Pontoon Bridge on the Appomattox River near Butler's Headquarters.

Signaling by Torches from General Butler's Headquarters.

There was nothing much to do, and Butler did it grandly. The general was celebrated as "a man of untiring industry and activity"; and, if his exertions were more pointless than profitable, at least they were picturesque. His camp was kept in a constant flurry of excitement with reports and counterreports of enemy activity. Signal towers were constructed so that his men on one side of the river would not lose a second in flashing the lack of news to those on the other. By day the signaling was done with flags, and at night torches were used. "The sign-language is made by three movements of a flag or torch—one to the right, one to the left and one downward to the front," admiring reporters noted. "This seems almost too simple to be intelligible, but the repeated and combined movements are so complicated as to make a complete alphabet, and full messages can be sent and comprehended." "The signaling is observed by means of a telescope. The messages from the high signal-tower on the other side of the river are read by the sergeant or officer at the telescope, and the reply is signaled by the man with the torch."

"I had erected a lookout in the neighborhood of two hundred feet high," Butler related proudly. "It was composed of trestle work. . . . It was a great annoyance to the enemy and of great usefulness to me. There was a nine-foot square space on the top to which observers could be drawn up in a large basket by means of a windlass. Once at the top of this lookout, a large portion of the peninsula, with all the works of the enemy, and my own lines . . . for . . . more than three miles, lay like a map under my eyes."

The soldiers called it the "Crow's Nest," and it was so placed as to reveal to the enemy the precise location of the large Federal battery at its base. "There were occasional duels between the Howlett House [Confederate] and Crow's Nest batteries which interested us as the mammoth shot passed to and fro," a Union diarist recorded. "The Howlett House battery has fired occasionally at our Crow's Nest observation tower, but never seriously damaged it. Our big battery has replied now and then, and when standing behind our guns we could see the shot as they arched to the other side. . . . The enemy tried to destroy our signal tower and we tried to destroy their guns, but nothing much resulted, except a big noise."

Crow's Nest at Dutch Gap Being Fortified with Ten-Inch Mortars.

Fort Mahone, in the Confederate Line Before Petersburg.

Meanwhile Beauregard's Confederates were desperately rushing to complete their entrenchments across the peninsula. "We not only erected a strong line of works in our front," wrote the historian of a South Carolina brigade, "but we assisted in throwing up powerful field fortifications some two miles below our camp. For nearly two months, a detail, varying from two hundred to three hundred and fifty men, was constantly at work here, except on Sunday, from eight o'clock, A.M., to four, P.M. These works were constructed according to rule—with a ditch in front of six feet depth and eight feet width, whence all the earth for the embankment was thrown; with an embankment of six feet height, twelve feet base, and four feet terre-plain; with a strong, neat revetement, and a banquette tread. These works would conceal troops marching behind them, would afford perfect protection from small-arms and ordinary field-artillery fire, and they could scarcely be stormed, on account of the ditch and the brush abatis in front.

"It was at this work that I had the strongest evidence of the exhaustion of the troops. Some men dug and shovelled well; but the majority . . . would pant and grow faint under the labor of half an hour. This was most strikingly the case when our meat ration failed. A pint of corn-meal could hardly keep men hearty. . . . If I am not mistaken, we had no meat for a whole week, once. The most pitiful shifts were employed to procure us meat. Canned beef, imported from England (!) was issued a few times, and at other times, small bits of poor, blue beef were doled out. Sometimes we had coffee, and now and then a spoonful of sugar. Tobacco, of the worst quality, was issued every month, at the rate of a fourth of a pound to the man. Each officer had one ration given him now, just as enlisted men. Once we had half a gill of whiskey issued to each man. It was amusing, as well as sad, to see the delight of the troops over this drop of comfort. All this time the enemy drank coffee, eat fat, fresh beef and good bread, and drank quantities of whiskey, as their roarings at night testified."

Confederate Quarters in Front of Petersburg.

Brigadier General Alfred H. Colquitt, C.S.A.

The days of quiet below Richmond were soon ended. On June 14 Grant ordered Butler to attack Petersburg while the Army of the Potomac was crossing the James River. Beauregard was desperate. The troops he had were good, like Colquitt's brigade, which had fought "gallantly, and with brilliant success," against Butler's earlier advance. But there were so few of them, and Lee's army was still north of the river.

Company E, 4th U.S. Colored Infantry, at Fort Lincoln.

At first Butler's assault went admirably, and the first line of Confederate defenses was taken. He had used Negro troops, against whom there was "a stupid, unreasoning, and quite vengeful prejudice . . . among the regular officers" of the army. When Butler was asked why he entrusted such responsibility to Negro soldiers, the abolitionist general, who was credited with coining the word "contrabands" to describe the escaped slaves who flocked to his lines, replied, "I knew that they would fight more desperately than any white troops, in order to prevent capture, because they knew . . . that if captured they would be returned into slavery."

On the night of June 15, when Grant's veterans crossed the James, they met "a mob of black troops, who were hauling some brass guns. They had attached long ropes to the limbers, and, with many shouts, were dragging them down the road. Some of them bore flaming torches of pine knots in their hands. They sang, they shouted, they danced weirdly. . . . They were happy, dirty, savagely excited. . . . The eager infantrymen asked: 'Where did you get those guns?' They replied: 'We'uns captured them from the rebels today.'" Many had doubted the valor of colored troops, but even the distrustful Theodore Lyman was obliged to admit: "Everyone gives great credit to the negroes for the spirit they showed. I believe there is no question their conduct was entirely to their credit."

For some unexplained reason "Baldy" Smith, who had led the assault, stopped after taking the first line of Confederate defenses, and by a desperate dash Lee was able to slip into Petersburg before the battle could be renewed. The fortifications which the Negro troops had captured remained in Federal hands. They were "superb, both in construction and position." "Much astonishment was expressed at the comparatively small loss attending the capture of these strong works," a Union diarist recorded. "Decently defended the whole of Grant's army could not have captured them."

Though Grant had lost the race, he was not willing to give up the prize. On the following days he ordered the attack renewed. On June 18, as the sun set, the infantry prepared for a final charge. "The charging cheer rang out loudly," a New York private recalled, "the line of blue-clad soldiers rushed forward, the Confederate pickets emptied their rifles, jumped from their rifle-pits, and ran for their main line, which was still silent excepting the artillery. This was served rapidly. . . . The line of blue swept on in good order, cheering loudly and continuously. They drew near to the Confederate earthworks. Canister cut gaps in the ranks. Then the heads of Lee's infantry rose above their intrenchments. I saw

Confederate Fortifications Around Petersburg.

Brigadier General Orlando Bolivar Willcox, U.S.A., and Staff Before Petersburg.

the glint of the sun on their polished rifle barrels. A cloud of smoke curled along the works. Our men began to tumble in large numbers. . . . The field grew hazy with smoke. Rifles were tossed high in the air. Battle flags went down with a sweep to again appear and plunge into the smoke. Wounded men straggled out of the battle. . . . The fire grew steadily fiercer and fiercer. . . . Night settled down, and the fight still went on. . . ."

The Confederate fire was murderous. "When this division commenced the final advance," reported General Willcox, "the ranks were reduced to less than 1,000 officers and men." Slowly the Federals were driven back, and the assault was abandoned. "All was done that men could do," Willcox explained.

[333]

Captain James H. Cooper's Battery, 1st Pennsylvania Light Artillery, Before Petersburg, June 21, 1864.

"I talked to some rebel prisoners and swapped food for tobacco," the New York private related of the day after the battle. "They were inclined to boast. . . . In truth they had torn us badly. One long-legged, dangling Cracker, with a broad, derisive grin on his face, which displayed his long, tobacco-stained teeth, said to me, drawlingly: 'Say, sonny, did you . . . chaps get a bellyful?' I assured him we had room for more, whereat he grinned and marched to the rear with his comrades."

After the failure on June 18 Federal strategists, amateur and professional alike, agreed: "The enemy is becoming well entrenched and it is evident that further movements in line of battle are impracticable. Siege operations must be commenced. . . . Sharp-shooting and picket-firing continues, to the imminent danger of every exposed head. It is evident enough that Grant's . . . well-planned capture of Petersburg has failed, and, again, because not promptly and resolutely executed."

Union Powder Magazine at Fort Brady on the James River.

Field Telegraph Station at Wilcox Landing near City Point.

From army headquarters at City Point, Grant had followed the fighting closely. His efficient signal and telegraph corps kept him in constant communication with his subordinates. "The moment the troops were put in position to go into camp all the men connected with this branch of service would proceed to put up their wires. A mule loaded with a coil of wire would be led to the rear of the nearest flank of the brigade he belonged to, and would be led in a line parallel thereto, while one man would hold an end of the wire and uncoil it as the mule was led off. . . . This would be done in rear of every brigade at the same time. The ends of all the wires would then be joined, making a continuous wire in the rear of the whole army. The men, attached to brigades or divisions, would all commence at once raising the wires with their telegraph poles. . . . While this was being done the telegraph wagons would take their positions near where the headquarters they belonged to were to be established, and would connect with the wire. Thus, in a few minutes longer time than it took a mule to walk the length of its coil, telegraphic communication would be effected between all the headquarters of the army."

From all parts of his vast army the same word came: Petersburg could not be taken by assault. Grant accepted the inevitable. "I now ordered the troops to be put under cover," he said, "and allowed some of the rest which they had so long needed. They remained quiet, except that there was more or less firing every day. . . . Thus began the siege of Petersburg."

Supplies were ordered for a protracted investment of the city. Grant's headquarters were at City Point, which when Butler landed had consisted "of a bluff some fifty feet high at the point where the Appomattox River empties into the James; the remnants of a wharf which had been consumed above the piles by fire; at the foot of the bluff a few shabby houses ranged along two or three short lanes or streets; and the spacious grounds and dilapidated house of one Dr. Eppes." Now it was converted into a modern port. Here came "old stern-wheelers, looking like huge sawmills afloat on the tide, huge black ocean steamers and little river boats, tugs dragging schooners loaded with rations for man or beast, and dispatch boats darting from one point to another"—all serving the army.

Wharf at City Point.

"And Grant has a railroad of his own, a sure-enough iron rail, all the way from City Point, around by the east and south of Petersburg, along the line that his army occupies," wrote an envious Confederate. "So vast are the resources and appliances of war at his command. They do not spare in means or men, but are lavish of both."

The military railroad was not ostentation on Grant's part. From the unhappy experience of McClellan and Burnside he had learned the lesson of the Virginia mud. "The railroad is completed and cars now run from City Point to the Weldon Road," a Union diarist recorded in September. "Grant's railroad, running in the rear of our lines, much of the way in sight of the Rebels, seems to annoy them exceedingly. Night before last they obtained a position from which they could shell a long bridge that spanned a ravine, and began to fortify. Last night our forces charged these works, . . . and captured the working party. I could plainly hear the shouts of triumph that announced their success."

U.S. Military Railroad Engine at City Point.

Army Teamsters near Butler's Signal Tower, Bermuda Hundred.

Still, most of the supplies for the Federal army were carried by mule-drawn wagons. "On each wagon was the Corps badge, with the division color and the number of the brigade, so at a glance it could be seen whether or not the wagon was in its place; the contents also of each wagon was plainly marked, whether of ammunition for artillery or for rations; if for rations, it was so marked, and just what the wagon contained—bread, pork, beans, coffee, sugar, etc. As soon as a wagon was emptied it was immediately sent to the rear to the base of supplies to take on another load."

Mules were thus as indispensable to the Civil War armies as generals—and sometimes more popular. One New York soldier recorded in his diary a heated session "upon the mule's patience, endurance and its value as an army auxiliary." After many hours the "symposium" broke up when a muleteer pronounced judgment: "Whoever says mules are easy to git along with is a liar, that is, providin' he has an intimate acquaintance with 'em; and as for stoppin' the use of swear words in handlin' 'em, it ain't fair to a mule with an army experience to begin learnin' him polite synonyms."

Bombproof Quarters of Fort Sedgwick.

After the failure of the assault, Union soldiers began digging in for a siege. About the center of the Federal position rose the heavily armed Fort Sedgwick, only three hundred yards from the Confederate Fort Mahone. Soldiers called them Forts Hell and Damnation. All along the line such earthworks were raised, "very workmanlike, handsomely sloped in front, and neatly built up with logs in the rear." "It is really a handsome sight," thought Theodore Lyman, "to get a view of half a mile of uniform parapet . . . and see the men's shelter-tents neatly pitched in the pine woods, just in the rear, while in front a broad stretch of timber has been 'slashed,' to give a good field of fire and break up any body of troops advancing to attack. It is quite interesting, too, to see a redoubt going up. The men work after the manner of bees, each at the duty assigned. The mass throw up earth; the engineer soldiers do the 'revetting,' that is the interior facing of logs. The engineer sergeants run about with tapes and stakes, measuring busily; and the engineer officers look as wise as possible and superintend."

Trenches and breastworks gave protection against Confederate muskets and ordinary field-pieces; but the Southerners resorted to "those confounded mortars, throwing those enormous shells up in almost a perpendicular direction, with such a peculiar aim that . . .

they would descend plump within our lines, tearing up the earth in a most frightful manner, and filling the air with death-dealing missiles by their explosions." "We soon guessed the remedy," a New York volunteer wrote, "and bomb-proofs were at once added to our trenches." "The bombproofs were irregularly constructed without square, plumb or level, and there was neither conformity in dimensions, nor in frontage. . . . Only in their covering did similarity exist. Crossed layers of logs surmounted with an abundance of earth constituted the roof. . . . After each fierce bombardment some of them had to be new-topped to render them inhabitable."

For the first few weeks the weather was hot and dry. "The earth seemed pulverized and the very air was filled with dust. It penetrated our clothing and mingled with our perspiration. We inhaled the 'sacred soil' with our breath, swallowed it with our rations and absorbed it through every pore. We could scarcely get sufficient water to drink," remembered a New York private. Then the rains came. "It was impossible to secure drainage of the entire line, and the heavy rains common to the South would soon flood the trenches. I have seen soldiers in the trenches up to their waists in water, with their ammunition about their necks—not for an hour, but for a day."

Fort Sedgwick, or Fort Hell.

Members of Company C, 1st Connecticut Artillery, at Fort Brady.

On the north side of the James, Fort Brady was erected to prevent the Confederate ironclads from slipping down the river to damage Grant's transports and supply ships at City Point. In October, when the Confederate flotilla tried to descend the river, the First Connecticut Artillery opened fire on the lead vessel. "Evidently taken by surprise, it took her some time to move," Captain Pierce proudly reported; and he had "the satisfaction of seeing sixteen shells strike her and burst before she was fairly under way. . . . In the meantime, the rams and ironclads, seemingly startled by the sudden attack, had got up steam, and moved further out into the stream. . . . Deeming the fire too hot to permit them to cross . . . , they gave up the attempt, and sought the shelter of the bank."

The Richmond *Dispatch* admitted that the Confederate vessels "weighed anchor and got out of range as quick as possible." The Confederate gunboats remained bottled up, and the siege went on.

Officers of Company C, 1st Connecticut Artillery, at Fort Brady.

Gunners of the Eighteenth Corps Protected by Mantelets.

"It would take a volume to describe our trench life," one Union veteran reminisced, "and words cannot picture the experiences of that long siege. At night the exhibition of 'fireworks' was grand. One battery would throw a few shot to get some desired range and this would be replied to from the other side. Another battery would join the dispute, and another, till from the Appomattox to the South Side Road, there would be a roar and blaze of artillery. The large mortar shells would mount to above the low-hanging clouds, and descending with increasing velocity, seemed like angry meteors falling from the skies. Their arched path could be distinctly seen at night by their burning fuses, crossing and interlacing each other as they went forth from side to side."

In both armies sharpshooters, using telescopic sights, alertly picked off enemy artillery-men who exposed themselves. For protection Union gunners placed "*mantelets,* . . . really nothing more nor less than rope-mats, heavily constructed, made to cover the embrasures, and having an aperture through which the gun's muzzle is thrust."

[344]

Union Sharpshooters of the Eighteenth Corps in Front of Petersburg.

"It was hell itself," a Pennsylvania corporal recalled, "and it is wondrous to me that so many of us survived the event. The over-taxing of the men in building rifle pits, batteries, forts and cover ways, in addition to the continuous sharpshooting; the evening and morning duels, which were so deadly in our front, being from one to two hundred yards apart and right in front of the city, was simply awful. One-half of the line would fire while the other worked on the pits or tried to sleep."

"After a while, by common consent, sharpshooting ceased at sundown. Pickets were posted in front of both armies, and consequently 'Reb' and 'Yank' would be within a short distance watching each other the night long. Men of both armies would crawl out of their 'holes,' stretch themselves and breathe the better air; sing, blackguard each other, etc. At about sunrise, the pickets having been withdrawn, the trenches policed and the sharpshooters in position, notice would be given by a shot from the first side ready and then woe to any exposed head."

Bombproof Quarters Behind the Union Lines at Petersburg.

"There was fighting more or less every day especially on our left," recalled John L. Cunningham, a New York volunteer. "Our tedious trench life was wearing us out; fatigue, dirt and vermin were depressing our spirits to a decidedly visible extent, so, for a little relief, it was arranged that we occasionally have a few days out of the trenches, by retiring to a pine wood a mile or so to our right and rear close down to the Appomattox. The enemy soon found our hiding place and commenced a nightly shelling of these woods from batteries across the river. This obliged us to make bomb-proofs even here for our protection. . . . These woods were also below our rear batteries, and we suffered from the bursting of poor shells intended for the enemy across the Appomattox, but prematurely exploding. Our bomb-proofs in the woods were dug some fifteen to twenty feet long and about four feet wide, with earth left for 'benches' along the side, like an omnibus, and deep enough for sitting upright. The excavation was covered with logs and these by the excavated earth —entrances at each end."

Unable to force Lee out of Petersburg, Grant sought to starve him out, and on June 22 dispatched General James H. Wilson with 5,500 horsemen to cut the railroads behind the Confederate lines. "The . . . road led us northwest to Sixteen-mile Turnout on the Southside Railroad," Wilson related, "which we struck about 2 P.M. without meeting any resistance whatever. . . . Fortunately we found two loaded freight trains at the station, disabled the two engines, burned sixteen cars of army supplies, the station, wood piles, water tank, sawmill and, besides, tore up the tracks and the sleepers, piled up the crossties, and burned them, which, in turn, heated the rails so that they were bent easily around the trees. . . . The hot weather favored us, for it made buildings, crossties, bridges, trestles, wood piles, cars, and stations so dry and inflammable that they burned like tinder, filling the air with clouds of cinders and smoke, and setting fire to the dry leaves and grass on both sides of the track." While returning to Grant's lines, Wilson was hotly attacked, but his casualties did not compensate Lee for "the heaviest blow of the kind that ever befell the Confederacy. . . . It was nine weeks . . . before a train from the south ran into Petersburg."

Wilson's Raid Against Lee's Lines of Communication, June, 1864.

"Things here are curiously dull," wrote Charles Francis Adams in July from Meade's headquarters; "there is nothing that I know of going on." Apparently the private soldiers were better informed than their officers, for at the same time a New York diarist reported "vague rumors of a wonderful mine being prepared under some portion of the enemy's line." Even the Confederates seemed to have guessed the Union intention. "On June 30," wrote General E. P. Alexander, "I became convinced that the enemy were preparing to mine our position at Elliott Salient," just across from Fort Morton. "At that point, incessant fire was kept up . . . , while a few hundred yards to the right and left the fire had been gradually allowed to diminish. . . . For several days I had expected to see zigzag approaches started on the surface. . . . When . . . nothing appeared, I became satisfied that their activity was underground."

In fact, the Federal soldiers had been digging for weeks. Colonel Henry Pleasants, whose regiment was composed mostly of Pennsylvania miners, had originally suggested the scheme, and Burnside strongly endorsed it. Though he had no great expectations of success, Grant "approved of it, as a means of keeping the men occupied." A gallery 510.8 feet long was dug, and the mine was charged with 8000 pounds of powder.

Fort Morton, Opposite the Crater.

Explosion of the Mine Under the Confederate Works at Sunrise, July 30, 1864.

The "calm and clear morning" of July 30 was chosen for the explosion, and, as usual, the artist Alfred R. Waud was on the scene. "The rebels were plainly visible sitting about, and strolling upon . . . their parapets, . . . enjoying the cool air, apparently unsuspicious," he reported. "On our side no unusual number of men was visible, the works and covered ways giving ample concealment. Nevertheless many anxious eyes were directed to the point of the expected explosion, speculating upon the cause of its delay. The fuse had failed, and it was but a short time before sunrise that the mine was sprung. With a muffled roar it came, and as from the eruption of a volcano . . . upward shot masses of earth, momently illuminated from beneath by the lurid flare. For a few seconds huge blocks of earth and other *débris,* mingled with dust, was seen in a column perhaps 150 feet in height, and then the heavy volume of smoke, which spread out in billowy waves on every side, enveloped all. . . ."

"The explosion made a crater 150 feet long, 97 feet wide, and 30 feet deep. . . . The bulk of the earth . . . fell immediately around the crater, mingled with the debris of 2 guns, 22 cannoneers, and perhaps 250 infantrymen. . . . The falling earth . . . formed a high embankment . . . all around the crater, with one enormous clod, the size of a small cabin, perched about the middle of the inside rim. . . ."

Scene of the Explosion. Saturday July 30th.   A. R. Waud—

Union Advance into the Crater After the Explosion of the Mine.

When charging Union soldiers "reached the crater they found that its sides were so steep that it was almost impossible to climb out after once getting in. . . . The crater was soon filled with . . . disorganized men, who were mixed up with the dead and dying . . . , and tumbling aimlessly about, or attempting to scramble up the other side. The shouting, screaming, and cheering, mingled with the roar of the artillery and the explosion of shells, created a perfect pandemonium, and the crater had become a cauldron of hell."

Desperate, Lee ordered Mahone to drive the enemy back from the crater. "If we don't carry it by the first attack," the Virginia brigadier promised him, "we will renew the assault as long as a man of us is left, or until the work is ours." "When we got to the walls of the fort [crater]," related one Alabama captain in Mahone's division, "Colonel J. H. King ordered the men near him to put their hats on their bayonets and quickly raise them above the fort, which was done, and, as he anticipated, they were riddled with bullets. Then he ordered us over the embankment, and over we went, and were soon engaged in a hand-to-hand struggle. . . . The . . . death battle continued until most of the Yankees found in there were killed." By midafternoon the Confederates were in possession of the crater; for the Union army the affair had been, as Grant admitted, "a stupendous failure."

Major General William Mahone, C.S.A.

Lieutenant General Jubal Anderson Early, C.S.A.

The full impact of Grant's failure before Petersburg was not felt in the North; there was another disaster more imminent. In June, Lee had ordered the "bad old man" of his army, Jubal A. Early, into the Shenandoah Valley, in the hope that he might repeat the Jackson successes of 1862. Residents cheered when they saw the "burly person, . . . neglected dress, . . . swarthy features, and grizzled hair" of "Old Jubilee," for they knew that his home was in western Virginia and that he would fight to protect it. There was need for fighting, for Federal troops under General Hunter, who had replaced the ineffectual Sigel, had pushed down the valley, "leaving a track of desolation rarely witnessed in the course of civilized warfare." Hunter was proud of his depredations. He reported in May: "On the 12th, I . . . burned the Virginia Military Institute. . . . I found here a violent . . . proclamation from John Letcher, lately Governor of Virginia, inciting . . . a guerilla warfare on my troops, and . . . I ordered his property to be burned. . . ."

Major General David Hunter, U.S.A.

Mosby and Some Maryland Members of his Battalion.

Hunter's ferocity can be explained in part by his fear. In the Valley he was operating in the land of John Singleton Mosby and his partisan raiders, who repeatedly disrupted Federal communications, destroyed supply bases, and captured unwary detachments. "In general," Mosby explained, "my purpose was to threaten and harass the enemy on the border and in this way compel him to withdraw troops from his front to guard the line of the Potomac and Washington." The "daring enterprise and dashing heroism" of his raids had won the highest praise from the most daring, dashing cavalier of them all. "His exploits," Jeb Stuart wrote to Lee, "are not surpassed in daring and enterprise by those of *petite guerre* in any age. Unswerving devotion to duty, self-abnegation, and unflinching courage, with a quick perception and appreciation of the opportunity, are the characteristics of this officer." "The gallant band of Captain Mosby shares his glory, as they did the danger . . . , and are worthy of such a leader."

When he heard of Early's arrival in the Valley, Mosby renewed his attacks on Hunter's communications. At Lynchburg the Federal general—"owing," as he claimed, "to a want of ammunition"—avoided meeting Early and retreated into the mountains of West Virginia. Down the Valley the road to Washington lay open.

Colonel John Singleton Mosby, 43rd Battalion, Virginia Cavalry.

Battery Rodgers on the Potomac River near Alexandria.

As Early marched north, pushing aside Sigel's troops near Harpers Ferry and crossing over into Maryland, Washington residents were "in a great tremble." To be sure, ever since McClellan's command the fortifications of the Capital had been constantly elaborated, until by 1864 they were "works, in comparison with which those of Richmond were the merest castle-building of children." "The line of works constituting the defenses of Washington at this time consisted of sixty-eight inclosed forts and batteries, encircling that city and Alexandria, mounting eight hundred and seven guns and ninety-eight mortars. Besides these, there were a number of unarmed batteries. The entire circuit, leaving out the works at the Chain Bridge and omitting the distance across the Potomac at Alexandria, was thirty-three miles."

But fortifications do not man themselves, and Washington had been stripped to rein-force Grant's army. Only the invalid corps, District of Columbia volunteers, and some untrained hundred-day recruits, just arrived from the Middle West, protected the Capital. Even when some fifteen hundred employees of the quartermaster's department were has-tily armed and the veteran reserves of the Washington and Alexandria vicinity were called out, it was still a feeble defense against Early's jubilant raiders. In this crisis Federal offi-cials seemed impotent. Far away before Petersburg, Grant appeared oblivious to the danger; Halleck was "in a perfect maze, bewildered, without intelligent decision or self-reliance," and Stanton was "wisely ignorant." Fearing the worst, Assistant Secretary of the Navy Fox had a vessel ready to transport the President from the Capital should it fall.

Magazine at Battery Rodgers.

Chain Bridge over the Potomac River near Washington.

The only force between the Capital and Early's approaching columns was a handful of raw troops under General Lew Wallace, who had hurried from Baltimore to the Monocacy River, directly across Early's line of advance. Courageously the little army waited for the Confederates to attack. On July 9, after preliminary skirmishing, the Southerners charged across a cornfield on the Union left. The gray line "started forward slowly at first," Wallace wrote; "suddenly, . . . arms were shifted, and, taking to the double-quick, the men raised their battle-cry," which rose "sharper, shriller, and more like the composite yelping of wolves than I had ever heard it. And when to these there were presently super-added a tempestuous tossing of guidons, waving of banners, and a furious trampling of the young corn that flew before them like splashed billows, the demonstration was more than exciting—it was really fearful." Driven from their first line, the Union troops firmly held their second position. "Between the two hostile lines there was a narrow ravine down which ran a small stream of limpid water. In this ravine the fighting was desperate and at close quarters. To and fro the battle swayed across the little stream, . . . and when the struggle was ended a crimsoned current ran toward the river." Finally Wallace retreated; he had been fighting not for victory but for time, and he had gained a precious twenty-four hours.

Major General Lew Wallace, U.S.A.

Men of Company K, 3rd Massachusetts Artillery, at Fort Stevens.

"The Rebels are upon us," exclaimed Secretary Welles. On July 11 Early's army was shelling Fort Stevens, on the Silver Springs road just at the outskirts of the Capital. Cabinet members, Congressmen, and curious ladies rushed out to watch the battle. President Lincoln himself "was in the Fort when it was first attacked, standing upon the parapet. A soldier roughly ordered him to get down or he would have his head knocked off."

Early knew the works were "feebly manned," but since they appeared to be "exceedingly strong . . . enclosed forts of heavy artillery, with a tier of lower works in front . . . pierced for an immense number of guns, the whole being . . . strengthened by palisades and abattis," he hesitated to assault in force. His delay was fatal, for the veteran Sixth Corps of the Army of the Potomac, now under Horatio G. Wright, was landing at the Washington wharf. In the second day's skirmishing the Confederates were beaten back. "The cannon in the Fort opened on them and . . . shelled them till they was in full retreat," an exultant Union soldier wrote, "and then the Sixth Army Corps went after them and run them clean out of hearing. A Wednesday morning we got up and there was not a Johney to be seen."

[360]

Major General Horatio Gouverneur Wright, U.S.A.

Return of Sheridan's Troops.

Washington had been saved, but Early was still a menace. From the Valley he sent out raiding parties into Maryland and Pennsylvania. On July 30, when the authorities of Chambersburg, Pennsylvania, refused to pay a levy of $100,000 in gold, the Confederates laid the greater part of that town in ashes and returned to the security of the Shenandoah. Grant attributed Early's successes to "interference from Washington." "It seemed to be the policy of General Halleck and Secretary Stanton to keep any force sent . . . in pursuit of the invading army, moving right and left so as to keep between the enemy and our capital; and, generally speaking, they pursued this policy until all knowledge of the whereabouts of the enemy was lost. They were left, therefore, free to supply themselves with horses, beef cattle, and such provisions as they could carry away from Western Maryland and Pennsylvania."

"I determined to put a stop to this," Grant wrote. What the Federal forces in the Shenandoah needed was a single, energetic commander, and he asked for "a small broad-shouldered, squat man, with black hair and a square head" named Sheridan. Washington demurred. Nobody doubted the ability of Phil Sheridan, who had reorganized the cavalry corps of the Army of the Potomac. Nor could any deny the daring of a general who in May, during the Wilderness fighting, led his men on a spectacular raid behind Lee's lines, defeating the Confederate cavalry and killing Jeb Stuart at Yellow Tavern. But the Irish general was only thirty-three years old, which Stanton thought "too young for so important a command." Grant insisted, "I want Sheridan put in command of all the troops in the field, with instructions to put himself south of the enemy and follow him to the death."

A Union Volunteer Cavalryman.

Those who expected speedy success from the new general were to be disappointed. Many of his troops in the Shenandoah were "fagged-out and demoralized." After their exhausting retreat through West Virginia, Hunter's men were "ragged, famished, discouraged, sulky, and half of them in ambulances. They have been marched to tatters, they say, besides being overwhelmed and beaten."

Major General Philip Henry Sheridan, U.S.A.

**Brigadier General Cuvier Grover's Second Division of the Nineteenth Corps
at the Battle of Opequon (Winchester), September 19, 1864.**

On September 16 Grant thought the troops ready and gave the order, "Go in!" Three days later Sheridan's army crossed the Opequon Creek near Winchester to hit Early's scattered forces. Faulty deployment broke the effect of the first Federal assault, and the Southerners complacently contemplated another victory. But in midafternoon General Crook began a flanking attack against the Confederate left. "I could not see this advance, but I heard it plainly enough," wrote John W. De Forest, of the Twelfth Connecticut, part of the Nineteenth Corps. "To our right, hidden from me by the isolated wood . . . , the broad blue wave surged forward with a yell which lasted for minutes. In response there arose from the northern front of the wood a continuous, deafening wail of musketry. . . . But the yell came steadily on and triumphed gloriously over the fusillade. . . . Of course we . . . longed to help. . . . Presently, looking to the left, we saw that the Vermonters were charging; and we jumped forward with a scream, the officers leading and the men hard after. We were all in a swarm, double-quicking for the wood and yelling like redskins, when we heard behind us stentorian shouts of 'Halt! Lie down!' There on our tracks were mounted officers, our brigadier among them, sent . . . to stop our wild rush for victory—or repulse. . . . The Twelfth was still rocking back and forth, fluctuating between discipline and impulse, when an officer of Sheridan's staff (a dashing young fellow in embroidered blue shirt, with trousers tucked into his long boots) galloped into our front from the direction of Crook's column, and pointed to the wood with his drawn sabre. It was a superb picture. . . . The whole regiment saw him and rejoiced in him; it flung orders to the winds and leaped out like a runaway horse. The wood was carried in the next minute." Hastily the Confederates retreated up the Valley.

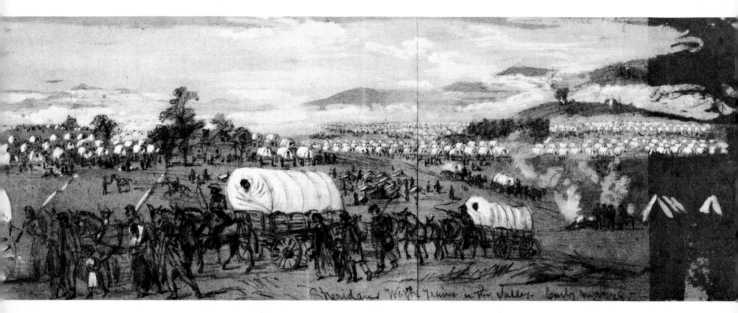

Sheridan's Wagon Trains in the Shenandoah Valley.

Pursuing Early up the Shenandoah, Sheridan struck him again on September 22 at Fisher's Hill, and "in an indescribable panic" the Confederates fled. "The stampede was complete," Sheridan reported, "the enemy leaving the field without semblance of organization, abandoning nearly all his artillery. . . ."

For the moment the Valley was free of Confederate troops; and Sheridan intended that it should remain so. "In pushing up the Shenandoah Valley," Grant had directed, "it is desirable that nothing should be left to invite the enemy to return. Take all provisions, forage, and stock wanted for the use of your command. Such as cannot be consumed, destroy." "Do all the damage to railroads and crops you can. Carry off stock of all descriptions and negroes, so as to prevent further planting. If the war is to last another year we want the Shenandoah Valley to remain a barren waste."

Sheridan's troops obeyed the order to the letter. "The atmosphere, from horizon to horizon, has been black with the smoke of a hundred conflagrations," an army reporter wrote, "and at night a gleam brighter and more lurid than sunset has shot from every verge. . . . Indiscriminating . . . , relentless, merciless, the torch has done its terrible business in . . . the valley. Few barns and stables have escaped. The gardens and cornfields have been desolated. The cattle, hogs, sheep, cows, oxen . . . have been driven from every farm. The poor, alike with the rich, have suffered. Some have lost their all. The wailing of women and children mingling with the crackling of flames has sounded from scores of dwellings. . . . The completeness of the desolation is awful."

Major General Thomas L. Rosser Attacking the Union Rear at Harrisonburg, Virginia, October 8, 1864.

Lee sent Early's battered army what reinforcements he could. When Tom Rosser arrived he was proclaimed the "Savior of the Valley"; but his brigade of cavalry was a pitiful caricature of the proud troops that had fought with Stuart. "Our horses are worn down," a Virginian complained, "and there is no source whence we can recruit. We have only pistols, sabres and old fashioned rifles, worn-out saddles, and none of the equipment in the way of portable furnaces, horse-shoes and other transportation requisite for efficient cavalry work; and above all, we have not enough food to keep the horses up."

An old cavalryman himself, Sheridan was jealous of the reputation which Rosser brought into the Valley. On October 8, the Federal general related grimly, when the Confederates "had the temerity to annoy my rear guard considerably . . . I concluded to open the enemy's eyes in earnest, so that night I told Torbert [the Federal cavalry commander] I expected him either to give Rosser a drubbing next morning or get whipped himself, and that the infantry would be halted until the affair was over; I also informed him that I proposed to ride out to Round Top Mountain to see the fight. . . . The engagement soon became general across the valley, both sides fighting mainly mounted. . . . The result was a general smash-up of the entire Confederate line, the retreat quickly degenerating into a rout the like of which was never before seen. For twenty-six miles this wild stampede kept up, with our troopers close at the enemy's heels."

Sheridan's Army Following Early Up the Valley of the Shenandoah.

On October 19 Early decided to risk another battle. At dawn he fell upon the Federal camp at Cedar Creek, while Sheridan was away in Winchester, and in a few minutes the whole army was in retreat. The roads north swarmed with "wagons, ambulances, pack mules, army followers and stray soldiers." "They were not running, not breathless and looking over their shoulders, but just trudging tranquilly rearward like a crowd hastening home from a circus."

It was a complete Confederate success, and the confident Southerners paused to loot the Union camp. Then Sheridan galloped up from Winchester, riding "down the pike at a tearing trot, swinging his cap and shouting . . . , 'About face, boys! We are . . . going to lick them out of their boots.'" By midafternoon he had rallied his ranks for a charge. Taken unprepared, the Confederates fell back in great disorder. "Regiment after regiment, brigade after brigade, in rapid succession was crushed, and, like hard clods of clay under a pelting rain, the superb commands crumbled to pieces. . . . The only possibility . . . was . . . unrestrained flight—every man for himself." At once Sheridan pursued, and the Confederates, "cowed by defeat and stupefied by fatigue," offered little resistance. "All the way to Strasburg the road was strewn with the leavings of a beaten and flying army." The Valley campaign was over.

During all the excitement in the Valley, the siege of Petersburg doggedly continued. After the failure of the June assaults and the fiasco of the crater, there were few major actions. Operations in the Shenandoah drained troops from both armies before Richmond, and it seemed that their role "must, for the present, be reduced to one purely of observation." "The army," a Michigan volunteer stationed near City Point wrote in his diary on October 15, "is pursuing a course of 'masterly inactivity.' Even the work of fortifying, which has been carried on with so much vigor during the past five months, is partially suspended. The hostile armies, separated by only a few rods of forbidden ground, are silently watching each other. Not a shot is fired, by day or night, along the front. The pickets, in some places not more than ten rods apart, are on the best of terms, exchanging newspapers, trading rations for tobacco, etc."

Union Railroad Battery in Front of Petersburg.

The Battle of Darbytown Road, Virginia, October 7, 1864.

Of course there actually were daily skirmishes and demonstrations all along the lines; but these had no major objectives and no important accomplishments. "The newspapers mentioned the affair of October 7 on the Darbytown road, and history will likely call it a reconnaissance in force," complained one of Hood's Texas Brigade; "but to me and fifty or a hundred others . . . who lost their lives or were wounded, it was a desperate assault by a small force upon well-manned earthworks, approachable only through open ground, and protected by a *chevaux-de-frise* made of felled timber. . . . A bullet struck my gun . . . ; another bored a hole in the lapel of my jacket. Catching sight of the Fifth Texas flag to my left and fifty yards or so ahead of me . . . , I made for it with all possible dispatch. But before I reached it its bearer . . . prudently sought protection from the storm of lead behind a tree scarcely as large around as his body, and within sixty yards of the breastworks. First one and then another . . . dropped in behind him, until seven or eight of us were strung out in a single file, your humble servant, as last comer, standing at the tail-end. . . . My companions . . . sensibly agreed that an instant and hasty retreat must be made. . . . I had not gone thirty feet when a bullet struck me in the foot. . . . If either wounded or killed, I always wanted it to be in a big battle."

During this period of the slow war, much interest was aroused on either side by inventions and ideas which might in some surprising way penetrate the enemy's lines and terminate the hostilities. Federal soldiers put much faith in their mortars. "In riding to Corps headquarters," a New York volunteer wrote, "I stopped for a while at our big mortar battery called 'The Petersburg Express,' which every half-hour or so sends its fifteen-inch spheroid shell into Petersburg. Even in the daytime we can, when standing behind the mortar, see it for a while as it arches high and drops out of sight. If there is not too much noise from other artillery the explosion in the city is sometimes heard. The mortar men have facetiously chalk-marked these shells to some 'made-up' street and number address for delivery in Petersburg."

Charles Francis Adams found the picture of a mortar crew so instructive that he sent a copy to his brother in England. "It gives a better idea of real military operations than any one picture I ever saw," he explained. "Here you see no fuss and feathers, no empty show; all is hard work by working men. In point of appearance and bearing the soldiers in this picture are fair specimens of men in the work of the field . . . rough, wiry, intelligent looking men."

Thirteen-Inch Mortar "Dictator" in Front of Petersburg.

Digging the Dutch Gap Canal.

Soldiers were more amused than excited by General Butler's canal at Dutch Gap on the James River below Richmond. "You will notice," Theodore Lyman wrote to his wife, "that the river at Dutch Gap makes a wide loop and comes back to nearly the same spot, and the canal is going through there. This cuts off five or six miles of river and avoids that much of navigation exposed to fire; and it may have strategic advantages if we can get ironclads through. . . . It was very worth seeing. Fancy a narrow ridge of land, only 135 yards wide, separating the river, which flows on either side; a high ridge, making a bluff fifty feet high where it overhangs the water. Through this a great chasm has been cut, only leaving a narrow wall on the side next the enemy, which is to be blown out with several thousand pounds of gunpowder. We stood on the brink and looked down, some seventy feet, at the men and the carts and the horses at work on the bottom. Where we stood, and indeed all over the ridge, was strewed thickly with pieces of shell, while here and there lay a whole one, which had failed to explode."

Dutch Gap Canal.

Still, Lyman had doubts about the value of the work. "I think when Butler gets his canal cleverly through, he will find fresh batteries, ready to rake it, and plenty more above it, on the river. The Richmond papers make merry and say it will increase their commerce." To one Confederate the "big ditch" seemed "the cleverest thing that Butler has done in these parts since his arrival here. . . . If it is true, he has done something of value, to perpetuate his name and fame to posterity. Virginia and Richmond, in future years, will thank Butler for his gratuitous service. If the canal is really a success, it will be a perpetual benefit to the navigation of the James for all time to come. What advantage the Federals hope to realize, however, from the said ditch, is not so clear. It will not put their iron-clads above Drewry's Bluff, and that, after all, is the military key to Richmond by water." The doubters were right, for the "canal was not of service during the war, but was subsequently enlarged and . . . became the usual channel for the passage of vessels."

After such slight diversions through the fall, both armies settled wearily into winter quarters before Petersburg. Soldier letters and diaries monotonously recorded: "Routine camp life; drilling, dress parades, a few alarms, some picket firing—quite comfortable considering the proximity of the enemy and the mud—much mud, deep mud!"

Again the huts that served to house the armies rose, and in this fourth winter of war the veterans had become expert at their construction. "Some of the barracks are better, some worse, according as to the material was at hand to build them," a Confederate private explained. "Elaborate or beautiful they are not. Original, unique, grotesque they are. They are picturesque also, and all more or less serviceable as temporary abodes of men who have no furniture to speak of, and but one object for a shelter over them, namely, *comfort*. . . . Our men have built them good log cabins, and we are near a forest, where there is plenty of fuel for fires. . . . The cabins are covered with slabs, but have no plank floors, and the bunks are placed on the sides of the cabins, one above another. We had no nails to fasten the roofs, and so the slabs are held in place by logs laid on top. Of course, the cabins are rough and unsightly enough, nothing like the neat ones that we had . . . when we had both plank and nails furnished us, and tools to work with."

Company B, 170th New York Infantry, in Front of Petersburg.

Company B of the U.S. Engineers in Front of Petersburg.

As one observed these hardened veterans encamped about Petersburg, it was hard to remember them as the raw recruits of 1861. "I have been noting for some time," a Union major wrote in January, 1865, "the visible 'ripening' of our boys. Of course their youthful spirit continues, for our regiment yet consists of young men. I suppose that the average age at enlistment was below twenty-two. What I mean is, the frivolous nonsense and thoughtlessness of 'just boys' has dwindled and there is growth in maturity after the manner of older men. The picnic idea of soldiering which characterized our earlier service has changed to considering it a serious business with a serious purpose. This aging process has been more rapid than it would have been in civil life; not so much in a physical sense— for we are stronger, more able to endure because of our training and experience—but in sober-mindedness and judgment. . . . The impulsiveness of raw, untrained and inexperienced soldiers is good, but the sober steadfastness of matured and trained men is better."

A Union Army Cook.

In spite of all their similarities, the two armies in the winter of 1864 presented the sharpest of contrasts as well. For the Federal troops it was a time of plenty. Each company had its own commissary, which was "nothing less than an immense grocery establishment. Coffee, tea, sugar, molasses, bacon, salt pork, fresh beef, potatoes, rice, flour, &c., were always kept on hand in large quantities, and of the best quality."

There was no standard method of preparing the food. "In new regiments," the historian of the 24th Michigan wrote, "it is customary to have a cook for each company, who with an assistant is detailed to prepare food for the men. Several large sized camp kettles form part of their outfit in which they boil the beef, pork, beans, etc. When the order 'Fall in for rations' is given, the men form in line with their tin cups and tin plates. The freshly cooked food is frequently all given out before some at the end of the line get any. . . . Sometimes the pork is fried in tin plates, sometimes . . . a slice is stuck on the end of a ramrod and held over the campfire. . . . Our bread is of cracker shape and thickness, about four inches square, and very hard—hence the name 'hardtack.' . . . To make it palatable it is soaked a few minutes in cold water, which leavens it to a pulp, and we then fry it on our tin plates, with a slice of pork. Hot water has no effect on the hardtack except to make it tough like leather. . . . The soldier likes nothing better than his coffee; without it he could not long endure field life."

Commissary Department of the 50th New York Engineers in Front of Petersburg.

For the Confederates, on the other hand, it was the worst winter of the war. "In some of the days to come," a Texan hoped, "I may be able to find pleasure in the recollection of the hunger experienced at Petersburg. Not that rations enough were not issued to keep body and soul together . . . , but the quantity was so distressingly disproportioned to the appetites and capacities of the recipients. As three days' rations for fifteen men the commissary-sergeant of the company usually drew seven pounds of rancid bacon. You would have been amused to see him distribute it. . . . I said it would have amused you, but . . . you would have seen behind the laugh and the joke, and detected the almost ravenous hunger of the gaunt and ragged men, who, like dogs for a bone, waited and watched so earnestly for their portions. The sole relief was in imagination, half a dozen of us getting together and describing the dinner we should like to have."

Confederate officers fared no better. "Our living is now very poor," a captain wrote; "nothing but corn-bread and poor beef,—blue and tough,—no vegetables, no coffee, sugar, tea or even molasses. . . . You would laugh, or cry, when you see me eating my supper,— a pone of corn-bread and a tin cup of water. We have meat only once a day. It is hard to maintain one's patriotism on ashcake and water."

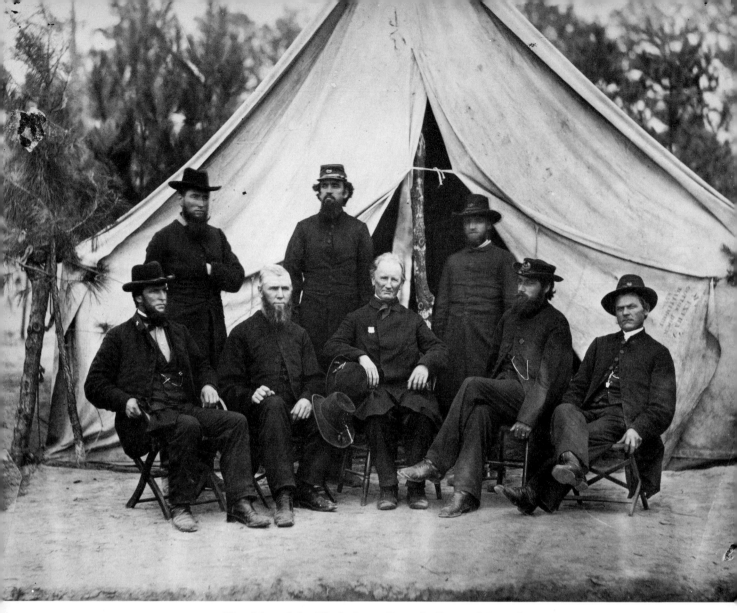

Chaplains of the Ninth Army Corps in Front of Petersburg.

As the winter months dragged by, soldiers thought much of hardships yet to come. Before spring there would be many a comrade wounded and many a friend dead. The 1860's were in the age of orthodoxy, and men in both armies turned naturally to religion for solace. Lee's army had seen an immense revivalist movement in the winter of 1863. "In every Confederate camp," General Gordon wrote, "chaplains and visiting ministers erected religious altars, around which the ragged soldiers knelt and worshipped the Heavenly Father into whose keeping they committed themselves and their cause, and through whose all-wise guidance they expected ultimate victory. . . . Not only on the Sabbath day, but during the week, night after night for long periods, these services continued, increasing in attendance and interest until they brought under religious influence the great body of the army." On a smaller scale a similar revival was now occurring in the Union ranks. "Our soldiers," one chaplain thought, "were as a class reverent. . . . Sick, wounded, or dying, soldiers welcomed the loving ministry of a chaplain. . . . If the chaplain came to his tent, the soldier loved to show him his home photographs, and to tell him of his latest home letters. Preaching to soldiers . . . enabled him to get a hold upon the men's respect and sympathies; and the pastoral work among the men at all times, in their tents, and as they marched and rested, was a yet more potent means of a chaplain's power over their hearts for good."

The less spiritual types put their trust elsewhere, and Lady Luck had her devotees in both camps. "Our officers," a Michigan volunteer wrote ironically, "are, during this temporary quiet, freely indulging in those refined tastes which army life is so well calculated to develop, by engaging in such innocent amusements and gentle recreations as horse racing, gambling, and their usual accompaniments, commissary whiskey, midnight revels and broken noses. . . . Last Saturday a very exciting contest came off between two blooded horses, owned by two 'bloods,' both Brigadier Generals. Another match is announced for tomorrow and another for Saturday. With such examples, is it any wonder that gambling is on the increase? So far as my observation goes, nine men of every ten play cards for money."

Such pursuits were perhaps less indicative of moral weakness than of war-weariness. Soldiers were becoming bored with a war which seemed pointless and endless. "Both sides are growing tired," a Richmond private wrote. "Were it left solely and exclusively to the men in the two armies, I believe peace would be made before Christmas."

Cockfighting at General Orlando B. Willcox's Headquarters Before Petersburg.

Major General William Tecumseh Sherman, U.S.A.

XIII. Victory in the West

Those in the North who watched only Grant's campaign of slaughter and stalemate had reason to be discouraged; but on other fronts in 1864 there were signs of success. Farragut's seizure of Mobile, the sinking of the *Alabama,* and Sheridan's victories in the Valley helped keep hope alive. Even more exciting was the news from Tennessee and Georgia.

Grant had left behind him in the West three veteran armies: the Army of the Tennessee, which had captured Vicksburg; the Army of the Cumberland, which had fought at Murfreesboro and Chickamauga; and the Army of the Ohio, which had served with Burnside at Knoxville. Clearly these forces required a single, vigorous leader, and Grant selected his most trusted lieutenant, William Tecumseh Sherman.

The new Western commander was one of the most picturesque figures of the war. "General Sherman is the most American looking man I ever saw," John Chipman Gray wrote, "tall and lank, not very erect, with hair like thatch, which he rubs up with his hands, a rusty beard trimmed close, a wrinkled face, sharp, prominent red nose, small, bright eyes, coarse red hands; black felt hat slouched over the eyes. . . . dirty dickey with the points wilted down, black old-fashioned stock, brown field officer's coat with high collar and no shoulder straps, muddy trowsers and one spur. He carries his hands in his pocket, is very awkward in his gait and motions, talks continually and with immense rapidity. . . . At his departure I felt it a relief and experienced almost an exhaustion after the excitement of his vigorous presence."

It was no small assignment that Grant gave his new Western commander. Hard blows at Vicksburg, Knoxville, Lookout Mountain, and Missionary Ridge had failed to demoralize the Confederates in the West. Instead, Sherman found: "No amount of poverty or adversity seems to shake their faith: niggers gone, wealth and luxury gone, money worthless, starvation in view within a period of two or three years, and causes enough to make the bravest tremble. Yet I see no sign of let up—some few deserters, plenty tired of war, but the masses determined to fight it out."

The irresolute, ineffectual Bragg had been removed from Confederate command; and in his place President Davis had reluctantly named Joseph E. Johnston, a favorite of the soldiers. During the winter months he had drilled and equipped his army so that by spring, though still far smaller than Sherman's host, it was resolute and formidable. At a review in April, a Confederate diarist related: "The army presented itself in the best condition that I have ever witnessed it, and the thousands of hardy soldiers marching to the note of the shrill fife and bass drum or the harmonious melodies of brass bands looked grand and cheering. . . . Everybody speaks in the highest terms of the discipline and spirits of the troops. All feel confident that the next battle will result in a great victory for this army."

Against the confident Confederates, Sherman began his advance on May 4. "All that has gone before," he wrote to his wife, "is mere skirmishing."

Major General William Farquhar Barry, U.S.A.

Sherman gathered about him able, devoted aides. The Army of the Tennessee—his "whiplash," as he fondly called it—he entrusted to McPherson; the Army of the Ohio was given to Schofield; and the unbreakable Army of the Cumberland remained under Thomas, "slow, but true as steel." For chief of artillery Sherman picked Barry, "a finer-looking man than his photograph . . . a West Pointer . . . a gentleman in all respects."

[382]

Major General John Alexander Logan, U.S.A.

Corps commanders were selected as carefully as army leaders. "Black Jack" Logan, "a low, heavy man, dark complected, bilious temperament," resembled "much the noted chiefs among the native Indians in the Western wilds." This prewar Democratic Congressman proved to be as adept at military maneuver as he had been in parliamentary tactics, and his men knew him as a sagacious, bold fighter.

Confederate Defenses at Etowah Bridge, Georgia.

Johnston's army lay near Dalton, in northwestern Georgia, behind formidable entrenchments. With his numerical superiority and his highly flexible line, Sherman outflanked the Confederate positions, forcing the Southern army to retreat to its next prepared position. At Tunnel Hill, at Resaca, at Etowah Bridge the same process was repeated.

As the Confederates retreated toward Atlanta, they destroyed the railroad along which Sherman had to advance, his one link with Chattanooga and the North. But with amazing rapidity the road was restored, and Union soldiers liked to joke about the Southerners' astonishment. "Jo Johns[t]on has got old Sherman fixed now," one Confederate soldier was supposed to have said, "and he will soon have to fall back for want of supplies as we have burnt all the bridges as we fell back."

But, replied another, "Sherman had duplicates of all those bridges before he started . . . and he can replace them."

"Yes," said the first Johnny, "but we have blown up the tunnel."

"Oh, you d—md fool, dont you know that he has a duplicate tunnel too?"

At every strategic point on the road back to Atlanta, Johnston had constructed earthworks; and the advancing Union armies learned to imitate them. "We cut trees and lay the trunks on top of one another in line," a Union soldier explained, "till we have built it up like a solid straight fence 3 feet high, then dig a ditch about 4 feet wide and two deep, throwing the dirt on the out side; then if we have time, dig another on the outside and fill up the dirt thicker. Then we cut poles—with a notch in the end on both sides—and lay the notched ends on the top of the logs. Then lay other logs called head logs in the notches. Then we can fire under the head logs and not expose ourselfs much."

At New Hope Church on May 25–28, when Sherman was injudicious enough to attack the Confederate defenses, he found that these earthworks were "as dangerous to assault as a permanent fort." After the battle a Confederate saw "within the small space of about one acre . . . over seven hundred dead men, all Yanks, and most of them within ten or fifteen yards of our line. Our men, as it seems, reserved their fire until they came within such deadly range that every shot took effect. . . . I shudder as I think of the mutilated forms. . . ." But what assault could not do, maneuver could. Sherman extended his line to the east, and Johnston, again outflanked, fell back.

Confederate Entrenchments at New Hope Church, Georgia.

The Confederates pulled back to prepared positions on Kenesaw Mountain, and on June 10 the advancing Union soldiers came in sight. "Kenesaw mountain," an Illinois major reported, "is, I should think, about 700 feet high, and consists of two points or peaks, separated by a narrow gorge running across the top of the mountain. The mountain itself is entirely separated from all mountain ranges, and swells up like a great bulb from the plain." For days Sherman attempted to maneuver Johnston out of his elaborate entrenchments upon the mountain and finally on June 27, for reasons still not entirely clear, decided to risk a direct assault.

On Kenesaw the Confederates were waiting. "Those of us that were sleeping late this morning (having been on picket three consecutive days) were aroused by the most terrific outburst of artillery that the enemy has yet treated us to," a Missouri Confederate related. "Every gun that could reach us was brought to bear on Little Kenesaw. We knew what the shelling foreboded—every man sprang to his arms . . . and in a moment all was ready. . . .

Union Entrenchments in Front of Big and Little Kenesaw.

Battle of Kenesaw Mountain, June 27, 1864.

"The artillery soon slackened its fire and we could hear the volleys delivered by our skirmishers as they met the first line of the enemy. . . . In a few minutes the enemy made their appearance, a solid line of blue emerging from the woods, a hundred yards below us. We gave them a volley that checked them where they stood. As this line was melting away under our steady fire, another pressed forward and reached the foot of the mountain. Behind this came yet another line, but our fire was so steady and accurate that they could not be induced to advance, though their officers could be plainly seen trying to urge them up the hill.

"Then came another column, the heaviest that had yet appeared, which made the final, as well as the most determined assault, and which stood their ground longer than the others. Some of these men came twenty or thirty yards up the side of the mountain, but they were nearly all shot down, which deterred the others from following. Our men shot with unusual accuracy, because they had the low stone breastworks, which we had constructed with so much labor, on which to rest their guns. . . . In three-fourths of an hour the attack was over and the Federals were gone, leaving large numbers of their dead lying at the bottom of the hill."

Battle of Kenesaw Mountain.

The assault, Sherman had to admit, "inflicted comparatively little loss to the enemy, who lay behind his well-formed breast-works. Failure as it was, and for which I assume the entire responsibility, I yet claim it produced good fruits, as it demonstrated to General Johnston that I would assault and that boldly."

Nevertheless, the Union commander returned to his flanking tactics, and again his numbers were decisive. Johnston retreated across the Chattahoochee River, and on July 5 pursuing Federal troops came within sight of Atlanta. "Mine eyes have beheld the promised land!" an Illinois major wrote to his wife. "The 'domes and minarets and spires' of Atlanta are glittering in the sunlight before us, and only 8 miles distant. . . . While riding at the extreme front . . . and eagerly pressing our skirmishers forward after the rapidly retreating rebels, suddenly we came upon a high bluff overlooking the Chattahoochee, and looking southward across the river, there lay the beautiful 'Gate City' in full view, and . . . such a cheer went up as must have been heard even in the entrenchments of the doomed city itself. In a very few moments Generals Sherman and Thomas (who are always in the extreme front . . .) were with us on the hill top. . . . Sherman stepping nervously about, his eyes sparkling and his face aglow—casting a single glance at Atlanta, another at the River, and a dozen at the surrounding valley to see where he could best cross the River, how he best could flank them."

But sight was far from conquest. On the day Sherman's army crossed the Chattahoochee, Jefferson Davis replaced Johnston with John Bell Hood, and the Federal general rightly "inferred that the change of commanders meant 'fight.'" On July 20 the Confederates lashed out at the Union lines along Peach Tree Creek, just outside Atlanta. "Each assault . . . was met gallantly by the whole line and hurled back," Thomas reported proudly, "our men not yielding a foot of ground. . . . The enemy, repulsed at all points, fell back to his works."

"What tremendous defences of Atlanta the rebs had!" exclaimed Major Hitchcock of Sherman's staff. "Forts, breast-works, ditches, *chevaux-de-frise* (saw them) and stockade on flank, unapproachable by musketry and protected by ground, etc., from artillery." Finding the defenses formidable, Sherman settled down for a siege.

Palisades and Chevaux-de-frise Guarding Atlanta.

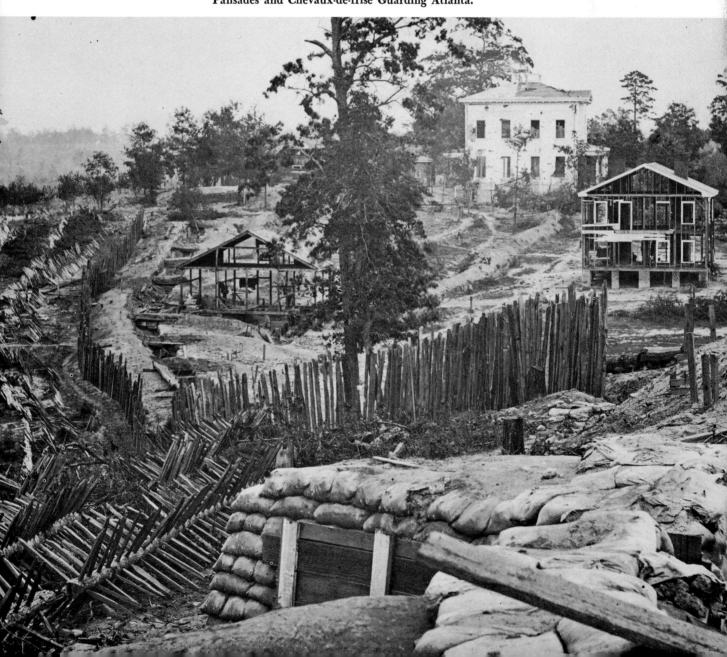

Confederate Defenses in Front of Atlanta.

Sherman's "irregular line of breast-works" extended "mile after mile, over hill and valley. . . . From several points the city was plainly visible," remembered an Illinois soldier, "and through openings in the forest the rebel forts and line of earthworks could be seen; at times thronged with men in gray. . . . The inevitable picket firing, as regular as the 'droppings' of a slow rain, reached the ears from the picket line. Men in blue, as busy as ants, were constantly moving hither and thither, in the rear of the main line. Light wreaths of smoke were visible where our cannons were at work, and little white 'puffs' were occasionally suspended in mid air by exploding rebel shells." "The Confederates had some large guns by which they were enabled to throw shells into our camp weighing sixty-four pounds," an Indiana sergeant related. "We called these shells 'camp-kettles.' We often watched these huge shells, as they arose from their guns in the hostile forts, describing their beautiful curves through the balmy air . . . and before they dropped among us . . . we could hear their screeching noise."

Posted in front of the main lines were pickets, grouped three or four together, who kept up a steady observation of the enemy and maintained a slight, irregular fire. There was much fraternization and surreptitious trading across the lines. One day when a Indiana soldier was returning from a scouting expedition, he was hailed, "Say, Yank, got anything to trade?"

Before him stood a lone Confederate. "As he stood in plain sight without a gun," the Hoosier related, "I was not alarmed. I had left my haversack some distance back and told him so. He said, 'Go and get it, I will wait for you.'

"I went back and got it, left my field glass and rifle but put my revolver where I could get it handy and went up to him. He still sat on a stone where I had left him. When I got to him there were two more lying down behind the rock. I stepped back ready for what might come, but said, 'Do you want to capture me?'

"'No,' said he, 'we wont hurt you. Got any coffee?'

"I had a little—about a pound—and gave it to him and he gave me some dog leg tobacco. And what pleased me more, a copy of a late Atlanta paper. After talking a while I said I must go and they all shook hands with me saying, 'Good luck, Yank! . . . I hope you wont git hurt in any of our fights.'"

Union Picket Post near Atlanta.

Major General Edward Moody McCook, U.S.A.

Of course the siege was not all amiable. Sherman sent out cavalry raiders to harass Hood's rear and break his supply lines. Venturing south of Atlanta, McCook "tore up two miles of track, burned two trains of cars, and cut away five miles of telegraph-wire." But soon "he found himself completely surrounded by infantry and cavalry. He had to drop his prisoners and fight his way out, losing about six hundred men."

Major General Joseph Wheeler, C.S.A.

After defeating McCook, the Confederate cavalry under Wheeler commenced a counter raid against Sherman's rail line to Nashville. The project was an audacious one —just what one would expect from a general who had sixteen horses killed under him during the war—but Wheeler "succeeded in burning the bridge over the Etowah . . . destroyed about thirty-five miles of railroad in the vicinity, and . . . , in addition, about fifty miles . . . in Tennessee."

Major General Alpheus Starkey Williams, U.S.A.

Using his other forces for flanking attacks, Sherman kept Thomas's Army of the Cumberland at the work for which it seemed best suited—the steady grinding away at Atlanta's defenses. Even the divisional commanders of that army shared its reputation of being more sedate than swift. "Pop" Williams, for example, "sitting his horse like a centaur . . . and holding firmly in his teeth the never-lighted stub of a cigar," was "sturdy, strong and imperturbable."

[394]

Major General John McAllister Schofield, U.S.A.

As a newcomer to his Army of the Ohio, Schofield had at first been distrusted by his men. Gradually, however, his canny, cautious fighting had won their toleration of his bookish tastes—and even of his red undershirts. "It's all right, boys," a private drawled. "I like the way the Old Man chaws his tobacco." Sherman, on the other hand, was disappointed. "Schofield is . . . slow and leaves too much to others," he complained.

Major General James Birdseye McPherson, U.S.A.

Closer to Sherman than either of the other army commanders was McPherson, as handsome as he was daring. On July 22 he was at headquarters when he heard firing from his troops. "He . . . jumped on his horse, saying he would hurry down his line and send me back word what these sounds meant," Sherman recalled. Approaching too close, he was killed by a skirmisher's bullet. "I have lost my right bower," Sherman grieved.

Union Soldiers in a Captured Confederate Fort Near Atlanta.

Day after day Hood struck out blindly at the Federal forces, only to be beaten back with bloody losses. Sherman edged south of the city to cut its last rail connections, and at Jonesboro he lured the Confederate army outside its defenses. "Oh, it was a glorious battle," an Illinois major wrote of the September 1 engagement. "Generals, Colonels, Majors, Captains and privates, all had to go forward together. . . . Not one instant did that line hesitate—it moved steadily forward to the enemy's works—over the works with a shout—over the cannon—over the rebels, and then commenced stern work with the bayonet, but the despairing cries of surrender soon stopped it, the firing ceased, and 1,000 rebels were . . . prisoners of war."

While Hood was fighting at Jonesboro, Atlanta was undefended, and Slocum's Twentieth Corps slipped into the city. On September 3 Sherman wired Halleck, "Atlanta is ours, and fairly won." The news could not have been more opportune. Announced just as the Democratic convention pronounced the war a failure, Sherman's victory helped carry the November elections for Lincoln.

Destruction of Rolling Mill and Hood's Ordnance Train on the Georgia Central Railroad.

"On the night of the 1st of September we withdrew from Atlanta," Hood was obliged to report to his superiors in Richmond. The Federal seizure of the railroad to Macon, he added, "necessitated the evacuation . . . at the earliest hour possible. . . . Notwithstanding full and positive instructions, delivered prior to the evacuation of the city, and ample time and facilities afforded to move all stores, cars and engines, the chief quarter master grossly neglected to send off a train of ordnance stores, and five engines, although they were on the track and in readiness to move. This negligence entailed the unnecessary loss of these stores, engines, and about eighty cars."

Brigadier General John Bell Hood, C.S.A.

When Atlanta fell, Hood wired Richmond for reinforcements. There were no troops, he was told. "No other resource remains." An ordinary man would have despaired, but not Hood. A magnificent human animal, six feet, two inches tall, he had lost the use of an arm at Gettysburg, a leg at Chickamauga; now he had to be strapped to his horse. But, as he drove himself, so would he drive his army. "As I became more and more convinced of our inability to successfully resist an advance of the Federal Army," he wrote, "I . . . concluded to resume active operations, move upon Sherman's communications, and avert, if possible, impending disaster from the Confederacy."

Battle of Allatoona Pass, Georgia, October 5, 1864.

On October 5 Hood fell upon a detachment under General J. M. Corse which Sherman had ordered to guard the railroad at Allatoona Pass. The Confederates demanded that the outnumbered garrison surrender "to avoid a needless effusion of blood." Corse replied, "We are prepared for the 'needless effusion of blood' whenever it is agreeable to you." "We . . . had what the boys called 'a hot time,'" a Tennessee volunteer wrote. "As our boys swarmed over the parapet the bayonet was freely used by both sides, officers firing their pistols, and many throwing sticks and stones. . . . This was, for the time engaged, the bloodiest fight we were ever in, and our loss was heavy. Corse's men fought like demons." The next day they were still holding out, and as Sherman rushed up with reinforcements, Corse signaled, "I am short a cheek-bone and an ear, but am able to whip all h—l yet!"

Major General Nathan Bedford Forrest, C.S.A.

"It will be a physical impossibility to protect the roads," groaned Sherman, "now that Hood, Forrest, and Wheeler, and the whole batch of devils, are turned loose without home or habitation." Clearly no force could guard every mile of his extended line against Forrest's swift and silent raiders. A "coarse Western man, ungrammatical whenever he opened his mouth, . . . but full of the generous fire of conflict," Forrest hated Yankees. During the war twenty-nine horses were shot under him, and he is supposed to have bragged, "I have with my own hand killed a man for every horse I lost in the war, and I was a horse ahead at its close." In the fall of 1864, moving parallel to Hood's force, Forrest was again on the loose. When he reached the Tennessee River he performed the astonishing feat of capturing a fleet of Union transports. The next thing Sherman knew "that devil Forrest" had manned the transports with his own "horse marines" and was "down about Johnsonville making havoc among the gunboats and transports."

**First Tennessee Colored Battery at Johnsonville, Tennessee,
November 23, 1864, on Its Way to Nashville.**

To protect Tennessee from Hood and Forrest, Sherman dispatched Thomas to Nashville and ordered all available troops in the state to his support. Later Schofield was sent
to join him. The Confederates saw the opportunity of fighting a divided enemy. At Spring
Hill on November 29 Hood planned to ambush Schofield's force; but by a night march
the Federals evaded the trap. Furious, Hood blamed his Second Corps commander,
Cheatham. The next day Hood still thought he had a chance to crush Schofield and ordered
battle at Franklin. "I do not like the looks of this fight," Cheatham protested; but he led
his men in the assault. "The Federal troops received the charging lines with steadiness
and courage. . . . The fire of small-arms and artillery was so heavy, constant, and incessant that great clouds of smoke 'hung like a pall of universal darkness' over that fatal
field. . . . Line after line was hurled on the works, but . . . the brave and heroic men
were repulsed with a loss of life fearful to contemplate. . . . The Confederate loss in the
battle was appalling."

Brigadier General Benjamin Franklin Cheatham, C.S.A.

Railroad Yards at Nashville.

By the narrowest of margins Schofield was able to elude the Confederates and to join Thomas behind the defenses of Nashville. Hood's army rapidly followed. "This morning," a Confederate diarist wrote on December 5, "we could distinctly hear the booming cannon at Nashville six miles distant. We moved on the pike for that city and when in two miles we could see the Yankee forts and their flags waving from the lofty hills around the city. Their heavy artillery opened upon my battery and threw some close shots as we passed in full view. I sought an eminence and with my opera glasses drew close to me the costly marble capitol of Tennessee on which waved the stars and stripes. The enemy's lines were strong, and yet they continued to work on them."

To the great distress of Lincoln, Grant, and Halleck, Thomas appeared to sit behind his fortifications in Nashville, doing nothing while Hood besieged him. Actually, the Union commander faced appalling difficulties. His army was still poorly integrated, and all his reinforcements had not yet arrived. Besides, the weather had turned abominably cold. "The soldiers suffered greatly for comfortable clothing," diarists recorded day after day. "The weather is cold and sleet is falling fast and thick. . . . Nature is clothed in winter's bleak costume—snow and ice. The soldiers stand around their fires warming one side while the other grows cold, and shed tears from the strong smoke that puffs in their eyes. . . . Our artillery carriages are frozen in the ground, and ice half an inch thick coats my brass guns. Don't want to fight in such weather as this. . . . This day will be remembered by the soldiery around Nashville as 'windy Sunday.' The winds have been sweeping all day long at the rate of 60 miles per hour, and the icy blasts are so piercing that it is impossible to keep warm."

Fort Negley, Nashville, Tennessee.

Colonel Stephen Dill Lee, C.S.A.

Hood made the unwise decision to entrench south of Nashville and wait for Thomas to attack, hoping, "if favored by success, to follow him into his works." On December 15 the slow-moving Thomas was ready. Directing his main attacks against the wings of the Confederate line, he had the garrison troops in Nashville keep up such a demonstration against General Stephen D. Lee's corps in the center that it "did not fire a shot during the day."

Major General John McArthur, U.S.A.

Meanwhile Union troops were advancing on both Confederate flanks. On the Federal right a "blue line, broken and irregular, but with steady persistence, made its way up the steep hillside against a fierce storm of musketry and artillery." McArthur's infantry division broke through one side of a salient at just the moment Wilson's cavalry breached the other. "In a moment the whole Confederate force in that quarter was routed."

Fortified Bridge Across the Cumberland River at Nashville.

That night Hood pulled back his army and re-formed his line in a shorter, more defensible position. "In front of his picket line large trees were felled, brush piled and obstructions of every kind interposed against the Federal advance. . . . They were still busy with pick-axe and spade when daylight revealed their new position." At six A.M. advancing Federal skirmishers "found themselves confronted by a strong picket line securely posted behind the barricade, and they knew it to be a hazardous undertaking to carry a position both naturally and artificially strong, but by a common impulse without orders they moved upon that treacherous line of fallen trees, behind which lay hundreds of Confederate marksmen. . . . They rushed forward in the desperate charge. . . . Suddenly a line of fire fringed the barricade, and volley after volley was poured upon the advancing line. Some were wounded. . . . Some were killed outright. . . . Others filled their places, and with cheering, rushed up the ascent, and charging with cold steel upon the barricades, finally drove every Rebel out of his hiding place. Then one long cheer relieved the pent up excitement of the reserves, and was wafted to the front as a testimonial of gratitude."

The main Confederate defenses still lay ahead. All morning Thomas felt out the enemy, waiting for the moment for a general assault. In the afternoon a dispatch from Hood was intercepted, "For God's sake, drive the Yankee cavalry from our left and rear or all is lost." Then Thomas calmly gave the word, "Order the charge."

"Thomas brought on an assault on our left," ran a Confederate report of what followed, "which was for a short time checked, but upon being re-enforced the enemy pierced the lines in front of General Bate's division, which shamefully broke and fled before the Yankees were within 200 yards of them. Then ensued one of the most disgraceful routs that it has been my misfortune to witness. All the batteries on the extreme left were captured, containing about 40 pieces of artillery, and hundreds if not thousands of the infantry fled in such shameful haste that they threw down their guns—their only means of defense. This occurred about 3 o'clock and every carriage, wagon, and ambulance was in a race to reach the Franklin Pike and the woods were thronged with stragglers." "I beheld for the first and only time," Hood admitted sadly, "a Confederate Army abandon the field in confusion." His army was not merely defeated; it was demolished.

The Union Line at Nashville, December 16, 1864.

The Last Train from Atlanta.

While Thomas was fighting the army of the Confederates, Sherman was engaged in operations against a more subtle foe—the morale of the South. By a slashing raid through the heart of Georgia, destroying valuable food crops just harvested and disrupting vital Confederate lines of communication, he proposed to bring the war home to the masses of the Southern population. "I can make the march," he told Grant, "and make Georgia howl!"

The first step was to reduce Atlanta in size and population so that it should have no military value if recaptured by the Confederates. Hundreds of families were ruthlessly uprooted, and the work of demolition began. Major Hitchcock recorded that orders were issued "to destroy all R.R. depots, large R.R., etc., warehouses, machine shops, etc., including all buildings of use to enemy: but no *dwellings* to be injured." "This P.M.," he wrote on November 15, "the torch applied, also sundry buildings blown up, with shells inside—heavy explosion, sundry lesser ones for several minutes following. Clouds of heavy smoke rise and hang like a pall over [the] doomed city."

Demolition of Railroad Depot in Atlanta.

Federal soldiers were ordered to destroy "all depots, car-houses, shops, factories, foundries &c., being careful to knock down all furnace chimneys, and break down their arches; fire will do most of the work." "Let the destruction be so thorough that not a rail or tie can be used again," Sherman directed. "My own experience demonstrates the proper method to be: To march a regiment to the road, stack arms, loosen two rails opposite the right and two opposite the left of the regiment, then to heave the whole track, rails and ties, over, breaking it all to pieces, then pile the ties in the nature of a crib work and lay the rails over them, then by means of fence rails make a bonfire, and when the rails are red-hot in the middle let men give the rail a twist, which cannot be straightened without machinery. Also fill up some of the cuts with heavy logs and trunks of trees and branches and cover up and fill with dirt."

In Washington, Lincoln was "anxious, if not fearful" about Sherman's plan, and even Grant doubted. In Sherman's own army some "weak knee'd brethren in shoulder straps" were "tendering resignations and clamoring for leaves on account of sick families, sick

Ripping up Railroad Tracks at Atlanta.

Sherman's Men Destroying the Railroad at Atlanta.

wives, &c." But in the ranks there was simple confidence. "We are told we are going on a great campaign," an Indiana volunteer wrote. "There are rumors that we are to cut loose and march South to the Ocean. We are in fine shape and I think could go anywhere Uncle Billy would lead."

On November 15, 62,000 select troops began the march to the sea. "Behind us lay Atlanta," Sherman remembered, "the black smoke rising high in air, and hanging like a pall over the ruined city. Away off in the distance . . . was the rear of Howard's column, the gun-barrels glistening in the sun, the white-topped wagons stretching away to the south; and right before us the XIVth Corps, marching steadily and rapidly, with a cheery look and swinging pace, that made light of the thousand miles that lay between us and Richmond. Some band, by accident, struck up the anthem of 'John Brown's soul goes marching on'; the men caught up the strain, and never before have I heard the chorus of 'Glory, glory, hallelujah!' done with more spirit, or in better harmony of time and place."

Major General Hugh Judson Kilpatrick, U.S.A.

Soldiers were ordered to "forage liberally on the country"—and they did. The most brutal foraging was performed by Sherman's cavalry, now led by Judson Kilpatrick, famed raider against Richmond. He permitted his men to loot but required them to save their ammunition. "Let the men catch and kill their hogs with their sabers," he ordered, "a weapon that can be used equally as well to kill hogs as rebels."

On December 9–10 Sherman was before Savannah. With a swoop his troops fell upon Fort McAllister, and at once his signal corps men got in touch with Dahlgren's fleet waiting offshore with supplies (see p. 278). When Sherman was rowed out, he related proudly, "General Foster and Admiral Dahlgren received me, manned the yards and cheered, the highest honor at sea."

Behind him lay the smoking ruins of Georgia. "We have . . . consumed the corn and fodder in the region of country thirty miles on either side of a line from Atlanta to Savannah," Sherman reported to Washington, "as also the sweet potatoes, cattle, hogs, sheep and poultry and have carried away more than 10,000 horses and mules, as well as a countless number of their slaves. I estimate the damage done to the State of Georgia and its military resources at $100,000,000; at least $20,000,000 of which has inured to our advantage, and the remainder is simple waste and destruction. This may seem a hard species of warfare, but it brings the sad realities of war home to those who have been directly or indirectly instrumental in involving us in its attendant calamities." To his wife Sherman put it even more simply: "We have devoured the land. . . . To realize what war is one should follow our tracks."

Signaling from Fort McAllister, Georgia, to Admiral Dahlgren's Flagship.

Sherman Reviewing His Army on Bay Street, Savannah, December, 1864.

After a brief siege Savannah fell; and with a flourish Sherman wrote to President Lincoln, "I beg to present you as a Christmas gift, the city of Savannah, with 150 heavy guns and plenty of ammunition, and also about 25,000 bales of cotton."

In the captured city Sherman rested and supplied his tired troops. His heart swelled with pride as his army marched past in review. "The procession as it marched along Bay street," one participant remembered, "seemed like a huge caterpillar of gorgeous colors slowly moving on innumerable legs, keeping pace to the strains of the martial music." Sherman thought no praise too high for these veterans. "Whether called on to fight, to march, to wade streams, to make roads, clear out obstructions, build bridges, make 'corduroy,' or tear up railroads, they have done it with alacrity and a degree of cheerfulness unsurpassed. A little loose in foraging, they 'did some things they ought not to have done,' yet on the whole they have supplied the wants of the army with as little violence as could be expected, and as little loss as I calculated."

Thomas's defeat of Hood and Sherman's capture of Savannah, coming almost simultaneously, were as Lincoln said "indeed a great success," for they ended effectual Confederate resistance in that part of the South. Already Sherman was planning further bold moves. "My experience is," he told the cautious Halleck, "that they are easier of execution than the more timid ones." He proposed another march—this time northward through the Carolinas against Lee's rear. "Every step I take from this point northward," he urged, "is as much a direct attack upon Lee's army as though we are operating within the sound of his artillery."

Halleck approved this plan for cutting "another wide swath through the center of the Confederacy"; and on February 1 Sherman crossed the river into South Carolina, "the hell-hole of secession." When Joseph E. Johnston, hastily recalled to Confederate command after Hood's debacle, heard that Sherman intended to march through flooded Carolina bottoms in the dead of winter, he was incredulous. "But when I heard that Sherman had not only started, but was marching through those . . . swamps at the rate of thirteen miles a day, making corduroy road every foot of the way," he said, "I made up my mind there had been so such army since the days of Julius Caesar."

Sherman's Troops Crossing the North Edisto River, South Carolina.

Lieutenant General Wade Hampton, C.S.A.

Hoping to check the oncoming Federals, Lee ordered Wade Hampton south. The wealthiest planter in South Carolina, Hampton had proved himself to be one of Lee's ablest lieutenants. When Stuart was killed he became chief of cavalry in the Army of Northern Virginia and was thought "as dauntless as Stuart and, if anything, a more distinguished-looking man." Now he came on a final, desperate effort to save the state that he so loved.

Ruins in Columbia, South Carolina.

On February 17 Sherman was in Columbia. "The whole army," he wrote, "is burning with an insatiable desire to wreak vengeance upon South Carolina. I almost tremble at her fate but feel that she deserves all that seems in store for her." That night the South Carolina capital was set on fire. Sherman asserted that Hampton's retreating troops by firing bales of cotton in the city were responsible; Southerners still believe that "Columbia was burned by the soldiers of General Sherman; that . . . for four hours they were seen with combustibles firing house after house without any affectation of concealment and without the slightest check from the officers." Regardless of responsibility, the result was only too clear. By the next morning two-thirds of the city was in ashes.

As Sherman advanced in the interior, the seaports fell, even Charleston, citadel of secession. Across South Carolina and into North Carolina the Federals pushed Johnston's minuscule defending army. Behind lay a land that would never forget Sherman. "My aim," he bragged, "was, to whip the rebels, to humble their pride, to follow them to their inmost recesses, and make them fear and dread us. 'Fear is the beginning of wisdom.'"

A Dead Confederate Soldier.

XIV. Appomattox

"You must not be surprised if calamity befalls us," Lee warned in early 1865. The new year brought no new hope to the Confederacy. Everywhere except before Richmond Southern armies were in retreat. Conscription brought in few new troops, and the project of enrolling Negroes in the Southern army was so belatedly and half-heartedly endorsed that it accomplished nothing. The fall of Fort Fisher meant complete strangulation by the blockade, and not even an offer to emancipate the slaves could secure the Confederacy foreign assistance. On the home front as the railroad system collapsed, civilians were going hungry; in Richmond meal was selling for $100 a bushel, bacon $13 a pound, and flour $1,500 a barrel. Peace sentiment was becoming stronger, and Governor Joseph E. Brown of Georgia defiantly threatened to secede from the Confederacy. "Where is this to end?" asked General Josiah Gorgas. "No money in the Treasury—no food to feed Gen. Lee's army—no troops to oppose Gen. Sherman—what does it all mean . . . ? Is the cause really hopeless? Is it to be abandoned and lost in this way?"

"Lee is about all we have . . . ," Gorgas sadly concluded. Yet a glance at the tattered veterans in the vermin-infested trenches about Richmond should have warned that not even Lee could continue to do the impossible. "The condition of our army was daily becoming more desperate," General Gordon wrote. "Starvation, literal starvation, was doing its deadly work. So depleted and poisoned was the blood of many of Lee's men from insufficient and unsound food that a slight wound which would probably not have been reported at the beginning of the war would often cause blood-poison, gangrene, and death. . . . It was a harrowing but not uncommon sight to see those hungry men gather the wasted corn from under the feet of half-fed horses, and wash and parch it to satisfy in some small measure their craving for food." Lee himself dared not hope; he could only promise, "I shall . . . endeavor to do my duty and fight to the last."

In the Union camps spring brought optimism. Sherman was approaching from the South. After giving a final defeat to Early's shattered troops in the Valley, Sheridan rode across Virginia to join Grant. Only Lee's army was left.

President Lincoln closely followed preparations for the spring offensive and more than once was at City Point, anxiously interested. It was not merely for victory that he hoped; he was looking to the years beyond, when conflict must be followed by reconciliation. Toward the Southerners he had no bitterness. "Let them once surrender and reach their homes," he assured Grant and Sherman, "they won't take up arms again. Let them all go, officers and all. I want submission, and no more bloodshed. Let them have their horses to plow with, and, if you like, their guns to shoot crows with. I want no one punished; treat them liberally all round. We want those people to return to their allegiance to the Union and submit to the laws. Again I say, give them the most liberal and honorable terms."

Union Troops in the Trenches Before Petersburg.

On March 26 Sheridan reached City Point, and Grant was ready to begin the final campaign of the war. By edging farther south of Petersburg and threatening the Southside Railroad, he forced Lee to stretch his attenuated line even more thinly. Then on April 1 in the battle of Five Forks Federal infantry and cavalry struck Lee's extended right wing. The Southerners resisted furiously. "A colonel with a shattered regiment came down upon us in a charge," a Northern newspaperman reported. "The bayonets were fixed; the men came on with a yell; their gray uniforms seemed black amidst the smoke; their preserved colors, torn by grape and ball, waved yet defiantly; twice they halted, and poured in volleys, but came on again like the surge from the fog, depleted, but determined; yet . . . while they pressed along, swept all the while by scathing volleys, a group of horsemen took them in flank. It was an awful instant; the horses recoiled; the charging column trembled like a single thing, but at once the Rebels, with rare organization, fell into a hollow square. . . . The horsemen rode around them in vain; no charge could break the shining squares, until our dismounted carbineers poured in their volleys afresh, making gaps in the spent ranks, and then in their wavering time the cavalry thundered down. The Rebels could stand no more; they reeled and swayed, and fell back broken and beaten."

[422]

"It has happened as I told them in Richmond it would happen," Lee said quietly. "The line has been stretched until it is broken." The right wing of the Confederate army was cut off from his main command. Left of the break-through the Southerners fell back upon inner fortifications running from the Appomattox River to the principal line of defenses. At the angle where the two lines joined, forming a salient nearest the Federal army, was Fort Gregg; and here 400 to 600 men of Cadmus Wilcox's division and Harris's brigade were put, to defend the position to the last extremity. "Slant fire, cross fire, and direct fire, by file and volley, rolled in perpetually, cutting down their bravest officers and strewing the fields with bleeding men. . . . their own artillery, captured from them, threw into their own ranks, from its old position, ungrateful grape and canister, enfilading their breastworks, whizzing and plunging by air line and ricochet; and at last bodies of cavalry fairly mounted their intrenchments, and charged down the parapet, slashing and trampling them, and producing inexplicable confusion. . . . A few more volleys, a new and irresistible charge, and a shrill and warning command to die or surrender, and, with a sullen and tearful impulse, . . . muskets are flung upon the ground. . . ."

Cheval-de-Frise and Dead Confederate Soldier.

**Bridge on the Appomattox River and Train of Cars and Workshop Burned by the
Confederates During the Evacuation of Petersburg.**

Petersburg was no longer tenable, and during the night of April 2 Lee's forces began
crossing to the north side of the Appomattox River, destroying the bridges as they withdrew.
Early the next morning Union troops swarmed over the fortifications and into the town.
At 4:28 A.M. the flag of the 1st Michigan Sharpshooters was hoisted upon the courthouse,
and the colors of the 2nd Michigan went up on the customhouse a few minutes later.
About eight o'clock Grant and Meade reached the city. "[We] took a position under cover
of a house which protected us from the enemies musketry which was flying thick and fast
there," Grant wrote. "As we would occasionally look around the corner we could see the
streets and the Appomattox bottom, presumably near the bridge, packed with the Confederate army. I did not have artillery brought up, because I was sure Lee was trying to
make his escape, and I wanted to push immediately in pursuit. At all events I had not the
heart to turn the artillery upon such a mass of defeated and fleeing men, and I hoped to
capture them soon."

Soon the Confederates were gone, and the victors looked curiously about the captured
city. "The outskirts are very poor, consisting chiefly of the houses of negroes, who collected,
with broad grins, to gaze on the triumphant Yanks," Theodore Lyman related with a
certain Massachusetts superiority, "while here and there a squalid family of poor whites

The Courthouse in Petersburg.

would lower at us from broken windows, with an air of lazy dislike. The main part of the town resembles Salem, very much, *plus* the southern shiftlessness and *minus* the Yankee thrift. Even in this we may except Market Street, where dwell the *haute noblesse,* and where there are just square brick houses and gardens about them, as you see in Salem, all very well kept and with nice trees. Near the river . . . the same closely built business streets, the lower parts of which had suffered severely from our shells; here and there an entire building had been burnt, and everywhere you saw corners knocked off, and shops with all the glass shattered by a shell exploding within."

Union Troops in Captured Fort Mahone.

From north of Richmond to south of Petersburg the entire Confederate line had been abandoned. It was hard for Union soldiers to believe that those frowning lines of fortifications were now empty. When a staff officer brought the news to the 20th Maine, cynical veterans shouted, "That's played out!" "Tell it to the recruits!" "Put him in a canteen!" "Give him a hard tack!"

But the news was true. Unopposed, the Federal troops marched across "that curious region of desolation . . . swept with the besom of destruction" which lay between the lines. "All landmarks are defaced," Charles Francis Adams found, "not only trees and fences, but even the houses and roads. It is one broad tract, far as the eye can reach, dotted here and there with clumps of trees which mark the spot where some Head Quarters stood, and for the rest covered with a thick stubble of stumps of the pine. You ride through mile after mile of deserted huts, marking the encampments of armies, and over roads now leading from nowhere, nowhither. . . . Forts, rifle-pits and abattis spring up in every direction, and in front of Petersburg the whole soil is actually burrowed and furrowed beyond the power of words to describe. There it all is, freshly deserted and as silent as death. . . ."

Curiously the Federals looked over the captured fortifications. The 7th Rhode Island regiment found near the Jerusalem Plank Road "a sixty-four-pounder Columbiad that had but just been mounted. Though in position it was spiked and stuffed with earth to the muzzle. A number of mortars were lying by spiked beside their beds. Among them we noticed more especially the 'Twin Sisters' (eight-inch), since they were most attentive to us. A more extended glance showed the Johnnies were troubled far more by our shells than we were by theirs, for the ground around the twins was literally honeycombed. . . . Some of the boys commenced amusing themselves with the big powder cylinders strewn around the huge gun, while others pretentiously sighted the piece and gave commands, still others watching meanwhile the flight of an imaginary projectile and congratulating the gunner on the surprising results of that lucky shot."

A Union Battery in a Captured Confederate Fort After the Fall of Petersburg.

There was little time for horseplay, because Lee's army was escaping. Haste was urgent, for if Lee joined Joseph E. Johnston in North Carolina the war would be protracted. "Let the thing be pushed," President Lincoln urged. But Grant did not need prodding. "Pursuit will be immediately made," he promised. Already Sheridan and the cavalry were far in advance, and Meade was ordered to "march immediately . . . up the Appomattox, taking the River road, leaving one division to hold Petersburg and the railroad." "In full tilt," the men sped along, "footing it, as if a lottery prize lay just ahead." "We never endured such marching before," said one veteran. "On every hand we could see indications that Lee's army would soon melt away. Prisoners were pouring into our lines by thousands; baggage wagons, artillery, mortars and baggage of all kinds, lined the roads along which the rebels were fleeing."

Muskets of Union Troops Stacked near the Railroad Station, Petersburg.

Ruins of Richmond Seen from Across the James River.

If Petersburg fell Richmond could not be defended. The Confederates had anticipated the necessity for evacuation, and when on April 2, while worshiping at St. Paul's Church, President Davis was handed Lee's telegram, "I advise that all preparation be made for leaving Richmond tonight," he quietly left the church to preside over the obsequies of the city. "Hastily the few remaining necessaries of the several departments were packed, and sent toward Danville, either by railroad or wagon. Ordnance supplies, that could not be moved, were rolled into the canal; commissary stores were thrown open, and their hoarded contents distributed to the eager crowds. And strange crowds they were. Fragile, delicate women staggered under the heavy loads they bore to suffering children at home; . . . and hoary-headed men tugged wearily at the barrels of pork, flour, or sugar they strove to roll before their weak arms. Later in the evening . . . fierce crowds of skulking men, and coarse, half-drunken women, gathered before the stores. Half-starved and desperate, they swore and fought among themselves over the spoils they seized."

Ruins of Richmond.

By morning the government was gone from Richmond, and army officers were burning supplies that might fall into enemy hands. "At dawn there were two tremendous explosions," a Confederate war department clerk recorded. "One of these was the blowing up of the magazine, near the new almshouse—the other probably the destruction of an iron-clad ram. But subsequently there were others. I was sleeping soundly when awakened by them. . . . At 7 A.M. Committees appointed by the city government visited the liquor shops and had the spirits (such as they could find) destroyed. The streets ran with liquor; and women and boys, black and white, were seen filling pitchers and buckets from the gutters. . . . At 8½ A.M. The armory, arsenal, and laboratory . . . which had been previously fired, gave forth terrific sounds from thousands of bursting shells. This continued for more than an hour. . . . The pavements are filled with pulverized glass. Some of the great flour mills have taken fire from the burning government warehouses, and the flames are spreading through the lower part of the city. A great conflagration is apprehended."

"The wildest confusion prevails," wrote a private in the Surry Light Artillery, which was trying to move through the city and across the river. "Along Main street . . . numberless women, reckless of personal danger, are tugging and pulling at parcels and goods thrown out from the depots where supplies had been stored. . . . It is difficult to make our way at all, through the crowds of excited humanity that throng the streets, and hinder travel with their burdens and loads of goods. An officer has to get in front of the Battery with drawn sword to make way for us. . . . By this time, an ocean of flame is dashing, as a tidal wave of destruction, from side to side, and roaring, raging, hissing about us, and leaping on from house to house, and from street to street, in very wantonness of wrath. Like a wild, mad steed, without any restraining hand to impede it, the flame bounds along, seeming to gloat in its great power to destroy. As the fire spreads, buildings are deserted, the helpless occupants dragging with them whatever they could of clothes or household goods. . . . Miles on miles of fire; mountain piled on mountain of black smoke; million on million of flying sparks, of hot ashes, of angry cinders; one ceaseless babel of human voices, crying, shouting, cursing; one mighty pandemonium of woe. . . ."

Ruins of the Gallego Flour Mills in Richmond.

Captured Confederate Cannon, Richmond.

That afternoon the mayor of Richmond requested the commander of the Federal troops outside Richmond to take possession of the city "with an organized force, to preserve order and protect women and children and property."

"This town is the Rebellion; it is all that we have directly striven for," Northerners thought, but when they entered the capital they found it a city of ruins. A few days later a journalist reported "no sound of life, but the stillness of a catacomb. . . . Says a melancholy voice: 'And this is Richmond.' We are under the shadow of ruins. From the pavements where we walk far off into the gradual curtain of the night, stretches a vista of desolation. The hundreds of fabrics, the millions of wealth, that crumbled less than a week ago beneath one fiery kiss, here topple and moulder into rest. A white smoke-wreath rising occasionally, enwraps a shattered wall as in a shroud. A gleam of flame shoots a grotesque picture of broken arches and ragged chimneys into the brain."

[432]

After the fall of Petersburg and Richmond came the chase. At every junction Lee must be headed off, so that he could not turn south and join Johnston. "The pursuit had now become swift, unflagging, relentless. Sheridan, 'the inevitable,' as the enemy had learned to call him, was in advance, thundering on with his cavalry, followed by . . . the rest of the Army of the Potomac. . . . The troops were made to realize that this campaign was to be won by legs; that the great walking-match had begun, and success depended upon which army could make the best distance record. . . . The columns were crowding the roads, and the men, aroused to still greater efforts by the inspiriting news . . . , were sweeping steadily along, despite the rain that fell, like trained pedestrians on a walking-track. As the general [Grant] rode among them he was greeted with shouts and hurrahs on all sides, and a string of sly remarks, . . . such as 'We've marched nigh twenty miles on this stretch, and we're good for twenty more if the general says so'; and 'We're not straddlin' any hosses, but we'll get there all the same.' "

Pontoon Bridge Across the Appomattox River at Petersburg.

First Union Wagon Train Entering Petersburg.

Under orders to move "regardless of every consideration but the one of finishing the war," Grant's army carried only three days' rations when it left Petersburg. It was impossible to bring up supplies fast enough, by river or by wagon train, for troops advancing so rapidly; but, hungry, wet, and tired, the Federal soldiers pushed on in pursuit. "We grew tired and prostrated," explained one veteran, "but we wanted to be there when the rebels found the last ditch of which they had talked so much."

Transporting Union Artillery down the James River, April, 1865.

Major General Cadmus Marcellus Wilcox, C.S.A.

Through "the week of flying fights" the Union army hounded the Confederates. At Jetersville, at Sayler's Creek, at Farmville, Lee found the enemy still pursuing, still preventing him from turning south to join Johnston. His army was disappearing. The veteran division of the dependable Wilcox, for instance, had numbered 6,946 on January 30; after Five Forks and Fort Gregg and the flight it had 2,681 officers and men.

Major General George Armstrong Custer, U.S.A.

Lee's only hope was to follow the railroad westward; but on April 8 Federal cavalry reached Appomattox station ahead of him. "A short time before dusk," Sheridan informed Grant, "General Custer, who had the advance, made a dash at the station, capturing four trains of supplies with locomotives. . . . Custer then pushed on toward Appomattox Court-House, driving the enemy. . . . If . . . the Fifth Corps can get up to-night we will perhaps finish the job in the morning."

The McLean House at Appomattox Court House.

There could be no escape, and on April 9 Lee had to surrender. In Wilmer McLean's house at Appomattox, in the parlor to the left of the hallway, he and Grant met. The Southern general "wore a new uniform of Confederate gray, buttoned to the throat, and a handsome sword and sash"; Grant "had on his single-breasted blouse of dark-blue flannel, unbuttoned . . . an ordinary pair of top-boots, with his trousers inside . . . spattered with mud." After a few minutes of conversation Grant wrote out his terms, and Lee accepted them. The entire Army of Northern Virginia was surrendered, to be released upon parole. Before leaving, the Confederate commander was obliged to request rations for his hungry men.

Then the party passed out to the porch. "Lee signaled to his orderly to bring up his horse, and while the animal was being bridled the general stood on the lowest step, and gazed sadly in the direction of the valley beyond, where his army lay—now an army of prisoners. He thrice smote the palm of his left hand slowly with his right fist in an absent sort of way, . . . and appeared unaware of everything about him. . . . The approach of his horse seemed to recall him from his reverie, and he at once mounted. General Grant now stepped down from the porch, moving toward him, and saluted him by raising his hat. He was followed in this act of courtesy by all . . . officers present. Lee raised his hat respectfully, and rode off at a slow trot to break the sad news to the brave fellows whom he had so long commanded."

April 12 was the day appointed for the surrender of Confederate arms. "When the head of each division column comes opposite our group," Union General Joshua L. Chamberlain wrote, "our bugle sounds the signal and instantly our whole line from right to left, regiment by regiment in succession, gives the soldier's salutation, from the 'order arms' to the old 'carry'—the marching salute. [General John B.] Gordon at the head of the column, riding with heavy spirit and downcast face, catches the sound of shifting arms, looks up, and, taking the meaning, wheels superbly, making with himself and his horse one uplifted figure . . . ; then facing to his own command, gives word for his successive brigades to pass us with the same position. . . . On our part not a sound of trumpet more, nor roll of drum; not a cheer, . . . but an awed stillness rather, and breath-holding, as if it were the passing of the dead! As each successive division . . . halts, the men face inward toward us across the road, twelve feet away; then carefully 'dress' their line. . . . They fix bayonets, stack arms; then, hesitatingly, remove cartridge-boxes and lay them down. Lastly . . . they tenderly fold their flags, battle-worn and torn, blood-stained, heart-holding colors, and lay them down; some frenziedly rushing from the ranks, . . . pressing them to their lips with burning tears. And only the Flag of the Union greets the sky!"

Union Soldiers at Appomattox Court House.

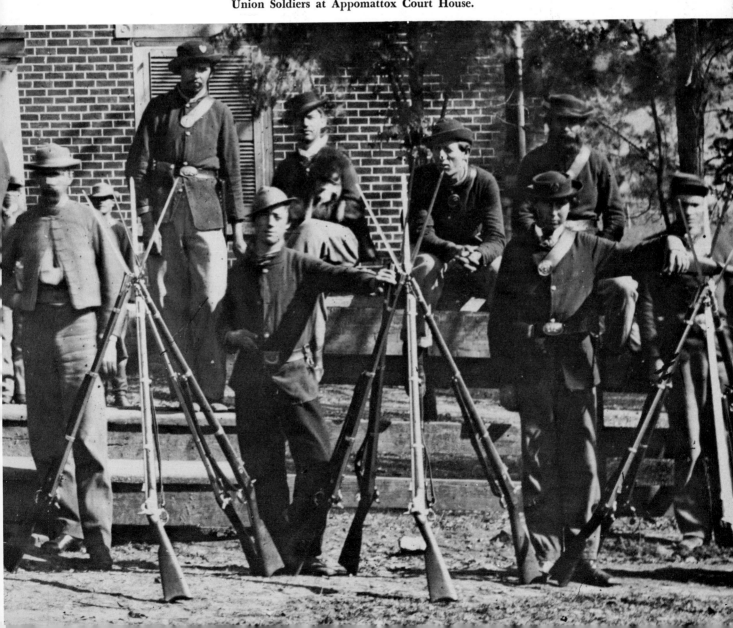

Lee After Appomattox—on the Porch of His Richmond Home with Major General
George Washington Custis Lee and Colonel Walter Taylor, April, 1865.

The Grand Review of the Union Armies in Washington—Artillery on Pennsylvania Avenue, May 24, 1865.

Picture Credits

CHAPTER IV

96 Julian Vannerson, 1863. Library of Congress.
98 Timothy H. O'Sullivan, 1862. Library of Congress.
99 Mathew B. Brady or assistant. The National Archives.
100 Timothy H. O'Sullivan, August 1862. Library of Congress.
101 Mathew B. Brady or assistant. Library of Congress.
102 Edwin Forbes, August 1862. Library of Congress.
103 Timothy H. O'Sullivan, 1862. Library of Congress.
104 Timothy H. O'Sullivan, August 19, 1862. Library of Congress.
105 Timothy H. O'Sullivan, August 27, 1862. The National Archives.
106 Timothy H. O'Sullivan, 1862. Library of Congress.
107 Mathew B. Brady or assistant. Library of Congress.
108 Edwin Forbes, August 1862. Library of Congress.
110 Mathew B. Brady or assistant. Library of Congress.
111 Unidentified. Library of Congress.
112 Unidentified. L. C. Handy Studios.
113 Pencil and wash drawing by Alfred R. Waud. Library of Congress.
114 Timothy H. O'Sullivan, 1862. Library of Congress.
115 Wash drawing by Alfred R. Waud, September 1862. Library of Congress.
116 Alfred R. Waud, September 1862. Library of Congress.
117 Mathew B. Brady or assistant. Library of Congress.
118 James F. Gibson, September 1862. Library of Congress.
119 Alexander Gardner, September 1862. Library of Congress.
120 Alexander Gardner, September 1862. Library of Congress.
121 Alexander Gardner, September 17, 1862. Library of Congress.
122 Alexander Gardner, September 1862. Library of Congress.
123 James Gardner, September 1862. L. C. Handy Studios.
124 Mathew B. Brady or assistant. Library of Congress.
125 Edwin Forbes. Library of Congress.
126 Attributed to George S. Cook. Library of Congress.
127 Whitehurst Gallery. Library of Congress.
128 Alexander Gardner, September 1862. Library of Congress.
129 Edwin Forbes, September 1862. Library of Congress.
130 Edwin Forbes, September 1862. Library of Congress.
131 Alexander Gardner, September 1862. Library of Congress.
132 Julian Vannerson. L. C. Handy Studios.
133 Pencil and wash drawing by Alfred R. Waud, September 1862. Library of Congress.
134 Mathew B. Brady or assistant. Library of Congress.
135 Alexander Gardner, September 1862. Library of Congress.
136 Alexander Gardner, September 1862. Library of Congress.
137 Alexander Gardner, October 3, 1862. Library of Congress.
138 James R. Chapin, 1862. Library of Congress.
139 George S. Cook. Heustis P. Cook, Richmond, Virginia.

CHAPTER V

140 Mathew B. Brady or assistant. Library of Congress.
142 Timothy H. O'Sullivan, February 1863. Library of Congress.
143 Pencil and wash drawing by Alfred R. Waud, December 1862. Library of Congress.
144 Pencil and wash drawing by Alfred R. Waud, 1862. Library of Congress.
145 (top) Pencil and wash drawing by Alfred R. Waud, 1862. Library of Congress.
(bottom) Mathew B. Brady or assistant, 1862. The National Archives.
146 Pencil and wash drawing by Alfred R. Waud, December 1862. Library of Congress.
147 Mathew B. Brady or assistant. Library of Congress.
148 Pencil and wash drawing by Alfred R. Waud, January 1862. Library of Congress.
149 Edwin Forbes, 1862. Library of Congress.

150 Mathew B. Brady or assistant. Library of Congress.
151 Timothy H. O'Sullivan, April 1863. Library of Congress.
152 Timothy H. O'Sullivan, March 1863. Library of Congress.
153 Timothy H. O'Sullivan, March 1863. Library of Congress.
154 Alexander Gardner, February 1863. Library of Congress.
155 Mathew B. Brady or assistant. Library of Congress.
156 Alexander Gardner, February 1863. Library of Congress.
157 Mathew B. Brady or assistant. Library of Congress.
158 Julian Vannerson. L. C. Handy Studios.
159 Edwin Forbes, April 1863. Library of Congress.
160 Edwin Forbes, 1863. Library of Congress.
161 Mathew B. Brady or assistant. Library of Congress.
162 Pencil and wash drawing by Alfred R. Waud, May 1863. Library of Congress.
163 George W. Minnes, made two weeks before Chancellorsville. The National Archives.
164 Pencil and wash drawing by Alfred R. Waud, May 1863. Library of Congress.
165 James Gardner, 1863. Library of Congress.
166 Captain A. J. Russell. Library of Congress.
167 Mathew B. Brady or assistant, December 1862. Library of Congress.

CHAPTER VI

168 Mathew B. Brady or assistant. Library of Congress.
170 Edwin Forbes, 1863. Library of Congress.
171 George S. Cook. Library of Congress.
172 Mathew B. Brady or assistant. L. C. Handy Studios.
173 Alfred R. Waud, July 1, 1863. Library of Congress.
174 Timothy H. O'Sullivan, July 1863. Library of Congress.
175 Unidentified. Confederate Memorial Hall, New Orleans, Louisiana.
176 Pencil and wash drawing by Alfred R. Waud, July 1863. Library of Congress.
177 Alexander Gardner, July 1863. Library of Congress.
178 Mathew B. Brady or assistant. Library of Congress.
179 Timothy H. O'Sullivan, July 1863. Library of Congress.
180 Alexander Gardner, July 1863. Library of Congress.
181 Alexander Gardner, July 1863. Library of Congress.
182 Mathew B. Brady or assistant. Library of Congress.
183 Attributed to James F. Gibson, July 1863. Library of Congress.
184 Edwin Forbes, July 1863. Library of Congress.
186 Pencil and wash drawing by Alfred R. Waud, July 1863. Library of Congress.
187 George S. Cook. L. C. Handy Studios.
188 Mathew B. Brady or assistant. Library of Congress.
189 George S. Cook. L. C. Handy Studios.
190 Mathew B. Brady or assistant, July 1863, Library of Congress.

CHAPTER VII

192 Edwin Forbes, September 1863. Library of Congress.
193 Alfred R. Waud, September 1863. Library of Congress.
194 Timothy H. O'Sullivan, 1863. Library of Congress.
195 Attributed to Timothy H. O'Sullivan. Library of Congress.
196 Alfred R. Waud, November 1863. Library of Congress.
197 Edwin Forbes. Library of Congress.
198 Edwin Forbes, February 1864. Library of Congress.
199 Alfred R. Waud, February 1864. Library of Congress.
200 Edwin Forbes, 1864. Library of Congress.
201 Edwin Forbes, January 1864. Library of Congress.
202 Timothy H. O'Sullivan, August 1863. Library of Congress.
203 Timothy H. O'Sullivan, August 1863. Library of Congress.

204 Edwin Forbes, August 1863. Library of Congress.
205 Timothy H. O'Sullivan, August 1863. Library of Congress.
206 Timothy H. O'Sullivan, April 1864. Library of Congress.
207 Mathew B. Brady or assistant, February 1864. Library of Congress.
208 Timothy H. O'Sullivan, March 1864. Library of Congress.
209 Timothy H. O'Sullivan, April 1864. Library of Congress.

CHAPTER VIII

210 Unidentified. Library of Congress.
212 Mathew B. Brady or assistant. Library of Congress.
213 Mathew B. Brady or assistant. Library of Congress.
214 William R. Pywell, February 1864. Library of Congress.
215 William R. Pywell, 1864. Library of Congress.
216 Unidentified. Library of Congress.
217 Pencil and wash drawing by Fred B. Schell, 1863. New York Historical Society.
218 Unidentified. Library of Congress.
219 Unidentified. Library of Congress.
220 William R. Pywell. Library of Congress.
221 Unidentified. The National Archives.
222 Fred B. Schell, July 1863. New York Public Library.
223 Mathew B. Brady or assistant. L. C. Handy Studios.
224 Mathew B. Brady or assistant. Library of Congress.
225 Unidentified. Library of Congress.
226 Unidentified. Library of Congress.
227 Unidentified. Library of Congress.

CHAPTER IX

228 Mathew B. Brady or assistant. Library of Congress.
230 Mathew B. Brady. L. C. Handy Studios.
231 Mathew B. Brady or assistant. Library of Congress.
232 Henry Lovie, 1863. New York Public Library.
233 Unknown. Miss Georgia Fleming, Bainbridge, Georgia.
234 Attributed to R. M. Cressey. Library of Congress.
235 Mathew B. Brady or assistant. L. C. Handy Studios.
236 Mathew B. Brady or assistant. Library of Congress.
237 Pencil and wash drawing by unidentified artist. Library of Congress.
238 Mathew B. Brady or assistant. L. C. Handy Studios.
239 Wash drawing by Alfred R. Waud, 1863. Library of Congress.
240 George N. Barnard. Library of Congress.
241 Unidentified, made at Chattanooga, 1863. Library of Congress.
242 Attributed to George N. Barnard, 1863. Library of Congress.
243 Unidentified. Library of Congress.
244 Mathew B. Brady or assistant. Library of Congress.
245 Lee. L. C. Handy Studios.
246 George N. Barnard, 1864. Library of Congress.
247 Attributed to George N. Barnard, 1863. Library of Congress.
248 Attributed to George N. Barnard, 1863. Library of Congress.
249 Mathew B. Brady or assistant. Library of Congress.
250 George N. Barnard, 1863. Library of Congress.
251 Unidentified artist. Library of Congress.
252 George S. Cook. Library of Congress.
253 Attributed to George N. Barnard, 1864. Library of Congress.

CHAPTER X

254 Mathew B. Brady or assistant. Library of Congress.
256 Mathew B. Brady or assistant, December 1864. Library of Congress.
257 Unidentified. Library of Congress.
258 (top) Watercolor by William Jorgerson. Chicago Historical Society.
(bottom) Watercolor by the Earl of Dunmore. Mariners' Museum, Newport News.
259 Unidentified. Library of Congress.
260 A. Dupertz, Kingston, Jamaica, 1863. Frederick H. Meserve Collection.
261 Unidentified. The National Archives.
262 Mathew B. Brady or assistant, made when Buchanan was a captain in the U. S. navy. Library of Congress.
263 James F. Gibson, July 1862. Library of Congress.
264 James F. Gibson, July 1862. Library of Congress.
265 Mathew B. Brady or assistant. L. C. Handy Studios.
266 Mathew B. Brady or assistant. Library of Congress.
267 Mathew B. Brady or assistant. Library of Congress.
268 N. O. Edwards or J. D. Edwards, February 1861. The National Archives.
269 Wash drawing by unidentified artist, 1861. Library of Congress.
270 Pencil and wash drawing by Alfred R. Waud, August 1861. Library of Congress.
271 Pencil and wash drawing by Alfred R. Waud, August 1861. Library of Congress.
272 Timothy H. O'Sullivan, February 1862. Library of Congress.
273 Mathew B. Brady or assistant. Library of Congress.
274 Samuel A. Cooley. Library of Congress.
275 George N. Barnard. Library of Congress.
276 Timothy H. O'Sullivan, April 1862. Library of Congress.
277 Timothy H. O'Sullivan, April 1862. Library of Congress.
278 Attributed to Samuel A. Cooley. Library of Congress.
279 S. R. Seibert, 1865. Library of Congress.
280 Unidentified. Library of Congress.
281 George S. Cook, 1863. Heustis P. Cook, Richmond, Virginia.
282 S. R. Siebert, 1865. Library of Congress.
283 George N. Barnard, April 1865. Library of Congress.
284 Mathew B. Brady or assistant. Library of Congress.
285 Unidentified. Library of Congress.
286 Unidentified. Library of Congress.
287 Unidentified. Library of Congress.
288 Mathew B. Brady or assistant. Library of Congress.
289 Haas & Peale, July 1863. Library of Congress.
290 Unidentified. Library of Congress.
291 Mathew B. Brady or assistant. Library of Congress.
292 George N. Barnard, April 1865. Library of Congress.
293 George N. Barnard, 1865. Library of Congress.
294 Alfred R. Waud, December 1864. Library of Congress.
295 Mathew B. Brady or assistant, April 1862. Library of Congress.
296 Timothy H. O'Sullivan. Library of Congress.
297 Timothy H. O'Sullivan. Library of Congress.

CHAPTER XI

298 Timothy H. O'Sullivan, May 1864. Library of Congress.
300 Alfred R. Waud, May 1864. Library of Congress.
301 Mathew B. Brady or assistant. Library of Congress.
302 Pencil and wash drawing by Alfred R. Waud, May 1864. Library of Congress.
303 Unidentified. L. C. Handy Studios.
304 Edwin Forbes, May 1864. Library of Congress.
305 George S. Cook. Heustis P. Cook, Richmond, Virginia.
306 Edwin Forbes, May 1864. Library of Congress.

307 Edwin Forbes, May 1864. Library of Congress.
308 Alfred R. Waud, May 1864. Library of Congress.
309 Mathew B. Brady or assistant. Library of Congress.
310 Timothy H. O'Sulllivan, May 1864. Library of Congress.
311 Timothy H. O'Sullivan, May 1864. Library of Congress.
312 Mathew B. Brady or assistant, May 1864. Library of Congress.
313 Timothy H. O'Sullivan, May 1864. Library of Congress.
314 Timothy H. O'Sullivan, May 1864. Library of Congress.
315 Timothy H. O'Sullivan, June 1864. Library of Congress.
316 Edwin Forbes, June 1864. Library of Congress.
317 Alfred R. Waud, June 1864. Library of Congress.
318 Mathew B. Brady or assistant. Library of Congress.
319 Alfred R. Waud, June 1864. Library of Congress.
320 Timothy H. O'Sullivan, June 13, 1864. Library of Congress.
321 Timothy H. O'Sullivan, May 30, 1864. Library of Congress.

CHAPTER XII

322 Mathew B. Brady or assistant, August 1864. Library of Congress.
324 Pencil and wash drawing by William Waud, October 1864. Library of Congress.
325 Pencil and wash drawing by Alfred R. Waud, July 1864. Library of Congress.
326 Pencil and wash drawing by William Waud, October 1864. Library of Congress.
327 Mathew B. Brady or assistant, 1864. Library of Congress.
328 Mathew B. Brady or assistant, July 1864. Library of Congress.
329 Timothy H. O'Sullivan, June 1864. Library of Congress.
330 Attributed to Julian Vannerson. L. C. Handy Studios.
331 William Morris Smith, 1865. Library of Congress.
332 Mathew B. Brady or assistant, July 1864. Library of Congress.
333 Mathew B. Brady or assistant, 1864. Library of Congress.
334 Timothy H. O'Sullivan, June 21, 1864. Library of Congress.
335 Mathew B. Brady or assistant, 1864. Library of Congress.
336 Mathew B. Brady or assistant, 1864. Library of Congress.
337 Mathew B. Brady or assistant, 1864. Library of Congress.
338 Mathew B. Brady or assistant, 1864. Library of Congress.
339 Mathew B. Brady or assistant. Library of Congress.
340 Alexander Gardner. Library of Congress.
341 Mathew B. Brady or assistant, July 1864. Library of Congress.
342 Mathew B. Brady or assistant, 1864. Library of Congress.
343 Mathew B. Brady or assistant, 1864. Library of Congress.
344 Alfred R. Waud, July 1864. Library of Congress.
345 Alfred R. Waud, July 1864. Library of Congress.
346 Attributed to Alexander Gardner, July 1864. Library of Congress.
347 Alfred R. Waud, June 1864. Library of Congress.
348 Mathew B. Brady or assistant, July 1864. Library of Congress.
349 Pencil and wash drawing by Alfred R. Waud, July 1864. Library of Congress.
350 Pencil and wash drawing by Alfred R. Waud, July 1864. Library of Congress.
351 Unidentified. Library of Congress.
352 Unidentified. Library of Congress.
353 Mathew B. Brady or assistant. Library of Congress.
354 Bendann Brothers. Maryland Division, United Daughters of the Confederacy and Maryland Historical Society, Baltimore.
355 Unidentified. L. C. Handy Studios.
356 Mathew B. Brady or assistant. Library of Congress.

357 Mathew B. Brady or assistant. Library of Congress.
358 William Morris Smith. Library of Congress.
359 Mathew B. Brady or assistant. L. C. Handy Studios.
360 William Morris Smith, August 1865. Library of Congress.
361 Mathew B. Brady or assistant. Library of Congress.
362 Winslow Homer. Addison Gallery of American Art, Phillips Academy, Andover, Massachusetts.
363 Alexander Gardner, October 1862. Library of Congress.
364 Mathew B. Brady or assistant, 1864. L. C. Handy Studios.
365 Pencil and wash drawing by Alfred R. Waud, September 19, 1864. Library of Congress.
366 Pencil and wash drawing by Alfred R. Waud, October 1864. Library of Congress.
367 Alfred R. Waud, 1864. Library of Congress.
368 Alfred R. Waud, September 1864. Library of Congress.
369 Mathew B. Brady or assistant, 1864. Library of Congress.
370 Pencil and wash drawing by William Waud, October 7, 1864. Library of Congress.
371 David Knox, October 1864. Library of Congress.
372 William Waud, October 1864. Library of Congress.
373 John Reekie, March 1865. Library of Congress.
374 Mathew B. Brady or assistant. The National Archives.
375 Timothy H. O'Sullivan, August 1864. Library of Congress.
376 Mathew B. Brady or assistant. Library of Congress.
377 Timothy H. O'Sullivan, November 1864. Library of Congress.
378 Mathew B. Brady or assistant, October 1864. Library of Congress.
379 Timothy H. O'Sullivan, August 1864. Library of Congress.

CHAPTER XIII

380 Mathew B. Brady or assistant. Library of Congress.
382 Mathew B. Brady or assistant. Library of Congress.
383 Mathew B. Brady or assistant. Library of Congress.
384 George N. Barnard, 1864. Library of Congress.
385 George N. Barnard, 1864. Library of Congress.
386 George N. Barnard, 1864. Library of Congress.
387 Pencil and wash drawing by unidentified artist. Library of Congress.
388 Pencil and wash drawing by unidentified artist. Library of Congress.
389 George N. Barnard, 1864. Library of Congress.
390 George N. Barnard, 1864. Library of Congress.
391 George N. Barnard, 1864. Library of Congress.
392 Mathew B. Brady or assistant. Library of Congress.
393 Unidentified. Library of Congress.
394 Mathew B. Brady or assistant. Library of Congress.
395 Mathew B. Brady or assistant. Library of Congress.
396 Mathew B. Brady or assistant. Library of Congress.
397 George N. Barnard, 1864. Library of Congress.
398 George N. Barnard, 1864. Library of Congress.
399 George S. Cook. Heustis P. Cook, Richmond, Virginia.
400 Pencil and wash drawing by unidentified artist. Library of Congress.
401 Unidentified. Library of Congress.
402 George N. Barnard, November 23, 1864. Library of Congress.
403 Unidentified. Library of Congress.
404 George N. Barnard, 1864. Library of Congress.
405 George N. Barnard, 1864. Library of Congress.
406 Unidentified. Library of Congress.
407 Unidentified. Library of Congress.
408 George N. Barnard, 1864. Library of Congress.
409 George N. Barnard, December 16, 1864. Library of Congress.
410 George N. Barnard, 1864. Library of Congress.
411 George N. Barnard, 1864. Library of Congress.

412 George N. Barnard, 1864. Library of Congress.
413 George N. Barnard, 1864. Library of Congress.
414 Mathew B. Brady or assistant. Library of Congress.
415 **Attributed to Samuel A. Cooley, 1864. Library of Congress.**
416 William Waud, 1864. Library of Congress.
417 William Waud, 1865. Library of Congress.
418 George S. Cook. Heustis P. Cook, Richmond, Virginia.
419 George N. Barnard, 1865. Library of Congress.

CHAPTER XIV

420 Attributed to Thomas C. Roche, April 1865. Library of Congress.
422 Mathew B. Brady or assistant, 1865. Library of Congress.
423 Attributed to Thomas C. Roche, April 1865. Library of Congress.
424 Alfred R. Waud, April 1865. Library of Congress.
425 John C. Roche or John Reekie, April 1865. Library of Congress.
426 Attributed to Thomas C. Roche, April 1865. Library of Congress.

427 Attributed to Thomas C. Roche, April 1865. Library of Congress.
428 John Reekie or Thomas C. Roche, April 1865. Library of Congress.
429 Mathew B. Brady or Alexander Gardner, April 1865. Library of Congress.
430 Alexander Gardner, April 1865. Library of Congress.
431 Mathew B. Brady or Alexander Gardner, April 1865. Library of Congress.
432 Mathew B. Brady or Alexander Gardner, April 1865. Library of Congress.
433 Alexander Gardner or Timothy H. O'Sullivan, 1865. Library of Congress.
434 John Reekie, April 1865. Library of Congress.
435 Mathew B. Brady or assistant, April 1865. Library of Congress.
436 Unknown. Library of Congress.
437 Mathew B. Brady or assistant. Library of Congress.
438 Timothy H. O'Sullivan, April 1865. Library of Congress.
439 Timothy H. O'Sullivan, April 1865. Library of Congress.
440 Mathew B. Brady, April 1865. L. C. Handy Studios.
441 Mathew B. Brady or Alexander Gardner, May 24, 1865. Library of Congress.

Reference Notes

These notes are not intended to serve as a bibliography of the Civil War; they do not even include all the works consulted in the preparation of this volume. Their purpose is simply to provide the interested reader citations for all direct quotations which appear in the text.

The following abbreviations have been used: *Cycle of Adams Letters* = W. C. Ford, ed., *A Cycle of Adams Letters* (1920); *H. W.* = *Harper's Weekly: A Journal of Civilization; Leslie's* = *Frank Leslie's Illustrated Weekly Newspaper; Meade's Hq.* = George R. Agassiz, ed., *Meade's Headquarters: Letters of Colonel Theodore Lyman* (1922); *O.R.* = *War of the Rebellion: A Compilation of the Official Records of the Union and Confederate Armies* (1880–1901), all references being to volumes in Series 1; *O.R.N.* = *Official Records of the Union and Confederate Navies in the War of the Rebellion* (1894–1922), all references being to volumes in Series 1; *Reb. Rec.* = Frank Moore, ed., *The Rebellion Record: A Diary of American Events* (1864–1868).

CHAPTER I

1 *Reb. Rec.*, I, 2 (doc.); M. R. Moore to Charles Sumner, Jan. 4, 1861, Sumner MSS., Harvard Lib.; R. P. Basler, ed., *Abraham Lincoln: His Speeches and Writings* (1946), 586–588.
3 Basler, *Lincoln Speeches*, 583; *O.R.*, I, 235, 297; U. B. Phillips, ed., *Correspondence of Robert Toombs* . . . (1913), 563.
4 Mary B. Chesnut, *A Diary from Dixie* (1905), 34–35; *H. W.*, April 20, 1861, p. 247.
6 MS. diary of Edmund Ruffin, April 12, 1861, Lib. of Cong.
7 *O.R.*, I, 12; J. F. Rhodes, *History of the United States* . . . (1895), III, 358, 382.
8 Carl Sandburg, *Abraham Lincoln: The War Years* (1939), I, 29.
9 *Reb. Rec.*, I, 30 (diary); N. Y. *Illustrated News*, May 11, 1861, p. 11.

10 Rhodes, *History of United States*, III, 367; *House Exec. Doc.* No. 15, 38 Cong., 1 sess. (1864), 9.
11 *Reb. Rec.*, I, 189 (doc.); *H. W.*, May 18, 1861, p. 317; Tyler Dennett, ed., *Lincoln and the Civil War* . . . (1939), 19; Rhodes, *History of United States*, III, 375n.
12 W. S. White, *A Diary of the War* (1883), 98.
13 Frank Moore, *The Portrait Gallery of the War* (1864), 115; W. S. White, *Diary*, 100.
15 J. H. Wilson, *Under the Old Flag* (1912), I, 66; *Reb. Rec.*, II, 313 (doc.).
16 *Reb. Rec.*, II, 313–314 (doc.); N. Y. *Illustrated News*, July 20, 1861, p. 194; J. E. Cooke, *Wearing of the Gray* (1867), 87.
18 *O.R.*, II, 441; Alfred Roman, *Military Operations of General Beauregard* (1884), I, 82.
19 *Reb. Rec.*, II, 36 (diary).
20 *O.R.*, II, 493; *Reb. Rec.*, II, 3, 106 (doc.).
22 *Reb. Rec.*, II, 103 (doc.); D. S. Freeman, *Lee's Lieutenants* (1944), I, 82.

23 W. H. Russell, *My Diary, North and South* (1863), II, 224; Charles Lanman, ed., *Journal of Alfred Ely* (1862), 7–15.

24 M. A. de W. Howe, ed., *Home Letters of General Sherman,* 209–210.

CHAPTER II

27 K. P. Williams, *Lincoln Finds a General* (1949), I, 104; *O.R.,* II, 316; W. H. Russell, *My Diary,* II, 268; *McClellan's Own Story* (1887), 82, 85, 83.

28 G. B. McClellan, *Report of the Organization . . . of the Army of the Potomac* (1864), 98–99; E. A. Walker, *Our First Year of Army Life* (1862), 54–56; description on reverse of stereotype pub. by War Photograph and Exhibition Co., Hartford.

29 Walker, *First Year,* 54–56.

30 *McClellan's Own Story,* 87; *B. & L.,* II, 113.

31 *McClellan's Own Story,* 69; R. G. Carter, *Four Brothers in Blue* (1913), 37.

33 *McClellan's Own Story,* 168; B. I. Wiley, *Life of Billy Yank* (1951), 164.

34 Susan L. Blackford, comp., *Letters from Lee's Army* (1947), 42; Edwin Forbes, *An Artist's Story of the Great War* (1891), II, 261; Frederic Denison, *Sabres and Spurs* (1876), 47; J. B. Polley, *A Soldier's Letters to His Charming Nellie* (1908), 15–16.

35 Polley, *Soldier's Letters,* 17, 19–20, 23; Denison, *Sabres and Spurs,* 47–48.

36 Denison, *Sabres and Spurs,* 47.

37 *H. W.,* Mar. 29, 1862, p. 203.

38 J. O. Casler, *Four Years in the Stonewall Brigade* (1893), 80.

39 Francis Goulding Woods to his family, Yorktown, Aug. 14, 1861, MS., Ga. Dept. of Archives and Hist., Atlanta.

40 G. A. Townsend, *Rustics in Rebellion* (1950), 50.

41 Bruce Catton, *Mr. Lincoln's Army* (1951), 110; J. F. Rhodes, *History of the Civil War* (1917), 126; *McClellan's Own Story,* 313–314.

42 *McClellan's Own Story,* 264–265; John Fitch, *Annals of the Army of the Cumberland* (1863), 265; Joel Cook, *The Siege of Richmond* (1862), 25.

43 F. M. Edge, *Major-General McClellan and the Campaign on the Yorktown Peninsula* (1865), 74–75.

44 Francis Goulding Woods to his family, Yorktown, April 16, 1862, MS., Ga. Dept. of Archives and Hist.; *McClellan's Own Story,* 286.

45 Comte de Paris, *History of the Civil War* (1876), II, 15–16.

46 *McClellan's Own Story,* 317; Thomas Kearny, *General Philip Kearny* (1937), 208, 226.

48 W. E. Baringer, "On Enemy Soil: Lincoln's Norfolk Campaign," *Abraham Lincoln Quar.,* VII (1952), 4–26.

49 *McClellan's Own Story,* 318; J. B. Gordon, *Reminiscenses of the Civil War* (1903), 53; Catton, *Mr. Lincoln's Army,* 109.

50 A. L. Castleman, *The Army of the Potomac* (1863), 143; Cook, *Siege of Richmond,* 88–89.

51 *McClellan's Own Story,* 362; T. L. Livermore, *Days and Events* (1920), 63; *O.R.,* XI, pt. 1, 655; J. R. Adams, *Memorial and Letters* (1890), 54.

52 *McClellan's Own Story,* 370; *H. W.,* June 21, 1862, p. 395.

53 *H. W.,* June 21, 1862, p. 395; *McClellan's Own Story,* 397.

54 *McClellan's Own Story,* 367.

55 B. W. Jones, *Under the Stars and Bars* (1909), 21.

56 Adams, *Memorial and Letters,* 55; Livermore, *Days and Events,* 67.

57 Adams, *Memorial and Letters,* 55; Livermore, *Days and Events,* 65, 69.

58 Cook, *Siege of Richmond,* 32, 35.

59 Cook, *Siege of Richmond,* 35–36.

61 *McClellan's Own Story,* 398; *Leslie's,* July 5, 1862, p. 227; Livermore, *Days and Events,* 65, 71.

62 Polley, *Soldier's Letters,* 53.

63 Catton, *Mr. Lincoln's Army,* 20; Jed Hotchkiss to his wife, May 26, 1862, MS., Lib. of Cong.

65 *Leslie's,* June 28, 1862, p. 198.

67 Cooke, *Wearing of the Gray,* 189.

69 *B. & L.,* II, 327.

70 C. A. Page, *Letters of a War Correspondent* (1899), 12; Polley, *Soldier's Letters,* 55.

71 *McClellan's Own Story,* 443; *B. & L.,* II, 386.

72 Alexander Gardner, *Gardner's Photographic Sketch Book of the War* (1865), I, opposite picture No. 17.

74 *H. W.,* Aug. 9, 1862, p. 503; Castleman, *Army of the Potomac,* 174.

77 W. R. Stilwell to "Dear Molly," July 4, 1862, MS., Ga. Dept. of Archives and Hist.

CHAPTER III

79 R. S. Thorndike, ed., *The Sherman Letters* (1894), 122, 128; *Battle-Fields of the South . . . by an English Combatant* (1863), I, 224; Rhodes, *History of United States,* III, 600.

80 *Dictionary of Am. Biog.,* II, 333; J. G. Nicolay and John Hay, eds., *Complete Works of Abraham Lincoln* (1905), VII, 85.

81 *B. & L.,* I, 273, 295; *Battle-Fields of the South,* I, 88; Dennett, *Lincoln and the Civil War,* 133.

82 Nicolay-Hay, eds., *Lincoln's Works,* VIII, 275.

84 Wilson, *Under the Old Flag,* I, 99.

85 Moore, *Portrait Gallery,* 65.

86 *B. & L.,* I, 347, 339; U. S. Grant, *Memoirs* (1885), I, facsimile facing p. 312.

87 *B. & L.,* I, 474; *H. W.,* April 26, 1862, p. 263.

88 *B. & L.,* I, 451–452.

90 *B. & L.,* II, 18–19, 26; *Reb. Rec.,* IV, 513–514 (doc.).

92 *Reb. Rec.,* IV, 511 (doc.); G. E. Belknap, ed., *Letters of Capt. Geo. Hamilton Perkins* (1901), 72–75.

94 *Reb. Rec.,* IV, 524 (doc.); *B. & L.,* II, 93; *H. W.,* May 24, 1862, p. 327; Belknap, *Perkins Letters,* 70; Rhodes, *History of United States,* IV, 93n.

CHAPTER IV

97 Williams, *Lincoln Finds a General,* I, 251; Dennett, *Lincoln and the Civil War,* 176; D. S. Freeman, *R. E. Lee* (1937), II, 261, 264; Blackford, *Letters from Lee's Army,* 114–115.

98 Herman Haupt, *Reminiscences* (1901), 45, 47.

99 Haupt, *Reminiscences,* 48–50.

100 *Reb. Rec.,* V, 552 (doc.).

101 Townsend, *Rustics in Rebellion,* 192.

103 *Leslie's,* Aug. 30, 1862, p. 358; Jed Hotchkiss to his brother, camp near Toddsburg, Va., Aug. 14, 1862, MS., Lib. of Cong.

104 *Harper's Mo.,* XXXV (1867), 704

105 *Harper's Mo.,* XXXV (1867), 712.

106 Haupt, *Reminiscences,* 83, 96, 104; Rhodes, *History of United States,* IV, 133.

108 Rhodes, *History of United States,* IV, 124.

109 *Leslie's,* Sept. 13, 1862, p. 387.

110 Casler, *Four Years in the Stonewall Brigade,* 162–163.

111 *O.R.,* XII, pt. 2, p. 737.

112 *O.R.*, XII, pt. 2, p. 746.
113 J. T. Durkin, ed., *John Dooley, Confederate Soldier* (1945), 22–24.
114 W. T. Lusk, *War Letters* (1911), 181; John Gibbon, *Personal Recollections of the Civil War* (1928), 70.
115 Heros von Borcke, *Memoirs of the Confederate War for Independence* (1938), I, 180, 185.
116 Freeman, *Lee*, II, 357; *H. W.*, Sept. 27, 1862, p. 618; von Borcke, *Memoirs*, I, 221–222.
118 Durkin, *John Dooley*, 31.
119 Durkin, *John Dooley*, 40–41.
120 *O.R.*, XIX, pt. 1, p. 122; *Gardner's Photographic Sketch Book*, I, opposite picture No. 22.
121 Durkin, *John Dooley*, 41.
122 Gordon, *Reminiscences*, 83–84; *B. & L.*, II, 640.
123 Thomas S. Taylor to his wife, Richmond, June 23, 1862, MS., Ala. Dept. of Archives and Hist., Montgomery.
125 Rhodes, *History of United States*, IV, 151; Wilson, *Under the Old Flag*, I, 109; Forbes, *Artist's Story*, 73.
126 Gordon, *Reminiscences*, 87.
127 Catton, *Mr. Lincoln's Army*, 299–304.
128 Durkin, *John Dooley*, 46–47.
129 *History of the Corn Exchange Regiment* (1888), 47; *Harper's Mo.*, XXXVI (1868), 284; *Reb. Rec.*, VI, 471.
130 *Reb. Rec.*, VI, 471. *Harper's Mo.*, XXXVI (1868), 284.
131 *Leslie's*, Oct. 11, 1862, pp. 45–46.
133 Freeman, *Lee*, II, 400–401; *Harper's Mo.*, XXXVI (1868), 285.
134 *H. W.*, Oct. 11, 1862, p. 655.
135 C. E. Davis, Jr., *Three Years in the Army* (1894), 150; E. W. Stone, *Rhode Island in the Rebellion* (1865), 154.
136 *Harper's Mo.*, XXXVI (1868), 286.
137 T. W. Hyde, *Following the Greek Cross* (1895), 107; Dennett, *Lincoln and the Civil War*, 53; John G. Nicolay and John Hay, *Abraham Lincoln: A History* (1904), VI, 177, 183; Abner Hard, *History of the Eighth Cavalry Regiment, Illinois Volunteers* (1868), 196.
138 E. A. Pollard, *Lee and His Lieutenants* (1867), 421–422; *McClellan's Own Story*, 660.

CHAPTER V

141 J. M. Favill, *The Diary of a Young Officer* (1909), 201; Moore, *Portrait Gallery*, 336; Williams, *Lincoln Finds a General*, II, 521; Freeman, *Lee*, II, 473; *Hist. of Corn Exchange Regiment*, 139; Lusk, *War Letters*, 274–275.
142 *Hist. of Corn Exchange Regiment*, 114; Favill, *Diary*, 203.
143 *H. W.*, Dec. 27, 1862, pp. 830–831.
144 *H. W.*, Jan. 3, 1863, p. 6; Dec. 27, 1862, p. 831.
146 Favill, *Diary*, 211–212.
148 *Hist. of Corn Exchange Regiment*, 160–161.
151 *H. W.*, Feb. 28, 1863, p. 130; *Hist. of Corn Exchange Regiment*, 188; W. H. Freeman, *Letters from Two Brothers* (1871), 69; Williams, *Lincoln Finds a General*, II, 562.
152 *Hist. of Corn Exchange Regiment*, 165; Livermore, *Days and Events*, 186.
153 H. N. Blake, *Three Years in the Army of the Potomac* (1865), 304–306.
154 Dennett, *Lincoln and the Civil War*, 46; Haupt, *Reminiscences*, 186.
156 Freeman, *Lee*, II, 484.
157 Williams, *Lincoln Finds a General*, II, 566.
160 Williams, *Lincoln Finds a General*, II, 577, 581; *Hist. of Corn Exchange Regiment*, 178; Favill, *Diary*, 233; L. P. Brockett, *Men of Our Day* (1868), 176.
162 Freeman, *Lee*, II, 462; *H. W.*, May 23, 1863, p. 331.
164 *H. W.*, May 23, 1863, p. 331; Rhodes, *History of United States*, IV, 263; Jed Hotchkiss to his wife, May 10, 1863, MS., Lib. of Cong.

165 Jed Hotchkiss to his wife, April 29, 1863, MS., Lib. of Cong.
166 Moore, *Portrait Gallery*, 323–324.
167 *H. W.*, May 23, 1863, p. 331; Favill, *Diary*, 235.

CHAPTER VI

169 Blackford, *Letters from Lee's Army*, 180–182; Freeman, *Lee*, III, 23, 34; Nicolay-Hay, *Lincoln: A History*, VII, 221; Favill, *Diary*, 242; Hyde, *Following the Greek Cross*, 140; *Life and Public Services of Major-General Meade* (1864), 59; Williams, *Lincoln Finds a General*, II, 675.
170 Freeman, *Lee*, III, 8; *Hist. of Corn Exchange Regiment*, 224–225.
172 *Meade's Hq.*, 21; Williams, *Lincoln Finds a General*, II, 672.
173 Bruce Catton, *Glory Road* (1952), 291; *Reb. Rec.*, VII, 117 (doc.).
174 S. M. Weld, *War Diary and Letters* (1912), 232; S. E. Morison and H. S. Commager, *Growth of American Republic* (1942), I, 720; Catton, *Glory Road*, 305; *Reb. Rec.*, VII, 117 (doc.).
175 Freeman, *Lee's Lieutenants*, III, 88, 110.
176 *Reb. Rec.*, VII, 88 (doc.); Favill, *Diary*, 242.
177 *Life and Public Services of Meade*, 55; Freeman, *Lee*, III, 72–73; *Reb. Rec.*, VII, 110 (doc.).
179 E. G. Taylor, *Gouverneur Kemble Warren* (1932), 125; Regis de Trobriand, *Four Years with the Army of the Potomac* (1889), 479.
180 Favill, *Diary*, 245–246; *Hist. of Corn Exchange Regiment*, 254; *Gardner's Photographic Sketch Book*, I, opposite No. 41.
181 Carter, *Four Brothers in Blue*, 324–325.
183 Taylor, *Warren*, 123, 128; Theodore Gerrish, *Army Life* (1882), 106–110.
186 Lasalle C. Pickett, *Pickett and his Men* (1899), xi; Durkin, *John Dooley*, 105–106.
188 Gibbon, *Personal Recollections*, 155–156, 159, 180.
189 D. E. Johnston, *The Story of a Confederate Boy* (1914), 211; Freeman, *Lee*, III, 155.
190 Dennett, *Lincoln and the Civil War*, 67.

CHAPTER VII

191 Blackford, *Letters from Lee's Army*, 200–201; *Meade's Hq.*, 31, 38, 5; Williams, *Lincoln Finds a General*, II, 769; Favill, *Diary*, 261; *B. & L.*, IV, 91.
192 *Meade's Hq.*, 17.
193 *Meade's Hq.*, 20–21.
194 George Meade, *Life and Letters of George Gordon Meade* (1913), II, 151; *Hist. of Corn Exchange Regiment*, 307–308.
195 *Meade's Hq.*, 29; J. D. Billings, *History of the Tenth Massachusetts Battery of Light Artillery* (1881), 108; Meade, *Meade*, II, 154.
196 *Meade's Hq.*, 43; Freeman, *Lee*, III, 193.
197 Forbes, *Artist's Story*, 97–98.
198 Forbes, *Artist's Story*, 41–42.
199 *Meade's Hq.*, 68–71.
200 *Meade's Hq.*, 78, 79; *Reb. Rec.*, VIII, 581 (doc.).
201 Forbes, *Artist's Story*, 225; O. B. Curtis, *History of the Twenty-Fourth Michigan* (1891), 214.
202 *Meade's Hq.*, 11–12; Wiley, *Billy Yank*, 199.
203 D. H. King and others, *History of the Ninety-Third Regiment New York Volunteer Infantry* (1895), 325; Wiley, *Billy Yank*, 226.
205 Forbes, *Artist's Story*, 21; Wiley, *Billy Yank*, 296–297.
206 G. A. Sala, *My Diary in America* (1865), I, 292–293.
207 *Meade's Hq.*, 65, 74; Sala, *Diary in America*, I, 294–295.

209 J. D. Billings, *Hardtack and Coffee* (1887), 49, 55–57; *Meade's Hq.*, 40–41.

CHAPTER VIII

211 *Meade's Hq.*, 81; J. C. Pemberton, *Pemberton: Defender of Vicksburg* (1942), 178; Grant, *Memoirs*, I, 437, 443; C. A. Dana, *Recollections of the Civil War* (1898), 30.
212 Wilson, *Under the Old Flag*, I, 135; Dana, *Recollections*, 72–73.
213 Wilson, *Under the Old Flag*, I, 175.
214 Grant, *Memoirs*, I, 442, 457, 542n.
215 O. H. Oldroyd, *A Soldier's Story of the Siege of Vicksburg* (1885), 25; Pemberton, *Pemberton*, 169.
216 *B. & L.*, III, 488; Oldroyd, *Soldier's Story*, 28; W. G. Smith, *Life and Letters of Thomas Kilby Smith* (1898), 296.
217 Smith, *Thomas Kilby Smith*, 295–296; A. Hugh Moss, *Diary* (1948), 26; J. L. Jones, *An Artilleryman's Diary* (1914), 73.
218 D. D. Porter, *Incidents and Anecdotes of the Civil War* (1885), 240–241; Oldroyd, *Soldier's Story*, 175; Mary W. Loughborough, *My Cave Life in Vicksburg* (1864), 61–62.
219 Moss, *Diary*, 29–30.
220 Moss, *Diary*, 39; *Reb. Rec.*, VII, 170 (doc.); W. R. Livermore, *The Story of the Civil War* (1933), Pt. III, Book 2, p. 389; G. W. Driggs, *Opening of the Mississippi* (1864), 137.
221 J. W. De Forest, *A Volunteer's Adventures* (1946), 105, 115, 116; Nicolay-Hay, *Lincoln's Works*, IX, 101.
222 Nicolay-Hay, *Lincoln: A History*, VII, 327; *Leslie's*, Aug. 1, 1863, pp. 305–306; Porter, *Incidents*, 218–219.
225 Pollard, *Lee and His Lieutenants*, 834–835; F. M. Flinn, *Campaigning with Banks* (1887), 108.
226 F. H. Harrington, *Fighting Politician: Major General N. P. Banks* (1948), 158–159; L. Van Alstyne, *Diary of an Enlisted Man* (1910), 317; A. H. Noll, *General Kirby-Smith* (1907), 225.

CHAPTER IX

229 *O.R.*, XXXI, Pt. 3, p. 297; Dana, *Recollections*, 110, 124–125; G. M. Sorrel, *Recollections of a Confederate Staff Officer* (1905), 200; John Beatty, *Memoirs of a Volunteer* (1946), 134.
231 Beatty, *Memoirs*, 77, 111.
232 J. H. Haynie, *The Nineteenth Illinois* (1912), 191, 194; Beatty, *Memoirs*, 156.
233 Beatty, *Memoirs*, 159.
234 Dana, *Recollections*, 128; Beatty, *Memoirs*, 175–176.
237 R. G. Caldwell, *James A. Garfield* (1931), 114; Sorrel, *Recollections*, 189; J. B. Hood, *Advance and Retreat* (1880), 61.
238 *H. W.*, VIII (Feb. 6, 1864), p. 85.
239 J. W. Bishop, *The Story of a Regiment* (1890), 109; T. F. Berry, *Four Years with Morgan and Forrest* (1914), 243.
240 Beatty, *Memoirs*, 250–251; W. F. G. Shanks, *Personal Recollections of Distinguished Generals* (1866), 268; Dana, *Recollections*, 118.
242 Bishop, *Story of a Regiment*, 117; Beatty, *Memoirs*, 259.
243 T. H. Williams, *Lincoln and His Generals* (1952), 285; *Reb. Rec.*, VIII, 191, 193 (doc.); Grant, *Memoirs*, II, 32.
244 Freeman, *Lee's Lieutenants*, III, 284.
245 James Longstreet, *From Manassas to Appomattox* (1896), 477; Freeman Cleaves, *Rock of Chickamauga* (1948), 190.

246 *Reb. Rec.*, VIII, 250 (doc.).
247 J. D. Cox, *Military Reminiscences of the Civil War* (1900), II, 30, 34; *Reb. Rec.*, VIII, 256–257 (doc.).
249 *Reb. Rec.*, VIII, 211–212 (doc.); Bishop, *Story of a Regiment*, 119.
250 Beatty, *Memoirs*, 263.
251 Dana, *Recollections*, 149; L. G. Bennett and W. M. Haigh, *History of the Thirty-Sixth Regiment, Illinois Volunteers* (1876), 526–529.
252 S. F. Horn, *The Army of the Tennessee* (1941), 156, 301, 303.
253 Dana, *Recollections*, 150; *O.R.*, XXXI, pt. 2, p. 69.

CHAPTER X

255 Gideon Welles, *Diary* (1911), I, 54; Chesnut, *Diary*, 140; R. M. Thompson and Richard Wainwright, eds., *Confidential Correspondence of Gustavus Vasa Fox* (1919), II, 381, 303; Russell, *My Diary*, I, 62.
256 J. R. Soley, *The Blockade and the Cruisers* (1885), 1; *B. & L.*, I, 614; Thompson-Wainwright, *Fox Correspondence*, II, 110.
257 *B. & L.*, I, 615; *Reb. Rec.*, I, 78 (doc.), *O.R.N.*, VI, 528–529.
259 F. B. C. Bradlee, *Blockade Running during the Civil War* (1925), 106; Soley, *The Blockade*, 156–157.
260 Raphael Semmes, *The Cruise of the Alabama* (1864), I, 98.
261 J. M. Kell, *Recollections of a Naval Life* (1900), 201, 193; *Reb. Rec.*, IX, 217.
263 B. E. Yerbey to his grandfather, Suffolk, Va., Mar. 11, 1862, MS., Ga. Dept. of Archives and Hist.; J. L. Worden and others, *The Monitor and the Merrimac* (1912), 10.
264 Worden, *Monitor and Merrimac*, 50, 55, 20; Edge, *Major-General McClellan*, 16.
266 Thompson-Wainwright, *Fox Correspondence*, I, 127; *O.R.N.*, XI, 601; Welles, *Diary*, II, 495–496.
267 Soley, *The Blockade*, 221.
268 Russell, *My Diary*, I, 296, 300.
269 Thompson-Wainwright, *Fox Correspondence*, I, 386; *Reb. Rec.*, I, 88–89 (diary).
270 D. D. Porter, *The Naval History of the Civil War* (1886), 45; *N. Y. Illustrated News*, Sept. 16, 1861, p. 314.
271 *N. Y. Illustrated News*, Sept. 16, 1861, p. 314; Porter, *Naval History*, 46; *O.R.N.*, VI, 173.
272 Thompson-Wainwright, *Fox Correspondence*, I, 65, 70, 117, 181–182.
274 *Reb. Rec.*, IV, 326 (doc.).
275 T. W. Montfort to his wife, Ft. Pulaski, Feb. 12, 1862, MS., Ga. Dept. of Archives and Hist.
276 T. W. Montfort to his family, Ft. Pulaski, Feb. 5 and April 5, 1862, MS., Ga. Dept. of Archives and Hist.; *Reb. Rec.*, IV, 452 (doc.).
278 W. T. Sherman, *Memoirs* (1876), II, 195, 197.
279 Welles, *Diary*, I, 264–265; Thompson-Wainwright, *Fox Correspondence*, I, 181; Dennett, *Lincoln and the Civil War*, 57.
281 *O.R.N.*, XIV, 75; Madeleine V. Dahlgren, *Memoir of John A. Dahlgren* (1882), 555–559.
282 *Reb. Rec.*, VI, 506 (doc.).
283 H. A. du Pont, *Rear-Admiral Samuel Francis du Pont* (1926), 180–181, 184; *O.R.N.*, XIV, 12.
285 Thompson-Wainwright, *Fox Correspondence*, I, 181, 168; Du Pont, *Du Pont*, 201; *O.R.N.*, XIV, 17, 6.
286 Welles, *Diary*, I, 311.
287 Dahlgren, *Memoir*, 352; Thompson-Wainwright, *Fox Correspondence*, I, 160.
289 Dahlgren, *Memoir*, 393, 399, 413; unidentified clipping in Edmund Ruffin diary, MS., Lib. of Cong.
290 Q. A. Gillmore, *Engineer and Artillery Operations against*

. . . *Charleston Harbor* (1865), 51, 80–81; *B. & L.*, IV, 73.

292 Chesnut, *Diary*, 258.

293 *The Burckmyer Letters* (1926), 363.

294 Porter, *Incidents*, 267; *H. W.*, Dec. 31, 1864, p. 835; R. D. Evans, *A Sailor's Log* (1901), 76.

295 Welles, *Diary*, II, 209; Porter, *Incidents*, 269, 272; Evans, *Sailor's Log*, 77–78.

296 Porter, *Incidents*, 273; Evans, *Sailor's Log*, 88–89.

297 Evans, *Sailor's Log*, 88–89; Porter, *Naval History*, 716; *B. & L.*, IV, 660–661.

CHAPTER XI

299 C. F. Adams, *Richard Henry Dana* (1890), II, 271–272; Grant, *Memoirs*, II, 122, 142–143; Taylor, *Warren*, 167; *Meade's Hq.*, 87; H. E. Wing in *Christian Advocate*, Jan. 2, 1913, p. 9.

300 Freeman, *Lee*, III, 290, 281; Page, *Letters of a War Correspondent*, 54.

302 W. P. Snow, *Southern Generals, Who They Are* (1865), 61; *Meade's Hq.*, 94; E. P. Alexander, *Military Memoirs of a Confederate* (1907), 506; *H. W.*, June 4, 1864, p. 358.

304 Horace Porter, *Campaigning with Grant* (1897), facsimile facing p. 104, 79.

305 D. A. Dickert, *History of Kershaw's Brigade* (1899), 357–358.

306 *Cycle of Adams Letters*, II, 138.

307 Gerrish, *Reminiscences*, 175–177; *Meade's Hq.*, 107–108.

308 *Meade's Hq.*, 109; Gordon, *Reminiscences*, 275, 279–280.

310 Porter, *Campaigning with Grant*, 127–129.

311 Grant, *Memoirs*, II, 237; Freeman, *Lee*, III, 385.

312 G. W. Bacon and E. W. Howland, *Letters of a Family during the War for the Union* (1899), II, 588–590; Welles, *Diary*, II, 31–32.

313 *Cycle of Adams Letters*, II, 131.

314 Porter, *Campaigning with Grant*, 85–86; Grant, *Memoirs*, II, 268; Gerrish, *Reminiscences*, 191; Freeman, *Lee*, III, 357.

315 Porter, *Campaigning with Grant*, 168.

316 *Meade's Hq.*, 101; Polley, *Soldier's Letters*, 245; Page, *Letters of a War Correspondent*, 94.

317 *Meade's Hq.*, 135–136.

319 Porter, *Campaigning with Grant*, 174; *Meade's Hq.*, 107; P. S. Michie, *Life and Letters of Emory Upton* (1885), 108–109.

321 *Cycle of Adams Letters*, II, 141–142; Grant, *Memoirs*, II, 284.

CHAPTER XII

323 *Cycle of Adams Letters*, II, 140–141; Welles, *Diary*, II, 45; E. M. Coulter, *The Confederate States of America* (1950), 375.

324 *Meade's Hq.*, 192; B. F. Butler, *Butler's Book* (1892), 649.

325 *B. & L.*, IV, 116.

326 *Meade's Hq.*, 192; Forbes, *Artist's Story*, 193; *H. W.*, Nov. 12, 1864, p. 734.

327 *Butler's Book*, 680; J. L. Cunningham, *Three Years with the Adirondack Regiment* (1920), 144.

329 J. F. J. Caldwell, *The History of a Brigade of South Carolinians* (1866), 196–197.

330 *O.R.*, XXXVI, pt. 2, p. 197.

331 *Butler's Book*, 672, 670; Frank Wilkeson, *Recollections of a Private Soldier* (1887), 158; *Meade's Hq.*, 162.

332 Cunningham, *Three Years*, 132; *Cycle of Adams Letters*, II, 154.

333 Wilkeson, *Recollections*, 169–171; *O.R.*, XL, pt. 2, p. 221.

334 Wilkeson, *Recollections*, 177–178; Cunningham, *Three Years*, 133.

336 Grant, *Memoirs*, II, 206–207.

337 Grant, *Memoirs*, II, 298–299; Livermore, *Days and Events*, 336; M. A. Haynes, *History of the Second Regiment New Hampshire Volunteers* (1865), 166-167.

338 Jones, *Under the Stars and Bars*, 240; David Lane, *A Soldier's Diary* (1905), 200–201.

339 E. J. Copp, *Reminiscences of the War of the Rebellion* (1911), 340; Cunningham, *Three Years*, 156–157.

340 *Meade's Hq.*, 240–241; Gerrish, *Reminiscences*, 203.

341 Cunningham, *Three Years*, 134–135 (order of sentences rearranged); W. P. Hopkins, *The Seventh Regiment Rhode Island Volunteers* (1903), 232.

342 *History of the First Connecticut Artillery* (1893), 116–117.

344 Cunningham, *Three Years*, 136; *H. W.*, July 30, 1864, p. 481.

345 G. W. Ward, *History of the Second Pennylvania Veteran Heavy Artillery* (1903), 76; Cunningham, *Three Years*, 136.

346 Cunningham, *Three Years*, 138.

347 Wilson, *Under the Old Flag*, I, 458–463.

348 *Cycle of Adams Letters*, II, 166; Cunningham, *Three Years*, 139; Alexander, *Military Memoirs*, 563–564; Grant, *Memoirs*, II, 307.

349 *H. W.*, Aug. 20, 1864, p. 542; Alexander, *Military Memoirs*, 569.

350 Porter, *Campaigning with Grant*, 264; N. M. Blake, *William Mahone of Virginia* (1935), 56; *So. Hist. Soc. Papers*, XXXIII (1905), 364–365; Grant, *Memoirs*, II, 315.

352 Pollard, *Lee and His Lieutenants*, 477–478; Rhodes, *History of United States*, IV, 496n.

354 C. W. Russell, ed., *The Memoirs of Colonel John S. Mosby* (1917), 149–150, 184, 270; *B. & L.*, IV, 493.

356 *Meade's Hq.*, 190; Lew Wallace, *An Autobiography* (1906), II, 701; E. S. Dudley, in *Sketches of War History, 1861–1865: Papers read before the Ohio Commandery of the Military Order of the Loyal Legion* (1888), 115.

357 Welles, *Diary*, II, 70.

358 Wallace, *Autobiography*, II, 768; Gordon, *Reminiscences*, 312.

360 Welles, *Diary*, II, 71; Dennett, *Lincoln and the Civil War*, 208; J. A. Early, *Autobiographical Sketch* (1912), 389–390; J. H. Cramer, *Lincoln under Enemy Fire* (1948), 27.

362 Grant, *Memoirs*, II, 317–318; *Meade's Hq.*, 82.

363 De Forest, *Volunteer's Adventures*, 163.

365 De Forest, *Volunteer's Adventures*, 186–187.

366 P. H. Sheridan, *Personal Memoirs* (1888), I, 465, 486; II, 38–40; Page, *Letters of a War Corespondent*, 269–270.

367 Blackford, *Letters from Lee's Army*, 253–254; Sheridan, *Memoirs*, II, 56–58.

368 De Forest, *Volunteer's Adventures*, 222, 214, 211, 229; Gordon, *Reminiscences*, 348–349.

369 *Cycle of Adams Letters*, II, 174; Lane, *Soldier's Diary*, 216.

370 Polley, *Soldier's Letters*, 264–266.

371 Cunningham, *Three Years*, 141; *Cycle of Adams Letters*, II, 205.

372 *Meade's Hq.*, 282–283.

373 *Meade's Hq.*, 213; Jones, *Under the Stars and Bars*, 238–239; *B. & L.*, IV, 575.

374 Cunningham, *Three Years*, 164; Jones, *Under the Stars and Bars*, 222–223.

375 Cunningham, *Three Years*, 164.

376 *Gardner's Photographic Sketch Book*, II, opposite No. 61; Curtis, *History of Twenty-Fourth Michigan*, 79.

377 Polley, *Soldier's Letters*, 250–251; Blackford, *Letters from Lee's Army*, 272.

378 Gordon, *Reminiscences*, 229–230; H. C. Trumbull, *War Memories of an Army Chaplain* (1898), 4–5.

379 Lane, *Soldier's Diary*, 217; Jones, *Under the Stars and Bars*, 224.

CHAPTER XIII

381 J. C. Gray and J. C. Ropes, *War Letters, 1862–1865* (1927), 427–428; Sherman, *Home Letters*, 287–288; W. A. Cate, ed., *Two Soldiers* (1938), 72.

382 Lloyd Lewis, *Sherman: Fighting Prophet* (1932), 381; *O.R.*, XXXVIII, pt. 5, p. 793; M. A. de W. Howe, ed., *Marching with Sherman* (1927), 23–24.

383 J. C. Wood, *Reminiscences of the War*, 132.

384 O. O. Winther, ed., *With Sherman to the Sea* (1943), 112–113.

385 Winther, *With Sherman to the Sea*, 109; Sherman, *Memoirs*, II, 55; Mrs. S. E. D. Smith, *The Soldier's Friend* (1867), 268.

386 Ill. State Hist. Lib., *Pubs.*, XXXV, 342.

387 R. S. Bevier, *History of the First and Second Missouri Confederate Brigades* (1879), 236–237.

388 *O.R.*, XXXVIII, pt. 1, p. 69; Ill. State Hist. Lib., *Pubs.*, XXXV, 346–347.

389 Sherman, *Memoirs*, II, 72; *O.R.*, XXXVIII, pt. 1, p. 156; Howe, *Marching with Sherman*, 55.

390 S. F. Fleharty, *Our Regiment* (1865), 100–101; D. B. Floyd, *History of the Seventy-Fifth Regiment of Indiana* (1893), 307.

391 Winther, *With Sherman to the Sea*, 113–114.

392 Sherman, *Memoirs*, II, 97.

393 Hood, *Advance and Retreat*, 199.

394 C. W. Boyce, *A Brief History of the Twenty-Eighth Regiment, New York State Volunteers* (1896), 62.

395 Lewis, *Sherman*, 350; *O.R.*, XXXVIII, pt. 5, p. 793.

396 Sherman, *Memoirs*, II, 76; Sherman, *Home Letters*, 302.

397 Ill. State Hist. Lib., *Pubs.*, XXXV, 360–361; *O.R.*, XXXVIII, pt. 5, p. 777.

398 *O.R.*, XXXVIII, pt. 3, p. 633; Hood, *Advance and Retreat*, 206, 208.

399 Hood, *Advance and Retreat*, 245–246.

400 Sherman, *Memoirs*, II, 147, 148–149; T. A. Head, *Campaign and Battles of the Sixteenth Regiment, Tennessee Volunteers* (1885), 145–147.

401 *O.R.*, XXXIX, pt. 3, p. 162; Pollard, *Lee and His Lieutenants*, 759–760; R. S. Henry, *'First with the Most' Forrest* (1944), 381.

402 Richard O'Connor, *Hood: Cavalier General* (1949), 237; R. W. Banks, *The Battle of Franklin* (1908), 30–31.

404 Cate, *Two Soldiers*, 162.

405 Cate, *Two Soldiers*, 165–166.

406 Hood, *Advance and Retreat*, 300; *B. & L.*, IV, 457.

407 *B. & L.*, IV, 458–459.

408 Bennett-Haigh, *Thirty-Sixth Regiment Illinois Volunteers*, 684–685.

409 Cleaves, *Thomas*, 265–266; Cate, *Two Soldiers*, 169; Hood, *Advance and Retreat*, 303.

410 Lewis, *Sherman*, 429; Howe, *Marching with Sherman*, 56–57.

412 *O.R.*, XXXIX, pt. 3, p. 680; XXXVIII, pt. 5, pp. 688–689.

413 E. S. Miers, *The General Who Marched to Hell* (1951), 214, 218, 223–224; Winther, *With Sherman to the Sea*, 133 (order of sentences changed).

414 Rhodes, *History of the Civil War*, 403; *O.R.*, XLIV, p. 485.

415 Sherman, *Home Letters*, 317, 298; *O.R.*, XLIV, 13.

416 *O.R.*, XLIV, p. 783; G. W. Pepper, *Personal Recollections of Sherman's Campaigns* (1866), 288–289; *Reb. Rec.*, IX, 7.

417 *O.R.*, XLIV, p. 809; Lewis, *Sherman*, 471; Cox, *Reminiscences*, II, 531–532.

418 M. W. Wellman, *Giant in Gray* (1949), text facing unnumbered illustration.

419 Rhodes, *History of the Civil War*, 424; Lewis, *Sherman*, 505; Sherman, *Memoirs*, II, 249.

CHAPTER XIV

421 Freeman, *Lee*, IV, 3, 21; F. E. Vandiver, ed., *The Civil War Diary of General Josiah Gorgas* (1947), 163–164, 172; Gordon, *Reminiscences*, 381–382; Porter, *Incidents*, 314.

422 Townsend, *Rustics in Rebellion*, 252–253.

423 Gordon, *Reminiscences*, 419; Townsend, *Rustics in Rebellion*, 257–258.

424 Grant, *Memoirs*, II, 454.

425 *Meade's Hq.*, 340.

426 Gerrish, *Reminiscences*, 247; *Cycle of Adams Letters*, II, 263–264.

427 Hopkins, *Seventh Regiment Rhode Island Volunteers*, 261.

428 *O.R.*, XLVI, pt. 3, 509, 512; *Meade's Hq.*, 356; Gerrish, *Reminiscences*, 251.

429 Freeman, *Lee*, IV, 49; T. C. DeLeon, *Four Years in Rebel Capitals* (1892), 356.

430 J. B. Jones, *A Rebel War Clerk's Diary* (1935), II, 467–468.

431 Jones, *Under the Stars and Bars*, 251–253.

432 A. H. Bill, *The Beleaguered City* (1946), 273; Townsend, *Rustics in Rebellion*, 262, 268.

433 Porter, *Campaigning with Grant*, 452–453, 457.

434 *O.R.*, XLVI, pt. 1, p. 549; Gerrish, *Reminiscences*, 251.

436 *O.R.*, XLVI, pt. 1, pp. 384, 1278.

437 *O.R.*, XLVI, pt. 3, p. 653.

438 Porter, *Campaigning with Grant*, 473–474, 485–486.

439 J. L. Chamberlain, *The Passing of the Armies* (1915), 260–262.

Index to the Portraits